A Simpler Guide to Gmail

An unofficial user guide to setting up and using your free Google email account

Ceri Clark

Ceri Clark | A Simpler Guide to Gmail

A Simpler Guide to Gmail: An unofficial user guide to setting up and using your free Google email account

Third Edition

Published by

Lycan Books

1 Monet Crescent, Newport, NP19 7PP

www.lycanbooks.com

Copyright © 2014 Ceri Clark

In association with Myrddin Publishing

ISBN-10: 1-909236-08-X
ISBN-13: 978-1-909236-08-0

All rights reserved. No part of this publication may be reproduced, stored in or introduced into a retrieval system, or transmitted, in any form, or by any means (electronic, mechanical, photocopying, recording or otherwise) without the prior written permission of the author. Any person who does any unauthorized act in relation to this publication may be liable to criminal prosecution and civil claims for damages.

Limited Liability/Disclaimer of Warranty: While best efforts have been used in preparing this book, the author and publisher make no representations or warranties of any kind and assume no liabilities of any kind with respect to the accuracy or completeness of the contents and specifically disclaim any implied warranties of merchantability or fitness of use for a particular purpose. Neither the author nor the publisher shall be held liable or responsible to any person or entity with respect to any loss or incidental or consequential damages caused, or alleged to have been caused, directly or indirectly without limitations, by the information or programs contained herein. Furthermore readers should be aware that internet sites listed in this work may have changed or disappeared from when this work was written to when it will be read. This work is sold with the understanding that the advice given herein may not be suitable for every situation.

Trademarks: Where trademarks are used in this book this infers no endorsement or any other affiliation with this book. Any trademarks used in this book are solely used for editorial purposes.

© 2014 Cover & Interior Design: Lycan Books

Photo element © Can Stock Photo Inc. / nasir1164

Dedication

My special thanks go to my family and friends for being so patient with me while I put this book together and of course my husband who looked after our toddler so I could finish this book.

Contents

Chapter 1 Introduction 1
    What Is This Book About? 1
    How Should I Use This Book? 1
    What is Gmail? 2
    Why Gmail? 2
Chapter 2 Opening Your Account 5
    Setting up your Google Gmail Account 5
        Filling in the form 8
        Choosing your username 8
        Choosing your password 9
        Birthday, gender, mobile phone and email address 10
        Word verification (prove you are not a robot) 10
        Location 11
        Terms of Service 11
        Create your Profile 12
            Adding your profile picture 12

Chapter 3 Getting Started 17
  Taking the Tour 17
    Importing mail and contacts 18
  Logging in 21
    Going directly there 22
    Adding Google as your homepage 23
  Reading Emails 25
  Viewing Attachments 27
  Turn off Chat 29
    Reactivating Chat 31
Chapter 4 Security 33
  Passwords 33
    Changing your password 33
  Two-factor authentication 34
    How to setup 2-step verification on Google 34
    Backup access 38
    Using Gmail or other Google Services on your mobile device(s) 40
    Accessing 2-step authentication after setup 43
    Using an Android app to gain verification codes 43
  Recognizing spam, scams and phishing emails 47
    It's too good to be true 48
    Your friend is on Vacation and asks you for money 48
    A stranger sob story 48
    An email sent to yourself 48
    Bad grammar and spelling 49
    Bank emails 49

The unsubscribe link	49
Chapter 5 Sending and Receiving Emails	**51**
Discussions	52
Replying and forwarding an email	54
Replying to a group	58
Composing an email	58
Formatting your email	59
Adding a link to your email	61
Spell Check	61
Deleting an email	63
Chapter 6 Address Book (Google Contacts)	**65**
How to add contacts using the Gmail website	65
Adding a contact using an email address	67
Manually Adding a Contact	67
Adding Pictures to Contacts	69
Filling in the fields	70
Editing Contacts	70
Groups	71
How to add a group	71
Importing and exporting contacts	73
Exporting Contacts	73
Importing Contacts	75
Chapter 7 Sorting Emails – No More Folders with Labels	**77**
Labels	78
Creating a Label	79
Circles	83

- Applying a Label 83
  - From the email list 83
  - From an opened email 85
- Spam 86

Chapter 8 Filters 89

- Creating a Filter 90
- Filters in Settings 93
  - How to get to Filters in the settings 93
  - Editing/changing a filter 93
  - Deleting a filter 94
  - Sharing filters with friends (exporting filters) 94
  - Adding filters given by friends (importing filters) 94

Chapter 9 Searching For, and In Emails 97

- Searching in your labels 99
- Searching for emails from a certain person 99
- Searching emails you have sent to people 99
- Subject Searching 99
- Searching for emails using keywords (Has the words…) 100
  - Removing emails from the search 100
- Finding emails with an attachment 100
- Searching through your Chats 101
- Searching by Size 101
- Searching emails by date 101

Chapter 10 Changing the Look and Feel 103

- Display Density 104
- Themes 106

Chapter 11 Under the Hood - Settings 109

General Settings 109

- Language 111
- Phone numbers 111
- Maximum Page Size 111
- Images 111
- Default reply behavior: 112
- Default text style: 113
- Conversation view 113
- Email via Google+ 114
- Send and Archive 114
- Stars 115
- Desktop Notifications 115
- Keyboard Shortcuts 116
- Button labels 117
- My Picture 117
- People Widget 118
- Create contacts for auto-complete 118
- Important signals for ads 118
- Signature 122
- Personal level indicators 129
- Snippets 130
- Vacation responder/Out of Office AutoReply 130
- Outgoing message encoding 131

Labels 131

Inbox 131

Default	132
Important first	135
Unread first	136
Starred first	137
Priority inbox	139
Accounts and Import	141
Change Account Settings	141
Import mail and contacts	142
Send Mail As	143
Check mail from other accounts (using POP3):	144
Using Gmail for work?	146
Grant access to your account:	147
Add additional storage:	147
Filters	147
Forwarding and POP/IMAP	148
Forwarding	149
POP Download	149
IMAP Access	150
Chat	151
Web Clips	151
Labs	151
Offline	152
Themes	152
Chapter 12 Google Accounts and Your Profile	155
Creating a Public Profile	157
Chapter 13 Keeping Your Email Under Control	161

Time management	161
Prioritize, prioritize, prioritize	162
Starring emails	162
Replying to messages	162
Replying with a Canned Response	164
Editing/Overwriting a Canned Response	164
Deleting Canned Responses	165
Using filters to automatically send Canned Responses	165
Using the inbox tabs	166
Using labels/folders as customized inboxes	166
Other Folders	167
Using filters with labels	168
Setting up filters from related email in your inbox	168
Unsubscribe from unwanted Newsletters	169
Signing up to Roll.me	171
Lastly find what works for you	172
Chapter 14 Introduction to Google+	175
Why use Google+?	176
How to get to Google+	176
Your Google+ homepage – an overview	177
Home (the stream)	177
Navigating Google+	177
The top navigation bar	177
The dropdown navigation menu	177
Home	178
Profile	178

People	178
Photos	179
What's hot	179
Communities	179
Events	179
Hangouts	179
Pages	179
Local	179
Settings	179
Your Profile	180
Setting up your profile	180
Adding a photo or cover	180
Adding Profile Information	182
Getting your personalized, custom profile URL	185
Hangouts	187
Reasons to use Hangouts	189
About Circles	189
Creating a Circle	191
Adding people to your Circles	195
Searching for a name you know	196
Searching for people using Communities	196
Searching by Tags	198
CircleShare	198
Creating a CircleShare or sharing a Circle	199
Deleting people and/or Circles	201
Deleting individuals	201

    Deleting Circles 201
Being social: liking, commenting and sharing 202
    +1 (Like) 202
    Commenting 203
    Sharing 204
Managing your posts 205
    Viewing Posts 205
    Viewing comments 207
    Posting 208
    Deleting posts 211
    Disabling Comments and reshares 212
Notifications 213
Searching on Google+ 215
    Searching for People 215
    Searching for subjects 216
Settings 217
    Who can interact with you and your posts 217
    Who can Hangout with you 218
    Shared Endorsements 219
    Notification delivery 219
    Manage Subscriptions 219
    Receive notifications 220
    Apps & activities 220
    Your circles 221
    Accessibility 221
    Photos and Videos 222

- Profile 223
- Hashtags 223
- Location Settings 224
- SMS Terms 224
- Disable Google+ 224
- Privacy 225
- Google+ app on your phone 226
  - Viewing your profile 227
  - Choosing your account 228
  - People Search 228
  - Notifications 229
  - Limiting the posts you see 230
  - Search 231
  - Posting 232
  - Settings 232
- Google+ extensions for the Chrome browser 233
  - Installing the extensions on Chrome 233
  - Circloscope 235
  - Replies and more for Google+ 235
  - Do Share 235
- Google+ Posting Cheat Sheet 235
  - Text Styling 235
  - Posting 236
  - Google+ Shortcut keys 236

Chapter 15 Chat 237
- Turning on Chat 237

Inviting a contact to chat	239
Older accounts	241
Contact availability	241
Blocking contacts	242
New account	242
Older account	243
Video, phone or text chat	243
Chapter 16 Tasks	245
Where to find Tasks	245
Adding a task	247
Completing a task	248
Deleting or removing a task	248
Actions	249
Indent and Unindent	249
Move up or down	250
Edit Details	250
Help	250
Show tips	250
Email task list	250
Print task list	250
View completed tasks	250
Sort by due date	250
Clear completed tasks	250
Organizing lists	250
Chapter 17 Netiquette	253
Chapter 18 Gmail on Your Android Device	255

The Gmail menu 256
Checking mail in the Gmail app 257
Composing mail in the Gmail app 257
Replying and forwarding to mail in the Gmail app 258
Browsing your email using Labels 259
Search your email 260
Settings 260
    General settings 260
        Gmail default action (Archive and delete options) 261
        Swipe actions 261
        Sender image 261
        Reply all 261
        Auto-fit messages 261
        Auto-advance 261
        Confirm before deleting, Confirm before archiving and Confirm before sending 262
    Email settings 262
        Inbox type 262
        Inbox categories 262
        Notifications and Inbox sound & vibrate 262
        Signature 262
        Vacation responder 262
        Sync Gmail and days of mail to sync 263
        Manage labels 263
        Download attachments 263
        Images 263

Adding another email account 264
Chapter 19 Advanced Features - Google Labs 265
Apps Search 266
Authentication icon for verified senders 266
Auto-advance 267
Canned Responses 267
Custom keyboard shortcuts 267
Google Calendar gadget 270
Google Maps preview in mail 270
Google Voice player in mail 270
Mark as Read button 271
Multiple inboxes 271
Picasa previews in mail 272
Pictures in chat 272
Preview Pane 273
Quick Links 275
Quote selected text 275
Right-sided chat 275
Smartlabels 276
Undo Send 276
Unread Message Icon 277
Yelp previews in mail 277

Chapter 20 Frequently Asked Questions (FAQ) 279
What was the address again to login to Gmail? 279
Help I've lost my password, what do I do now? 279
Where do I go to change my password? 281

Do I need a special browser to use Gmail?..281
How do I print email?...281
How do remove the 'extra' inboxes like updates, social and promotions?........281
How do I remove email addresses when I Reply to All? 283
How do I increase the size of the text in my browser and my Android phone?
....284
Glossary..285
Index..289
About the Author...297
More from Lycan Books & Myrddin Publishing: 298

Chapter 1 Introduction

What to expect in this Chapter:

- What Is This Book About?
- How Should I Use This Book?
- What Is Gmail?
- Why Choose Gmail?

What Is This Book About?

This book is about Google's answer to email, the instant online way to communicate over the internet. It is written to help new users learn the basics and discover features that are far and above better than the closest competition. This book assumes the reader knows the basics of using a computer and has used a browser.

How Should I Use This Book?

If you have never used Gmail before then the first few chapters explain how to set up your account, how to keep your account secure and the basics of sending and receiving email. Following this there are tips on using the excellent tools that will make organizing your email a breeze. If this is you, the book is designed so that you can dip in at your level.

For the purposes of this guide I have made a few assumptions. The first is that you have (or at least have access to) a computer, you are familiar with using a mouse and know what the internet is.

A small disclaimer at this point. Gmail is constantly evolving and while this book is as accurate as could be made possible at the time of publication, Gmail can and will change. Features will be added and others taken away, however the principles will remain the same.

In the e-book version of this book, the images may appear smaller due to restrictions laid down by retailer and/or download costs. I have tried to write the book in such a way that the images illustrate a point rather than show you how to do a task. For example I will tell you where on the screen a button is and the image will be there as a visual clue but you should be able to find it from the written instructions.

If you have bought this book as a Kindle book, I recommend downloading the Kindle for PC/Mac programs from Amazon (free) to view the book from your computer. You will be able to click on links and the images will be of better quality.

What is Gmail?

Gmail is Google's answer for providing free online email. There are a myriad of other email solutions on the internet, some of them are free, others charge and a few are a combination of the two. Google likes to do things differently and they've improved how I deal with my correspondence. With the use of labels, filters, contacts and even labs, you will find that Gmail can almost be your own personal secretary, and best of all, it is free!

Why Gmail?

In my opinion, Google offers the best service for email. My reasons are:
- Easy to use
- Nothing to install

- Over 15 gigabytes of space (enough for a lifetime of email, although it is/can be shared between other Google services)
- Spell Checking
- Address Book (Contacts)
- Mobile access (for your iPhone or Android mobile phone, although any phone capable of using a browser can use it)
- Possibly *the* best spam (unwanted email) protection in the world!
- Your username and password for Gmail works for all the other free Google services like Search, YouTube, Chrome and Google+ etc.

So what are you waiting for, open an account today!

Chapter 2 Opening Your Account

What to expect in this Chapter:

- Where to go to join Gmail
- First Steps In Setting Up Your Google Account
- Choosing Passwords

Setting up your Google Gmail Account

First the easy bit. Head over to the account set up page. As in (a) in Figure 1 below, type in your address bar: http://mail.google.com

Ceri Clark | A Simpler Guide to Gmail

Figure 1 Creating an account

Google will redirect you to the right place. Please click on *Create an account* (b) as shown in Figure 1 above.

You will then be taken to the page as illustrated in Figure 2 below to open a Google Account:

Opening your Account

Figure 2 Sign-in form

Tip

Opening a Google account doesn't just give you email, by creating this account you can use all Google services with one username and password.

Filling in the form

Please make sure you fill in all the boxes you can in the form. Your mobile number is requested for security reasons. If you cannot get into your account for any reason in the future, Google can send you a text message so you can get back in. The same with your email address. If the one you are creating will be your only email address, don't worry, you will still be able to get an account.

Choosing your username

Your username will be your new email address. I recommend choosing something that you won't be embarrassed about later. You may apply for jobs or be using this email address in your business. Fluffywuffychocolateguzzler may sound funny and may even be free when you type it in but future employers or business contacts may not be so impressed!

The idea is to create an address of the form <username>@gmail.com where you are picking the <username> bit before the @ symbol. You can use letters, numbers and periods (full stops).

When you put in your desired username, Google will automatically check to see if it is available, if not the following will appear:

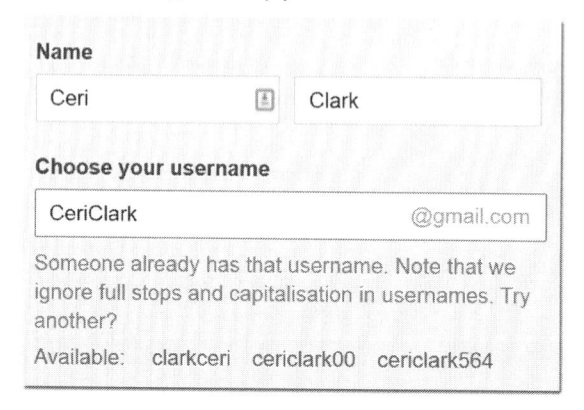

Figure 3 Username not available

Notice the nice people at Google have given you a few pointers below your choices for some names that *are* available? You can choose one of those but being a bit more creative can look more appropriate (read professional) than putting a number on the end. For example if you have put in your abbreviated first name, then your full first name may be more suitable or even putting in your middle name.

Type in different variants or choose one of their suggestions until you find one that is available.

Choosing your password

Next choose a password, making sure that it is strong. There are a few schools of thought when it comes to thinking up passwords. Here I am going to cover four ways.

No.1:
The simplest one to remember is choosing three random words which mean something to you but would be impossible to guess for an outsider. For example, if your favorite food is cake, your favorite vacation was in Hawaii and you just love baseball, then as much as my spell check hates it, cakeHawaiibaseball could be considered an excellent password.

No.2:
Another way to choose a password is by using a combination of letters, numbers and special characters. Using everyday words can make it easy to remember. For example, *Elephantsrock* is bad, *El3ph@nt5r0ck* is strong. To get El3ph@nt5r0ck, (if you haven't already worked it out), I replaced an e with 3, the a with @, s with 5 and o with 0 (zero). All the replacement numbers look like their letter counterparts to make it easy to remember.

No.3:
The third way is to choose a phrase which you will remember and take the first letters of each word. For example, **The scariest movie I have seen is Omen**! Once you have settled on a phrase just add a special character and number, I saw the film when I was about 9 so that's the number I will choose here. This password would be TsmihsiO!9.

No.4:
Another way to choose a password is similar to the above method but involves an aid. Those familiar with the movie, *Unknown* with Liam Neeson may recognize

this. If you have a favorite book then choose a passage and from that passage choose a word. For example, if the word is in the 22nd line on page 150. Two words along and the word is mammoth, the word would be 150222mammoth, or any combination of these elements that is easy for you to remember.

Tip

If you are like me and are liable to forget passwords, a good way to cheat is to use a service such as LastPass. Sign up at lastpass.com and use their service to either generate passwords for you or to remember passwords you have made. You will need one password to use LastPass but the service will remember all your other login information and can automatically log you in to websites. This way you can have different passwords for all the websites you visit and only have to remember the one! The service will also warn you when websites have been known to be compromised and ask you to change your password for them.

Birthday, gender, mobile phone and email address

The first two are self-explanatory, although if you are hyper-sensitive about your birthday I have known people to put a different birthday in. If you do this, remember what you entered!

Your mobile phone will be used to text a code to prove who you are when resetting your account if you have forgotten your password. You will also be contacted by your email address if you have a separate one. It is recommended that you put an accurate mobile phone and email address when you sign up.

Word verification (prove you are not a robot)

Otherwise known as CAPTCHA this is required to stop people using computers to automatically create 100s of accounts for spamming people (sending unwanted email). Type in the word you see or click on the microphone icon to hear an audio version (middle picture beside the text box).

Opening your Account

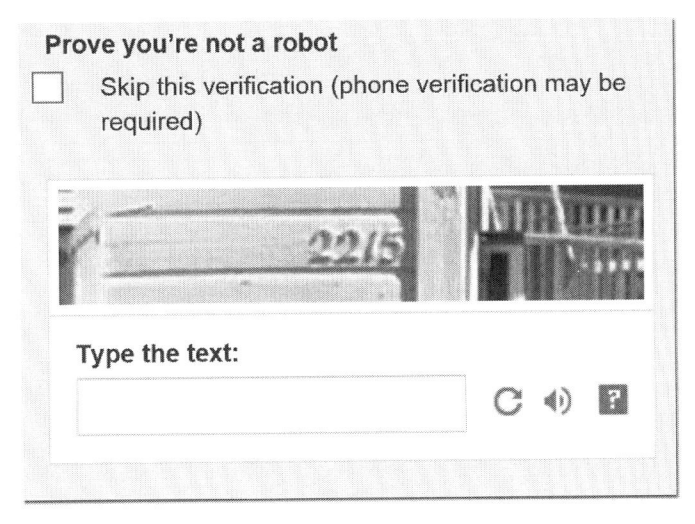

Figure 4 Word Verification section

If you can't make out what the number is, you can ask for another picture by clicking on the circular arrow. By clicking on the question mark, Google will explain what the symbols mean and how, by using the word verification, you are helping them digitize books.

Of course you can skip this step altogether by verifying over the phone by checking the box in front of 'Skip this verification'.

Location

Choose the country where you currently reside. This will make sure that your emails have the correct date and time for where you are. If the wrong location is set it could look like you are time travelling in the past to send emails (the time difference between the UK and USA for example. Another reason to choose the right location is to make sure you have the right terms and conditions for your country.

Terms of Service

Make sure you read the Google Terms of Service and then click on *Next step*.

Ceri Clark | A Simpler Guide to Gmail

Create your Profile

The first screen will show you how you will appear in all Google Services and Google will invite you to add a photo or go to the next step.

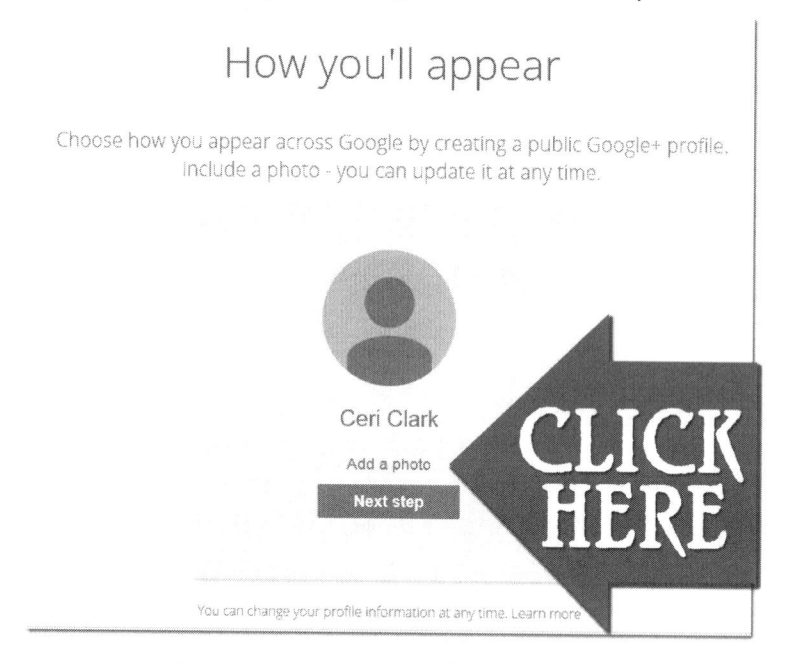

Figure 5 How your profile will appear

Adding your profile picture

Click on *Add a photo* to show other people how you look. This will appear in services like Google+, on emails that you send to people and even on your friend's phones in your contact information (when they put your email address into the contact information).

Opening your Account

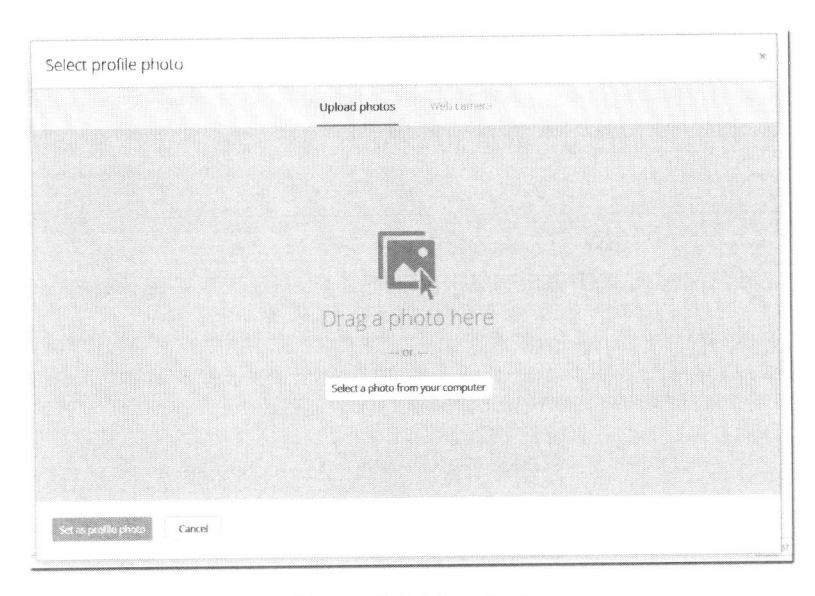

Figure 6 Add a photo

Go into your file explorer and find a flattering picture and drag it using your mouse on to the open Windows Explorer window. You will be given the option to edit your photo before it is accepted.

You can also browse for your file on your computer by clicking on *Select a photo from your computer* and finally you can use your webcam to take an instant photo by choosing the tab labelled Web camera!

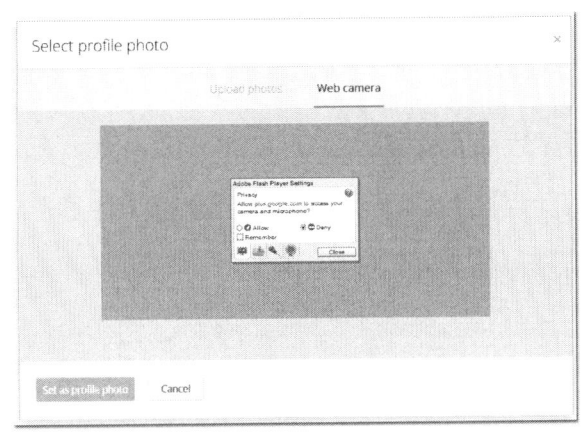

Figure 7 Allow Adobe Flash

13

Ceri Clark | A Simpler Guide to Gmail

If you do use your webcam you may need to allow Adobe Flash to use your camera. Click on Allow and Close. I never choose remember for this kind of thing as I want to know what is using my camera but then I can be known as slightly paranoid!

Click on the red button with the camera symbol and Take a snapshot written on it. You can do this as many times until you get the result you want.

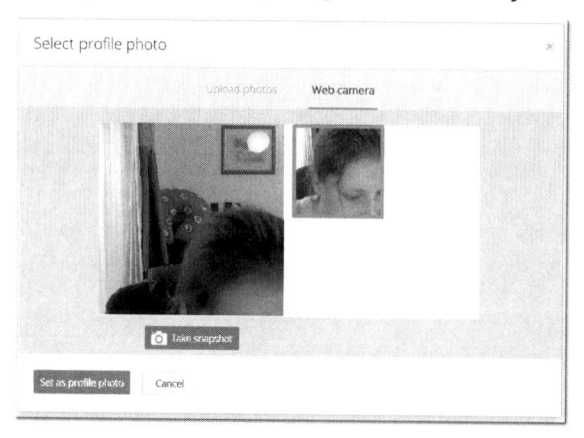

Figure 8 Choose your snapshot

When you are happy with one of the photos, click on it to select it and click on the blue button, Set as profile photo.

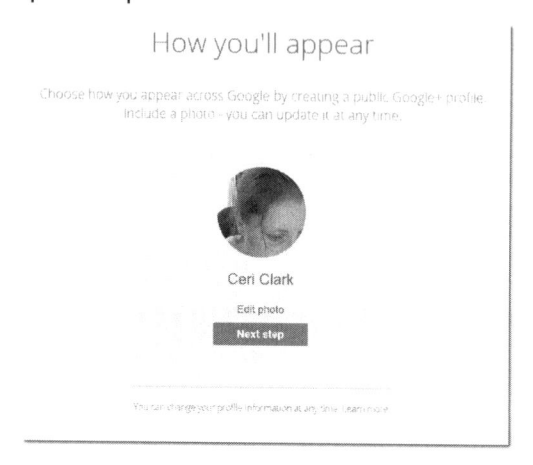

Figure 9 How your photo will look

If you click on Next Step before clicking on *Add a photo* you will just be taken straight to the welcome screen. You can change your profile picture later.

Opening your Account

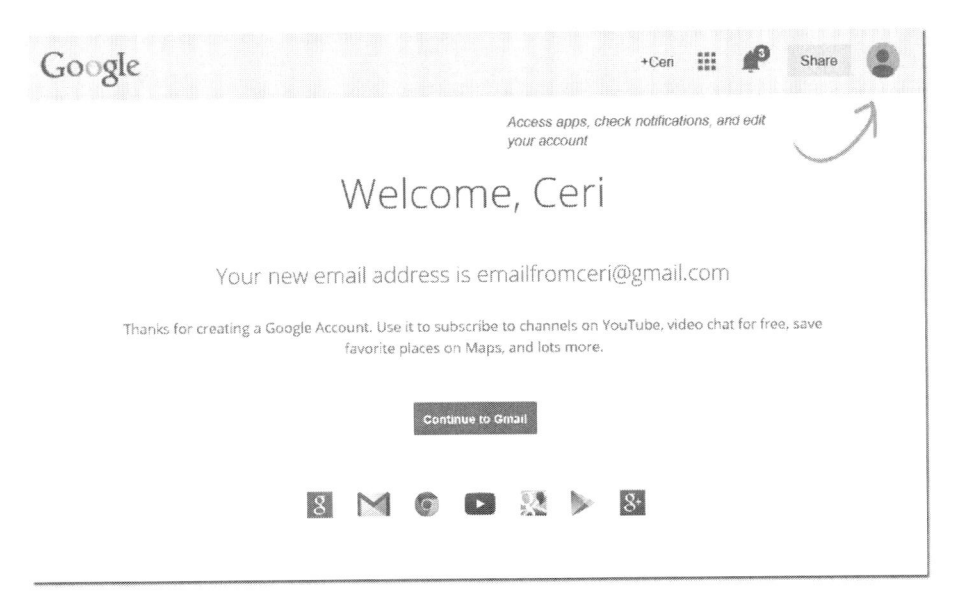

Figure 10 Welcome Screen

Select the blue button *Continue to Gmail* to get started.

Chapter 3 Getting Started

What to expect in this Chapter:

- First Steps In Setting Up Your Google Account
- Taking the Tour
- Choosing Passwords

Taking the Tour

The first thing you might see is a Google tour, which talks about new features that Google has implemented but also helps you to import mail and contacts within the tutorial. I recommend you have a look at this.

If the tutorial doesn't pop up automatically or you close it by accident, click on the gear symbol on the top right of the screen under your profile picture and choose *Take the Tour*.

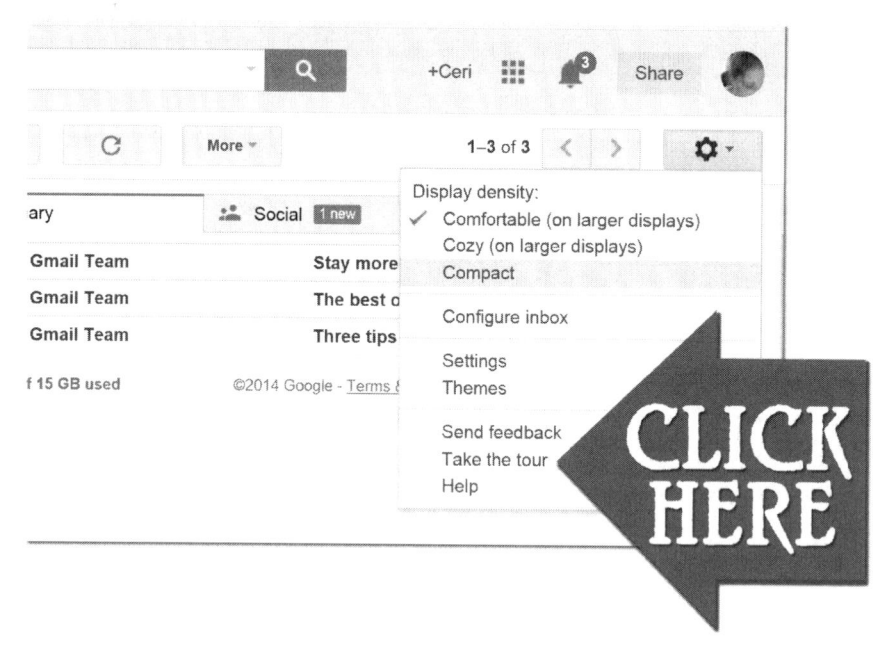

Figure 11 How to turn on the tour

The following pop up will appear inviting you to import your mail and contacts.

Figure 12 The tour popup over the home screen

Importing mail and contacts

When you click on Import mail and contacts within the tour. Google will metaphorically take you by the hand to import these from other email accounts you may already have.

Getting Started

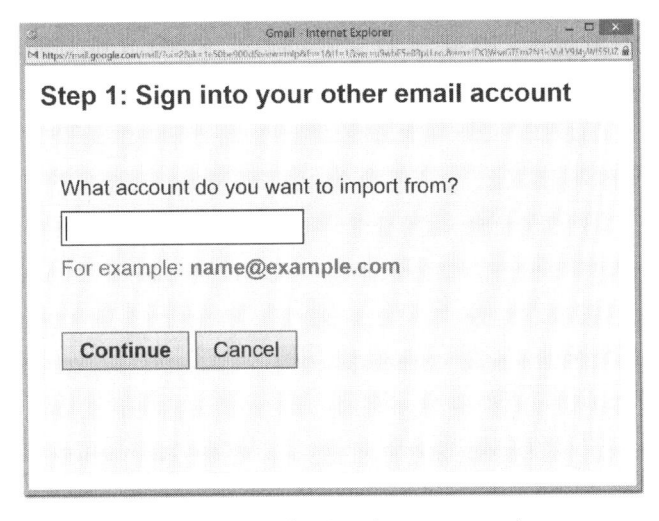

Figure 13 Letting Google sign into your other account

Type in your name in the box and click on continue.

Figure 14 Adding your password

Then choose what you would like to be imported into your new Google account. The importing of your data is done by another party so you cannot have your email imported for more than 30 days, however you can have your mail brought into Google indefinitely through the settings which I will explain later. I would therefore not bother with the third option as you might get your emails duplicated.

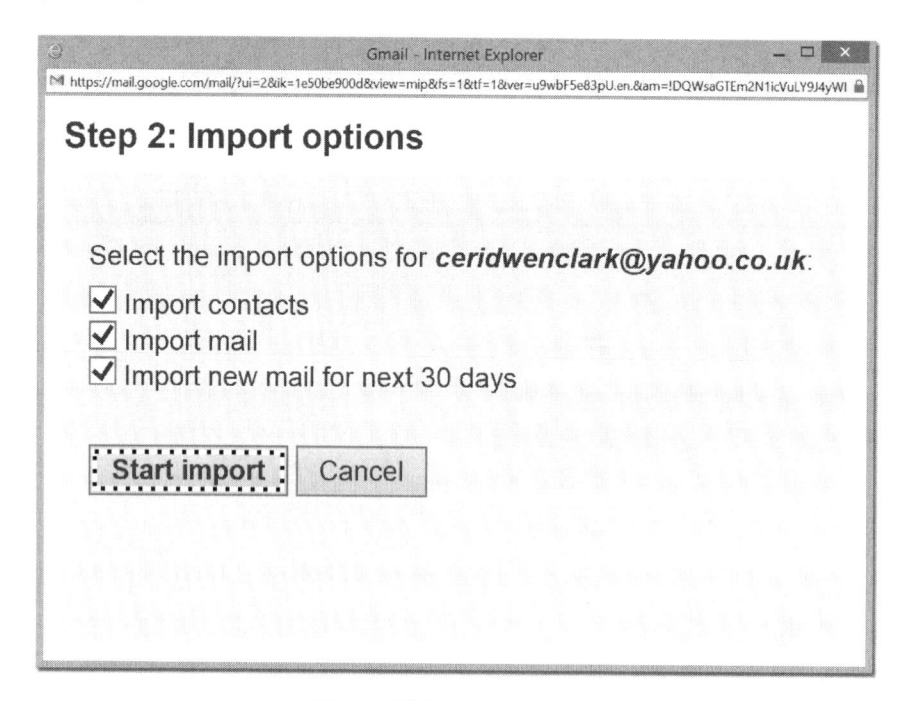

Figure 15 Import options

Click *Start import* and then *OK* on the next screen and your email and contacts will be automatically imported into Gmail.

Getting Started

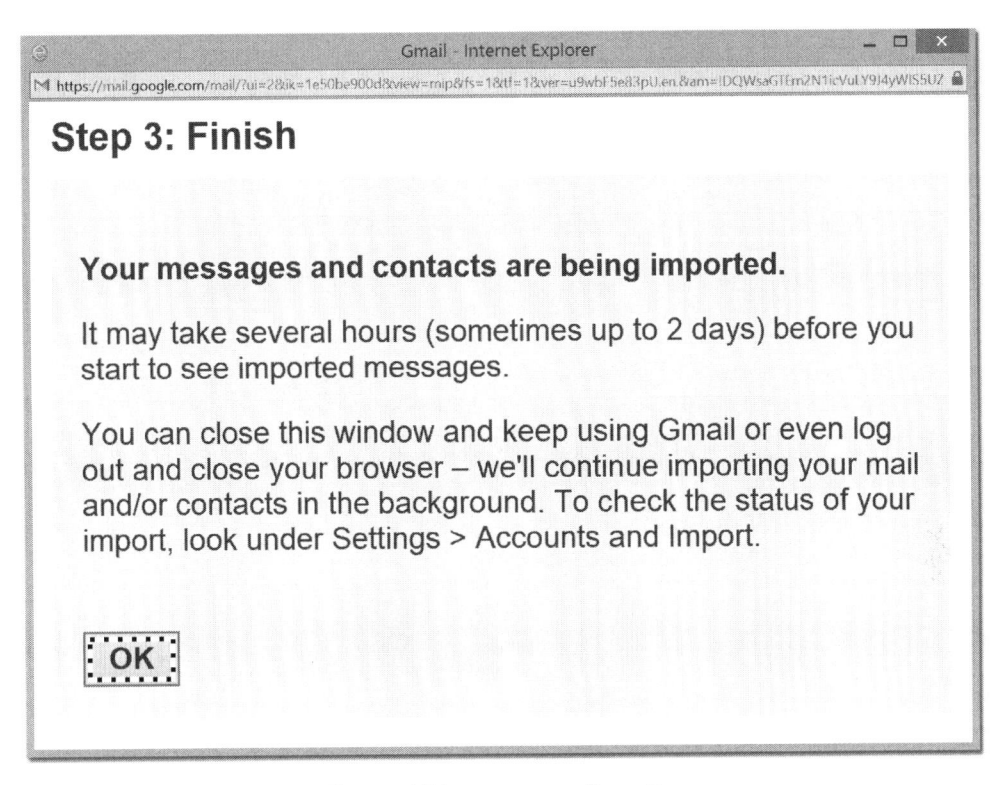

Figure 16 Imports confirmation

As the Yahoo account was new and created specifically for this book, my emails and contacts were imported within seconds. The time it takes to import your mail and contacts will vary depending on how many you have to transfer.

Click through the rest of the tour to get a broad overview of the features that Google offers.

As you can see there are three emails even before you've told all your best mates about your new address and imported your old email. These hold links to customizing the look and feel, importing your contacts and old email from other email services and using your mobile phone to see your email.

Logging in

Sometime has flown by and you haven't checked your email. You click open your browser, probably Internet Explorer, Chrome or Firefox. The horror, it's logged you out, how do I check it now?

Going directly there

Depending on if you bought this as a paperback or e-book, you could type in the following website address or highlight and copy it

http://mail.google.com

...and paste it into the address bar. Press *Enter* on your keyboard (otherwise known as *Return*) and you will be taken directly there.

Figure 17 Address bar

Fill in the boxes as in Figure 18, click on *Sign in* and you will be in to your email.

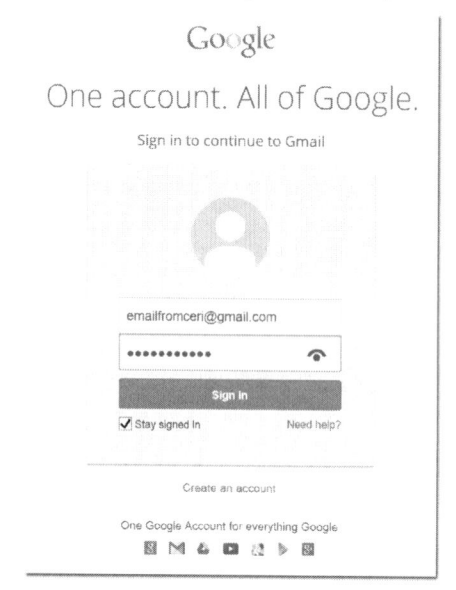

Figure 18 Signing in

Tip

Check the box next to *Stay signed in* to avoid typing in your password every day. Remember do NOT do this if you use a shared computer as other people would then have access to your account.

Adding Google as your homepage

If the first thing you do each day is check your Gmail account and search in Google, I recommend setting Gmail and Google as two separate tabs as your homepages. If you are using Internet Explorer click on the little gear wheel on the top right of your window, choose *Internet Options* and then choose *Use current* in the *Home page* section. Once you have done this click on *Apply* then *OK*.

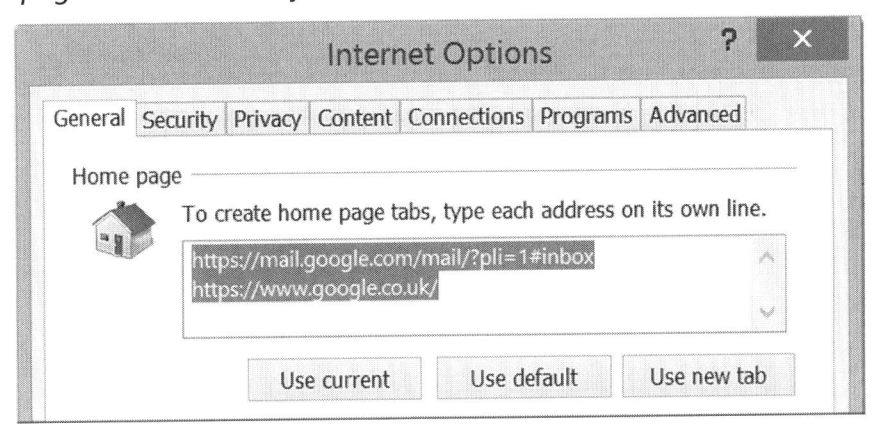

Figure 19 Putting Gmail as your homepage

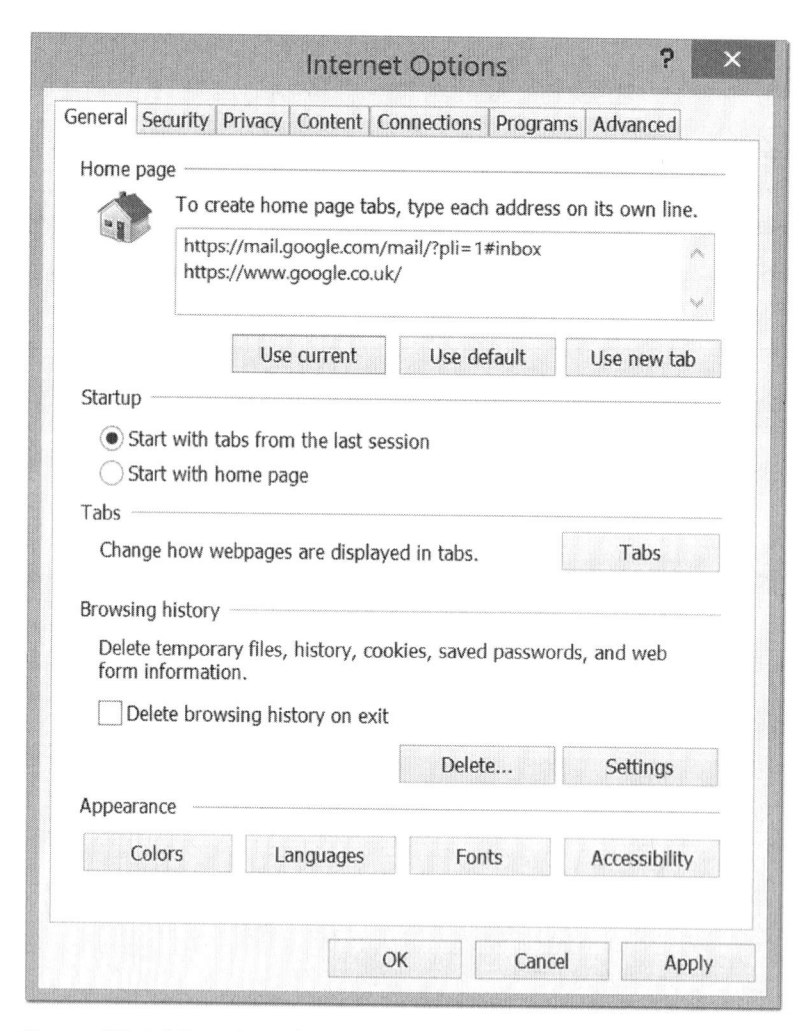

Figure 20 Adding Gmail and Google Search to your home pages.

These two pages will be the first pages you see when you load your browser. Selecting the little house icon on the top right of your browser will also bring up these pages from now on.

Getting Started

Figure 21 The home pages when Internet Explorer loads for the first time or the home icon is selected.

Reading Emails

This is the reason you created the account, right? Well this couldn't be simpler. As with every other email service out there, you just click anywhere on the email. The emails are displayed with who sent it first, the subject (what the email is about) and then the date it arrived. I'm interested in looking at my emails on my mobile so I click on the *The best of Gmail, wherever you are* email.

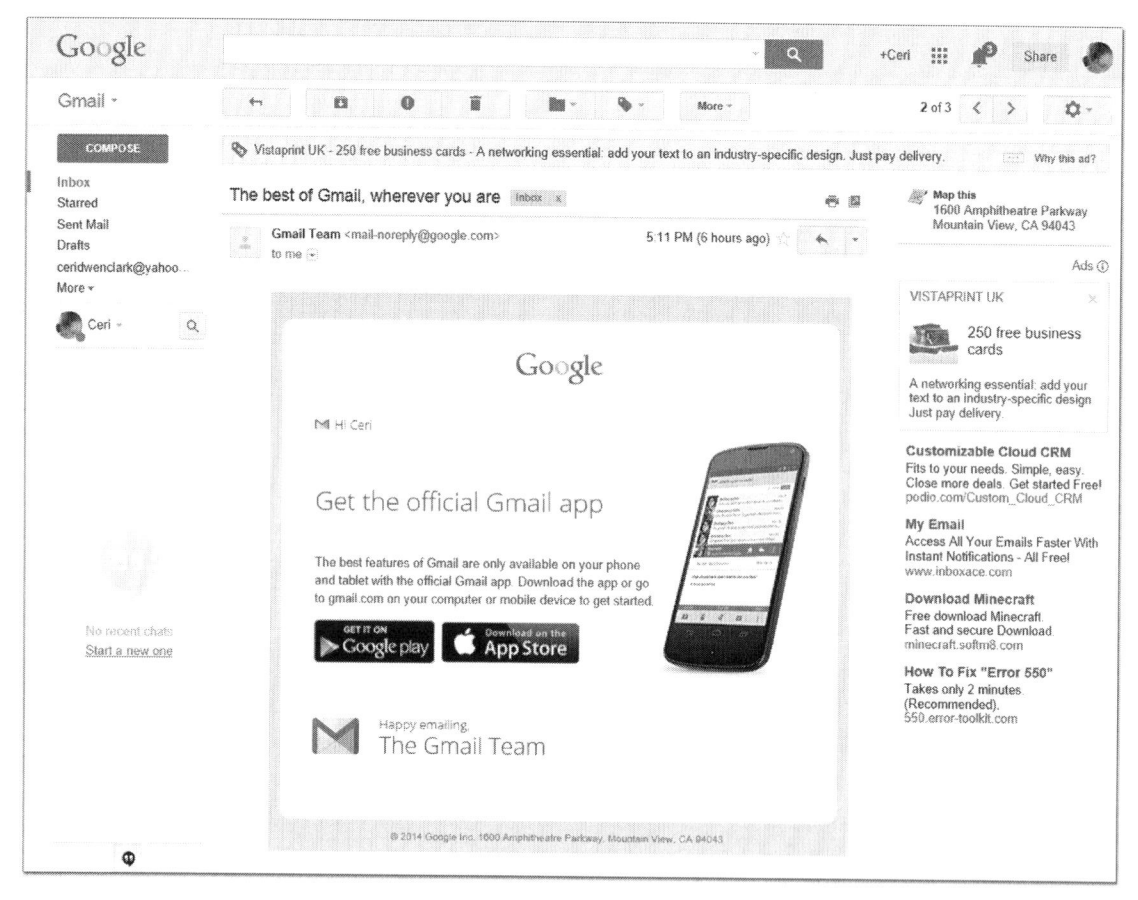

Figure 22 An example email

Images are sometimes blocked by Google. This is done to protect your computer but you can change this by changing the settings. If you would like to see the images in a particular email and it is blocked, Google will let you know as shown in Figure 22.

Figure 23 Displaying images in emails

Click on *Display images below* to see the email as it was meant to be viewed.

Getting Started

Once you have read the email, you can click on inbox, the Gmail logo, archive or delete to send you right back to the home screen.

Notice that once you have read an email, it is no longer bold.

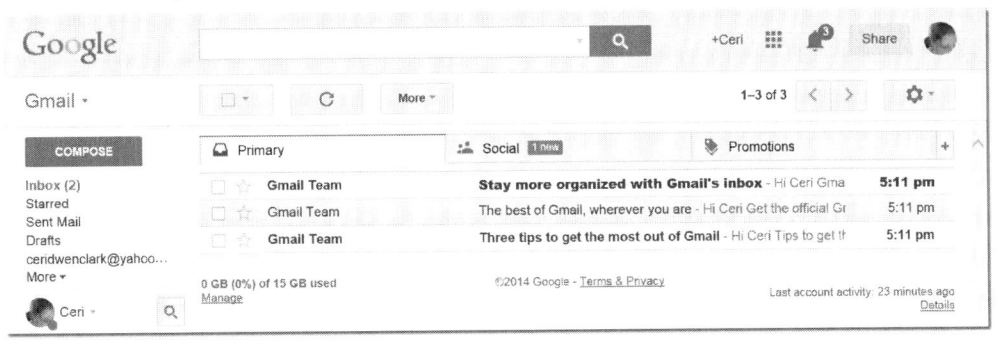

Figure 24 A read email greys out

To delete the email, click on the small box to the left of the email and then click on the picture of a bin/trash can above it. If you hover your mouse over the pictures, a little message pops up telling you what the picture means. I will go into more detail in the next chapter.

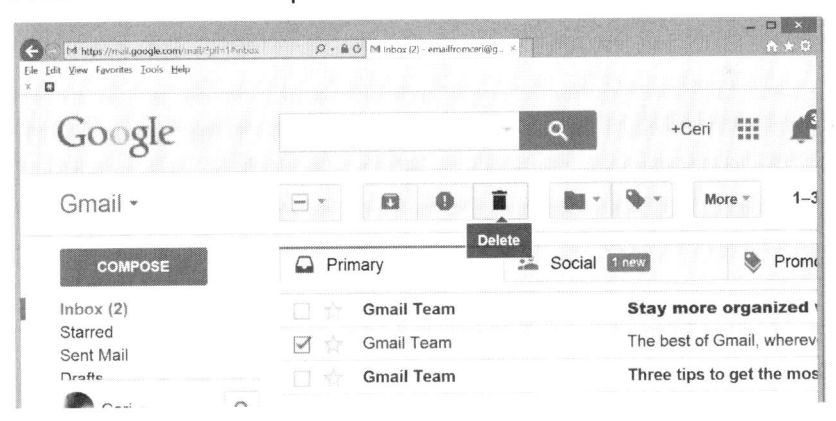

Figure 25 Trashcan image for deleting emails

Viewing Attachments

With Gmail you can look at attachments from right inside your browser. This means that if you don't have the software on your computer then you can still see most documents. You can view these documents as long as you have a) access to the internet and b) access to a browser.

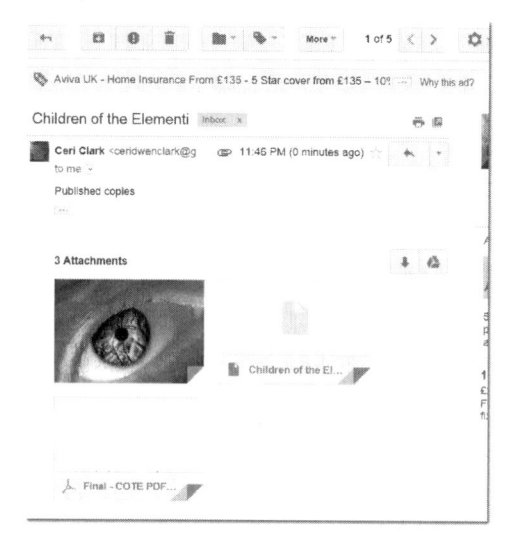

Figure 26 Attachments as they appear in an email.

Figure 26 shows how Google displays what documents are attached to the email. To view the options available you will need to hover your mouse over the pictures. As you can see, you can download them individually or all of the attachments at the same time.

Getting Started

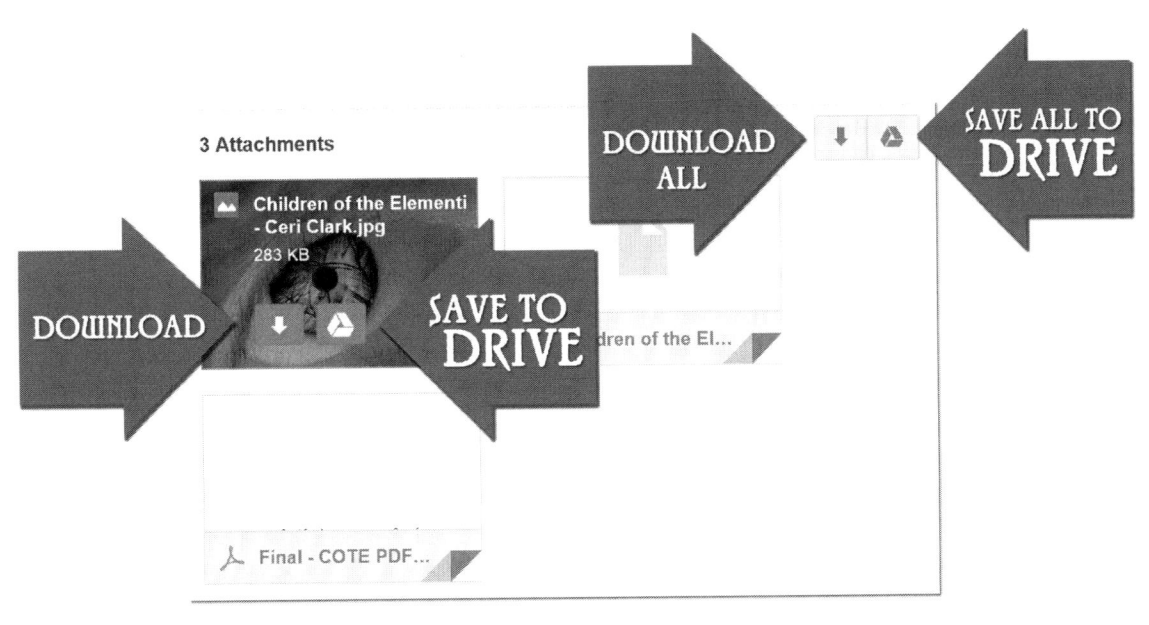

Figure 27 Attachment options

You can also get a preview of images by clicking on the images and they will load in your browser. If Google does not support the attachment file type, for example, a Mobi file, you can download the file on to your computer and use software from there. In this case Kindle for PC or Calibre.

Turn off Chat

If you are new to Google then there is plenty of time to find out more but to reduce the risk of information overload I recommend you turn off Chat

You can always reactivate it later, but for now there's so much to concentrate on.

First, go to the gear wheel at the top right of the screen, this is the main settings button, and then click on *Settings* as in figure 27.

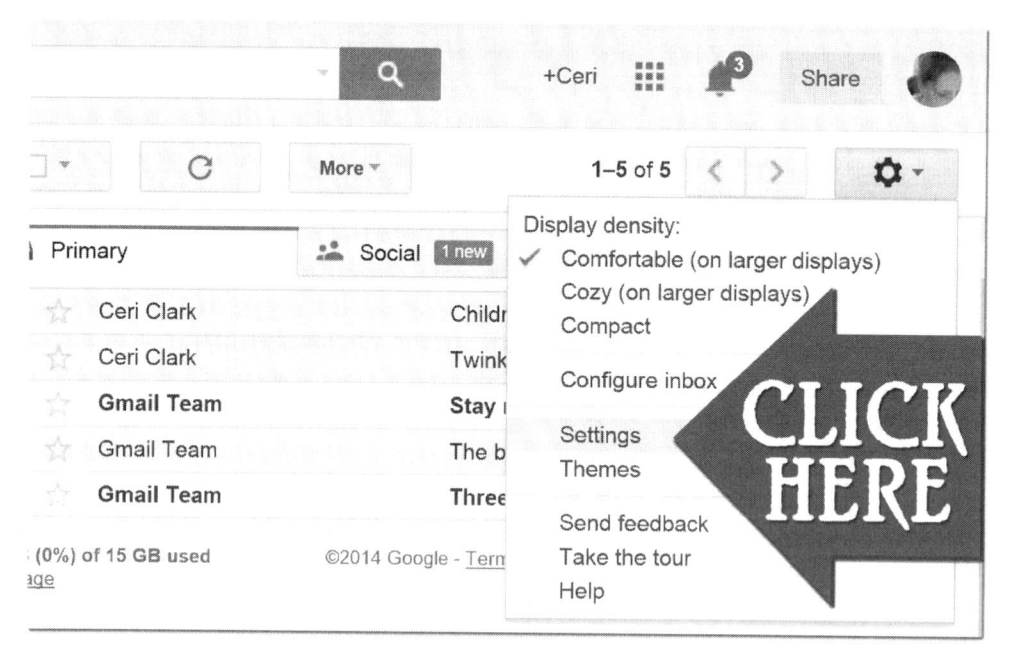

Figure 28 Location of settings button

A dropdown menu will appear when it is clicked on allowing you to choose *settings* to get the following screen.

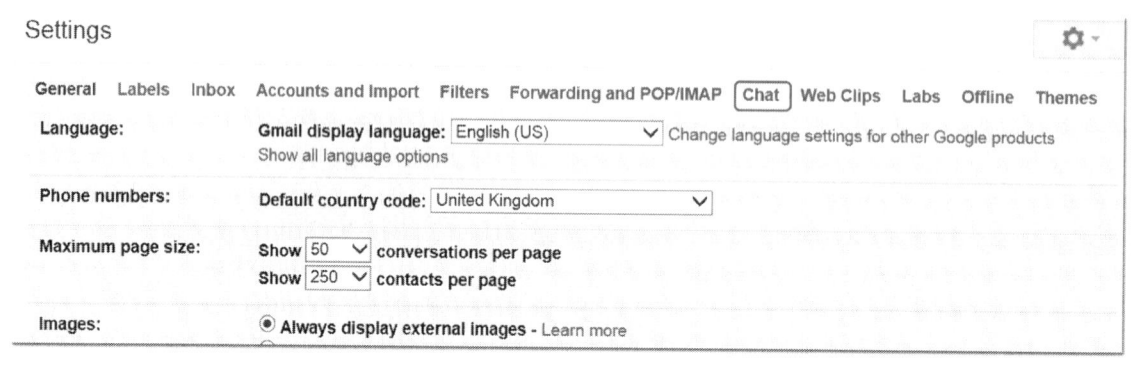

Figure 29 Chat settings

Go to the circled location labelled *Chat* (as above) to get all the settings relevant to Chat. Turn chat off by choosing *Chat off* and then clicking *Save Changes* at the bottom of the screen.

Reactivating Chat

If you would like to do this later, follow the steps in turning it off but choose *Chat on*.

Chapter 4 Security

What to expect in this Chapter:

- Passwords
- How to set up 2-step verification
- Spam and phishing

Securing your Google account is very important. The sum of all your emails, posts, contacts and other data can help someone to take advantage of you or use your details for their own use. Identity theft is a growing problem on the internet and you need to protect yourself as much as possible.

Passwords

I go into detail about this in *Chapter* 2 in the section called *Choosing your password*. Please read this for ways of choosing your password.

Changing your password

To change your password at any time, go to the settings page (the gear icon on the top right of the screen), then *Accounts and Import*. The *Change Password* link is the first item in the page as seen below.

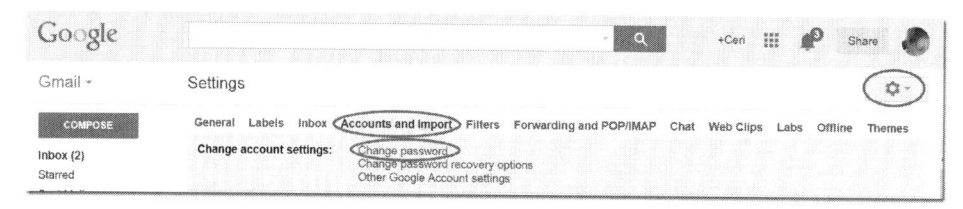

Figure 30 Password change location

Two-factor authentication

Changing your password regularly is a good way of securing access to your account, but remembering hundreds of passwords, constantly changing, can be a headache. Google's two-step verification can be an elegant solution to this for access to their website.

2-step verification/authentication is an extra step to make sure that access to your information, files and folders is restricted to you. Instead of relying just on a password (which can be discovered by nefarious means by hackers), a second device is used which you always have on you such as a phone or tablet computer. Any would-be infiltrator, bent on your destruction would need to have your password AND your phone to gain access to your account.

How to setup 2-step verification on Google

Go to your profile picture and click on it, then click on *Account* as seen below.

Security

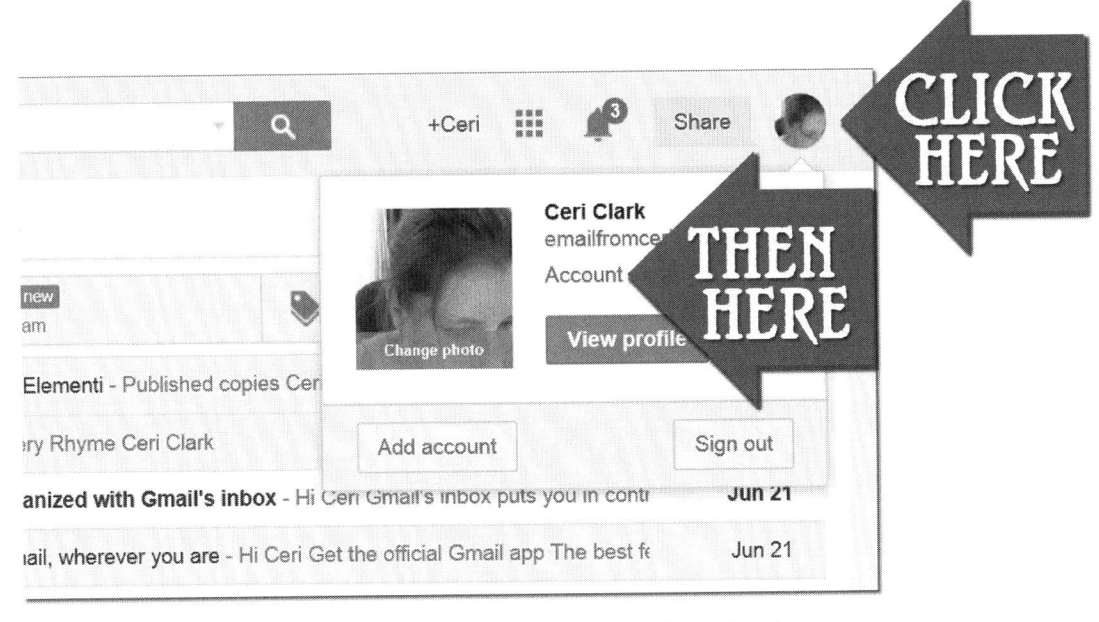

Figure 31 Go to your Account from Settings

Choose *Security* in the top navigation bar and then look down the page for the section labelled *Password* and click on *Setup* as seen in the next graphic.

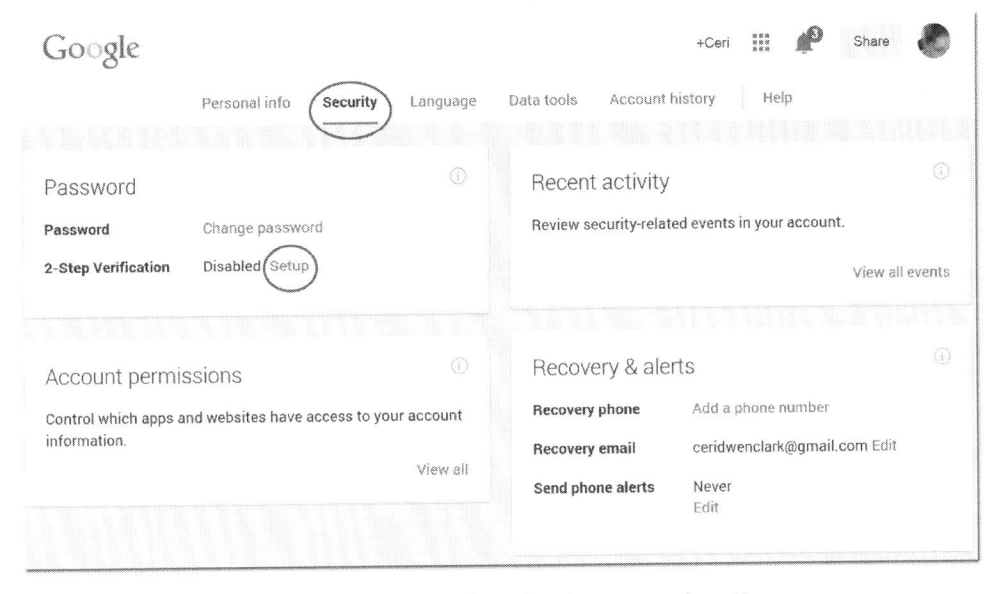

Figure 32 factor authentication setup location

The following page will load.

35

Ceri Clark | A Simpler Guide to Gmail

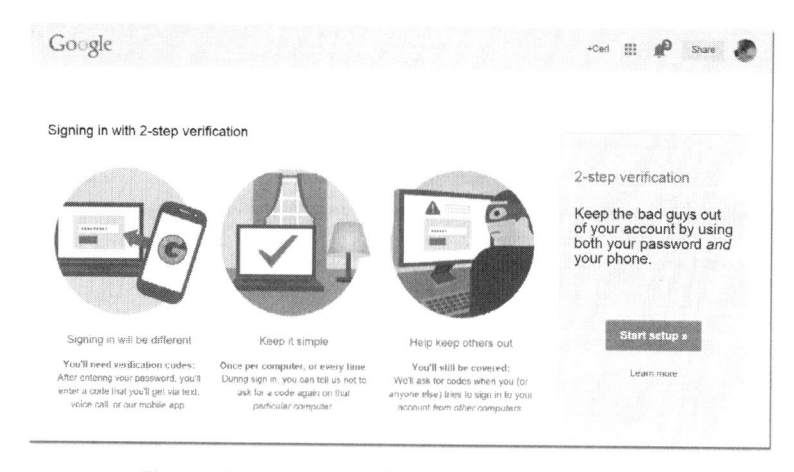

Figure 33 2-step verification welcome screen

Click on *Start Setup* in the box on the right of the screen and you will be directed to login in again. Once you do you will be taken to the page to setup the verification.

Type in your mobile/cell number in the space provided (making sure the correct flag is chosen to represent your country code i.e. stars and stripes for the US and the Union Jack for the UK) as illustrated in the next figure. Next, choose how you want the code to be sent to you. I chose SMS text verification. Click *Send code* and the code will be texted to you.

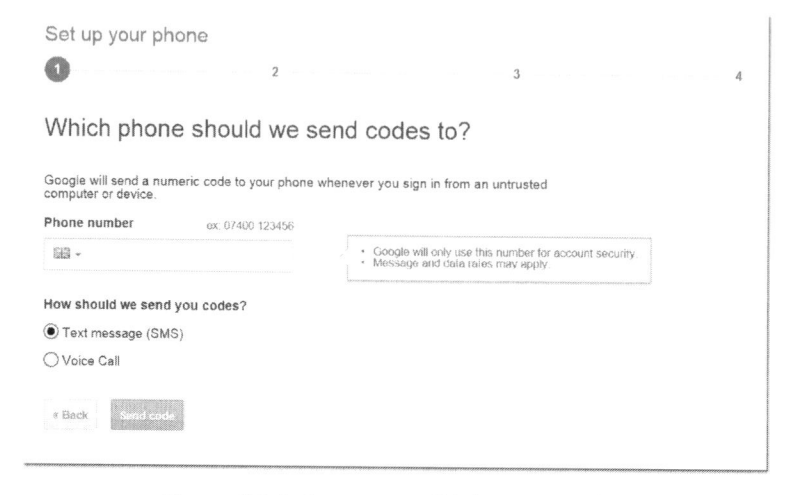

Figure 34 Enter your cell/phone number

Security

Take the code from your phone and enter it in the space provided in the form and click *Verify*.

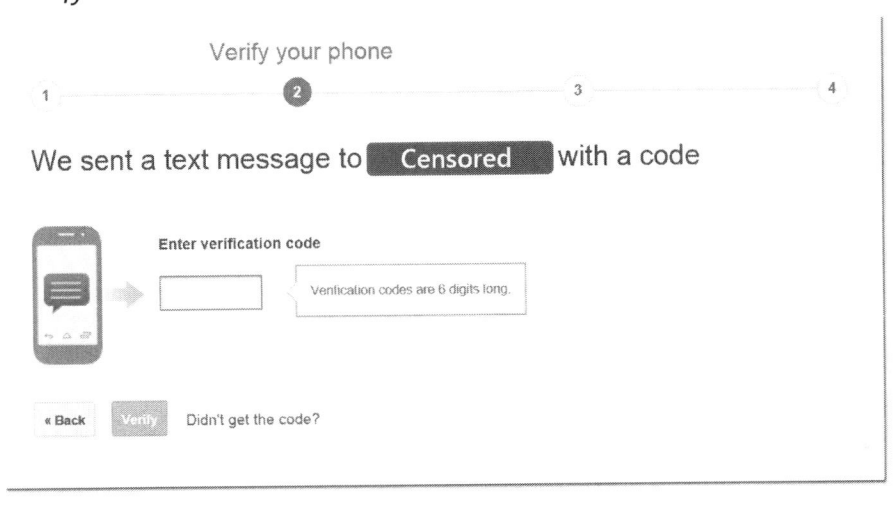

Figure 35 Enter the verification code

Check your phone and put in the code that was sent to you in box provided. Google will then ask you if you trust the computer that you are on. If you share a computer, say in a student house or an internet café then you will uncheck the box that says *Trust this computer*.

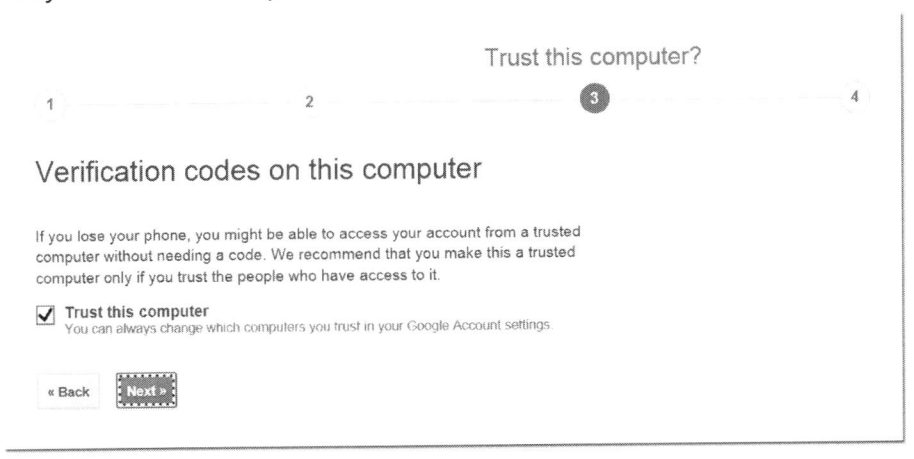

Figure 36 Do you trust the computer you are on?

Lastly for the setup, confirm if you trust the computer and that you understand that you will need to use special codes if you use other computers.

Ceri Clark | A Simpler Guide to Gmail

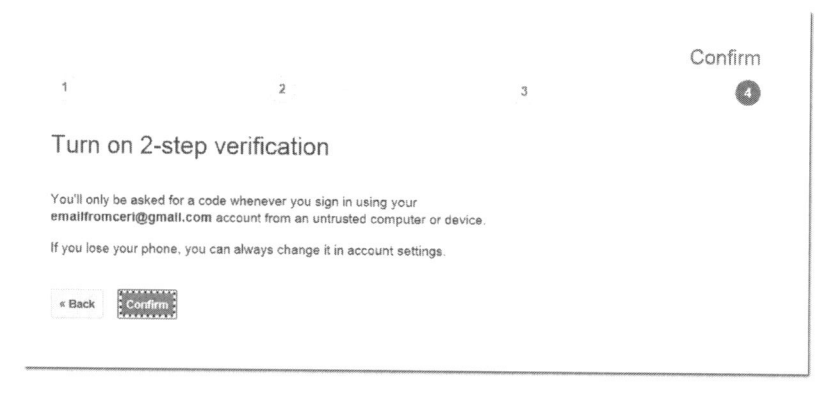

Figure 37 Confirmation

The following page will load:

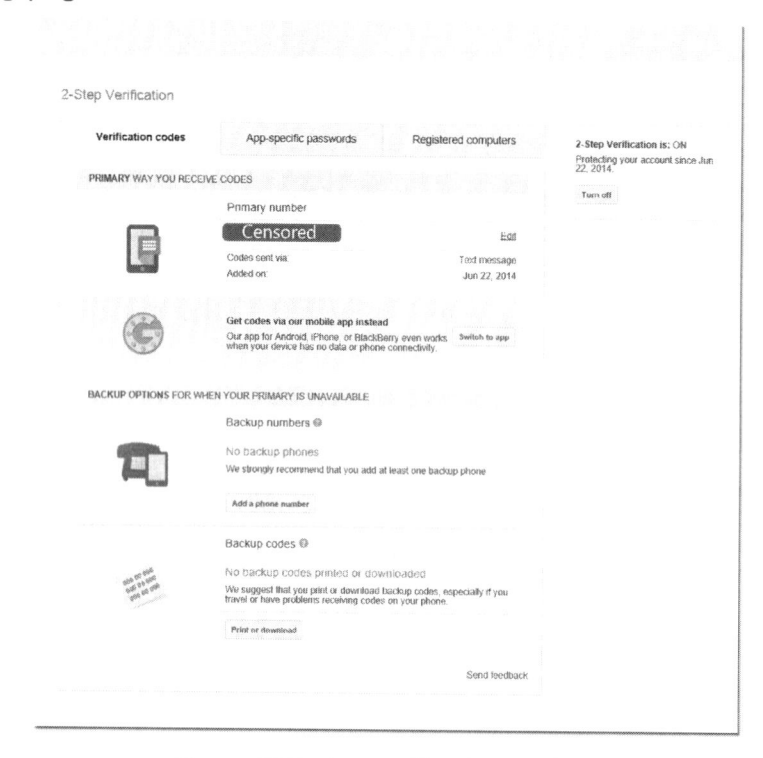

Figure 38 2-step verification settings

Backup access

Of course the main point of 2-step verification is to make it impossible to access your Gmail accounts but you don't want to be locked out of your own accounts

38

Security

either. This is why adding a backup phone and having backup codes will be a life saver when you really want access but you can't receive text messages or you don't have the authenticator app on a smartphone.

To add a backup phone number, click on *Add a phone number*. The rest is self-explanatory.

To get Backup codes, click on *Print or download* and a list of back up codes will be generated as in the next figure.

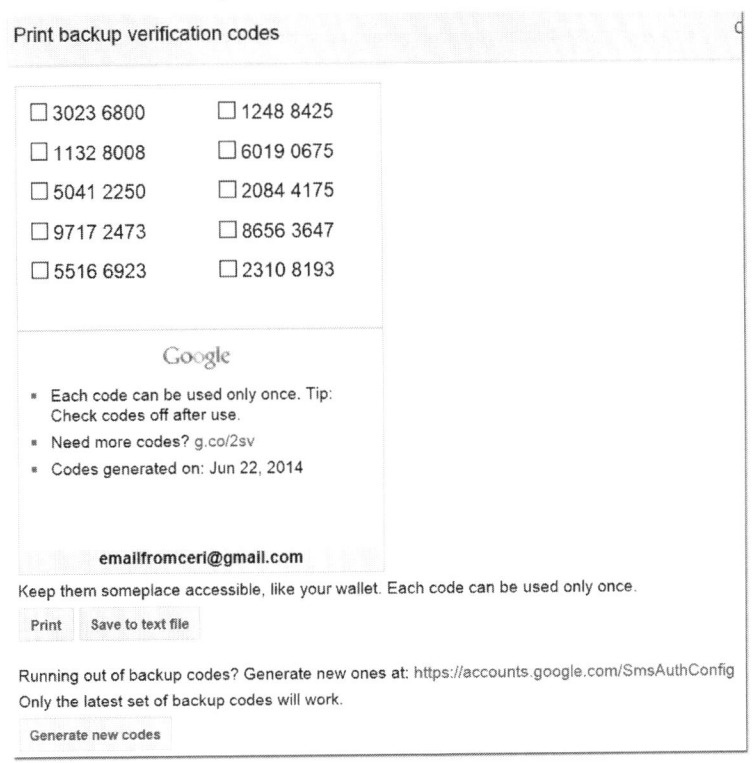

Figure 39 2-step verification settings

You can print these or save them to a text file.

Don't lose these and remember each code can only be used once. To generate more application specific codes simply click *on Generate new codes*.

39

Ceri Clark | A Simpler Guide to Gmail

Using Gmail or other Google Services on your mobile device(s)

If you use apps on mobile devices for any Google service, you will need to have application specific passwords for applications which aren't compatible with 2-step verification, to be able to access Google from them. *If you only access Google from your computer you do not have to worry about application specific passwords.*

You will need to generate some passwords that will only need to be inputted once for each application on a device. Click on *App specific passwords* tab on the top of the page and then *Manage application specific passwords*.

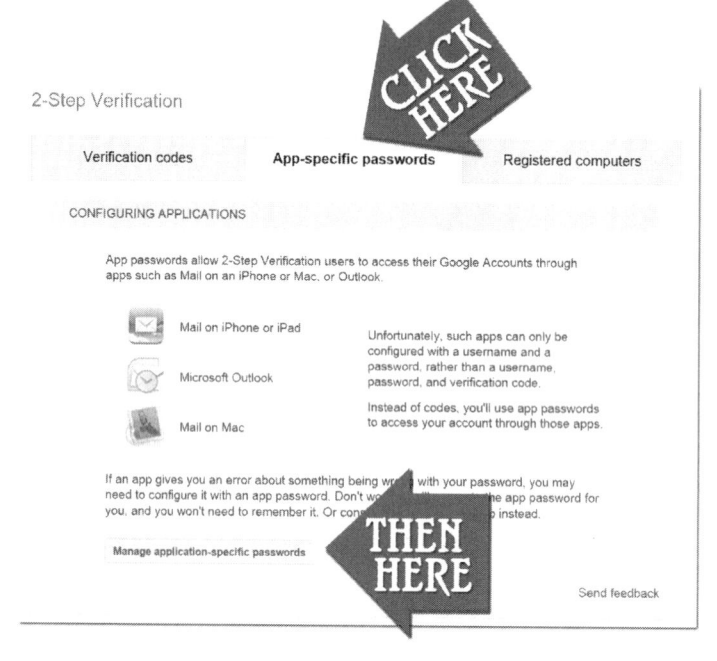

Figure 40 Manage your passwords for your mobile device(s).

You will of course be asked to login again.

I sometimes use my Gmail account on my smartphone and tablet using an email application. To generate a password for this, I typed *MailDroid Phone* (MailDroid or K9 are good 3rd party email applications) in the box provided on the page that loaded.

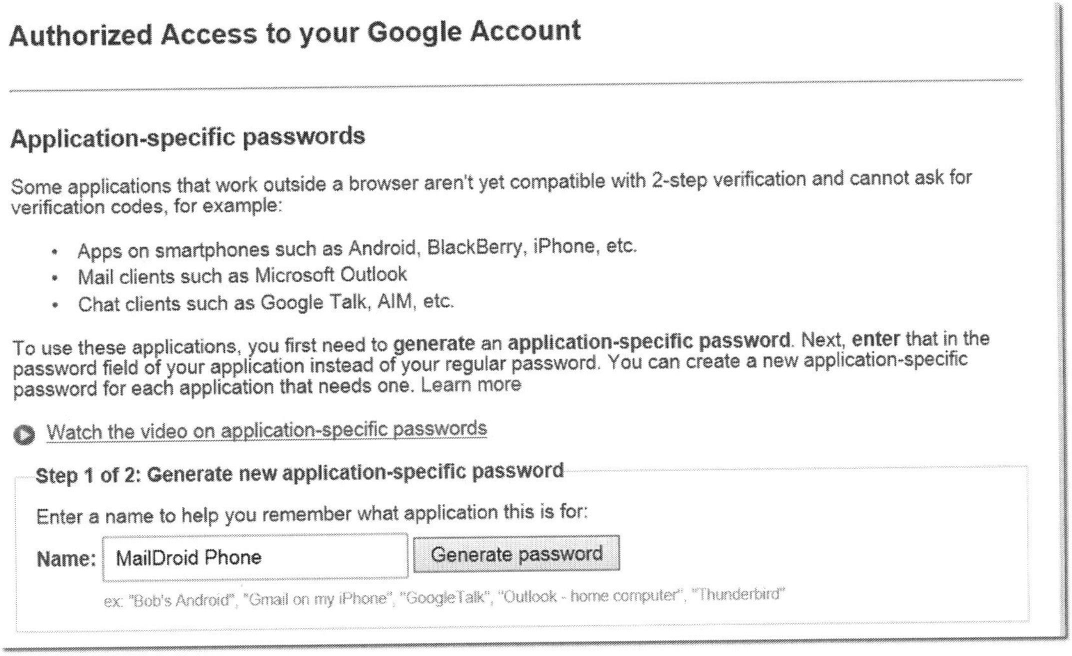

Security

> **Authorized Access to your Google Account**
>
> **Application-specific passwords**
>
> Some applications that work outside a browser aren't yet compatible with 2-step verification and cannot ask for verification codes, for example:
>
> - Apps on smartphones such as Android, BlackBerry, iPhone, etc.
> - Mail clients such as Microsoft Outlook
> - Chat clients such as Google Talk, AIM, etc.
>
> To use these applications, you first need to **generate** an **application-specific password**. Next, **enter** that in the password field of your application instead of your regular password. You can create a new application-specific password for each application that needs one. Learn more
>
> ▶ Watch the video on application-specific passwords
>
> ┌─ **Step 1 of 2: Generate new application-specific password** ──────────
> │ Enter a name to help you remember what application this is for:
> │
> │ Name: [MailDroid Phone]   [Generate password]
> │
> │   ex: "Bob's Android", "Gmail on my iPhone", "GoogleTalk", "Outlook - home computer", "Thunderbird"
> └──

Figure 41 Generating passwords for apps

Once you have typed the application name click on *Generate password*. On the next screen your one time only password will appear as illustrated in the next figure:

> **Authorized Access to your Google Account**
>
> **Application-specific passwords**
>
> ┌─ Step 2 of 2: Enter the generated application-specific password ─
> │ You may now enter your new application-specific password into your application.
> │ Note that this password grants complete access to your Google Account. For security reasons, it will not be
> │ displayed again:
> │
> │   pbdw wrpi akeo txws
> │   No need to memorize this password.
> │   You should need to enter it only once. Spaces don't matter.
> │
> │ [Done]
> └─
>
> **Your application-specific passwords**   **Creation date**   **Last used date**
> MailDroid Phone   Jun 22, 2014   Unavailable   [Revoke]

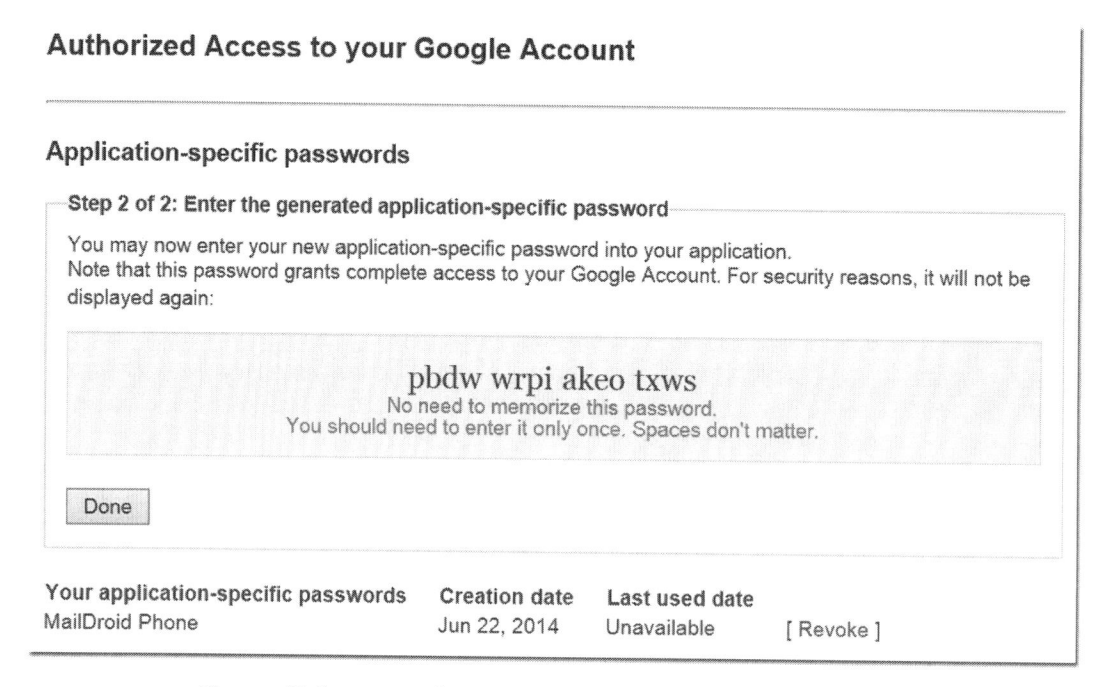

Figure 42 2-step authentication passwords generated screen

Notice that the application that you specified appears at the bottom of the screen? This is the beginning of a list of passwords you will have to generate for every application on all your mobile devices that you want to connect to Google. Click on *Done* to generate more passwords.

Google allows you to *Revoke* the password at any time by logging into your account. By doing this, if you lose your phone/tablet or other device then you can delete the passwords stopping anyone from accessing your account from that device.

If you have more than one device where you use the same application (for example, K9 on a tablet *and* a phone) I would recommend that you put the device name in the application name you chose. For example you could use K9Phone or K9Tablet depending on your preference.

Now that you have your password, type it in to the password field of the application that you want to use.

For MailDroid, I clicked on the email address, chose *Edit* and typed in the confirmation code without spaces into the password field. I was able to refresh the email as normal.

A word of warning, if you use MailDroid or another application that downloads your email, even if you use 2-step verification, someone can still access information already downloaded on to your phone. Even if there is a generated password in the application, information already on there can still be accessed but they won't be able to download new emails, therefore 2-step authentication should not be used as a replacement for password protecting your device and enabling encryption.

Accessing 2-step authentication after setup

To get back into your 2-step authentication go to:

Your profile picture > Account > Signing in > 2-step Verification

Using an Android app to gain verification codes

Every 30 days you will be asked to re-login, this also happens if you use a computer you haven't used before. You can get codes by SMS or using an Android app (Authenticator). This section explains how to use *Google Authenticator*.

First install "Google Authenticator" from Goggle Play (this used to be called Android Market) on your Android device, or App Store on your iPhone.

Ceri Clark | A Simpler Guide to Gmail

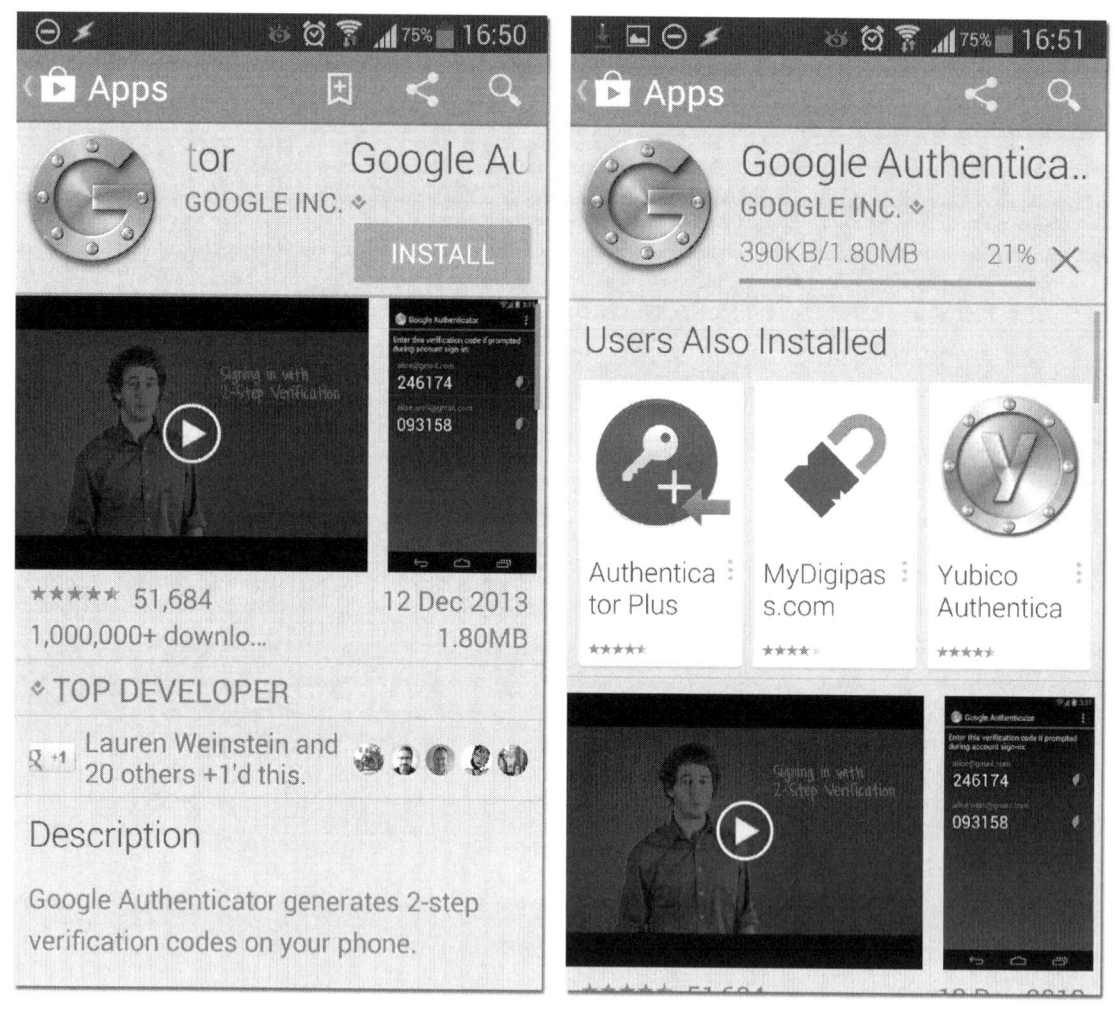

Figure 43 Google Authenticator in Google Play

Next go back to your 2-step verification administration panel by going to *Your profile picture > Account > Signing in > 2-step Verification*

As you we will be using Google authenticator, first click on *Switch to app* as seen in figure 44.

44

Security

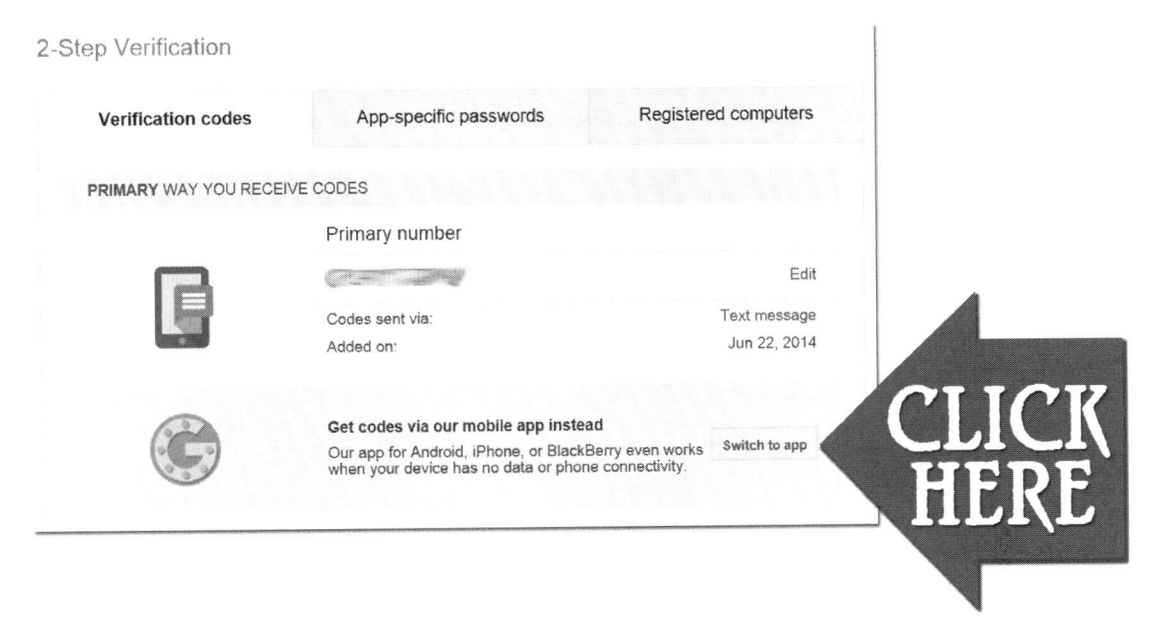

Figure 44 Switch to Google Authenticator

Then select the phone type from the options that pops up. In my case it was Android.

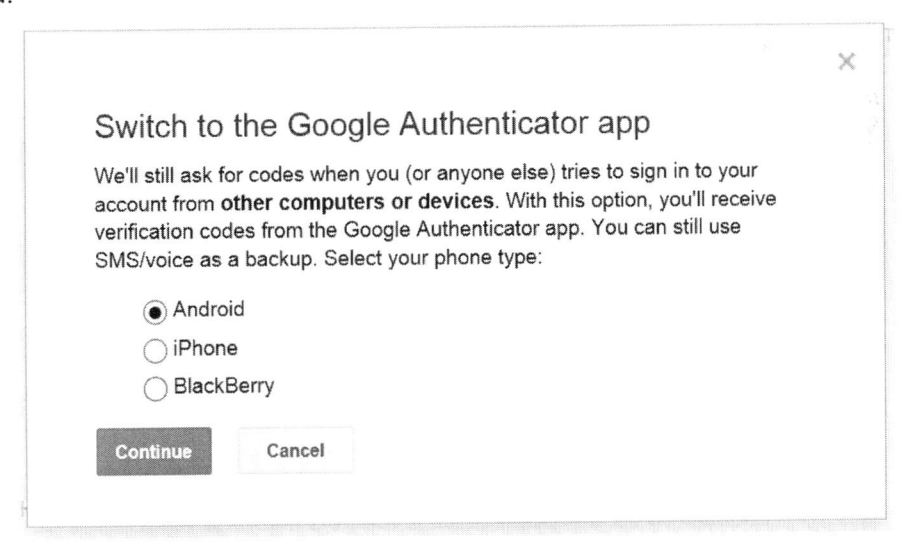

Figure 45 Select your device from the list

If you are using an iPhone or Blackberry, follow the on-screen instructions for those devices. Click on *Continue*.

45

A page will load with a barcode.

Figure 46 Mobile app authentication page

Go back to your mobile device and choose *Scan a barcode*. You can also use the code obtained earlier when setting up the 2-step verification initially but the barcode is easier (Especially if you forget the code).

Google's or another barcode scanning application will load. If you don't have a barcode reader already on your device, Google will suggest one and direct you to download it.

Use the camera on your device to view the barcode on the computer screen. Google Authenticator will then give you a unique code to type into the *code* at the bottom of the barcode page on your computer.

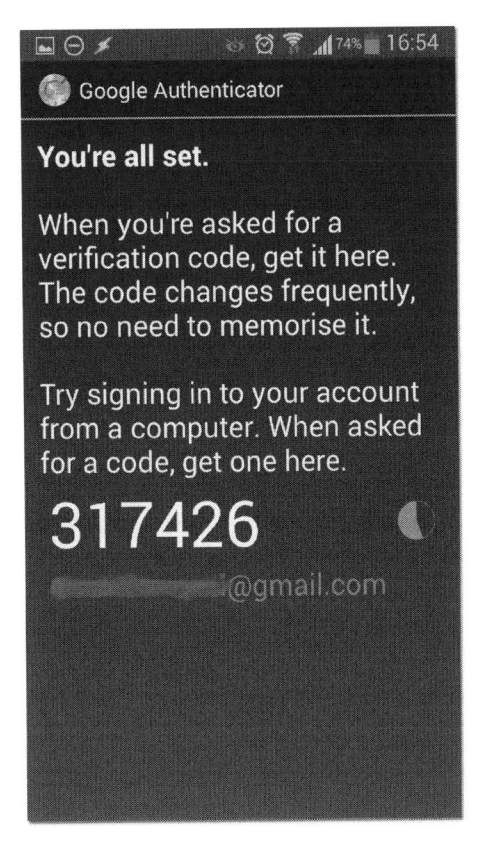

Figure 47 Google Authenticator code from a mobile device

After you click *Verify* on your computer you will receive a message to say your Android device is configured.

If you find that it doesn't work after a few attempts check the time and time-zone is correct on your mobile device.

Recognizing spam, scams and phishing emails

Spam, scams and phishing emails can be a security risk. They change all the time as the spammers/phishers get more sophisticated as time goes on but there are some things that make these messages stand out. This section is just some of the things you can look out for.

It's too good to be true

If you receive an email from a Nigerian prince/princess letting you know that they are in trouble but they will give you several million but only if you give them your bank details - this can be a good indication.

Another famous email scam is a foreign lottery/competition letting you know that you have won millions! This would be great but if you have never bought a ticket, but how likely is this actually to be true?

There are variations on these themes but they usually involve offering a large amount of money in unlikely circumstances.

Your friend is on Vacation and asks you for money

This is a scam where your friend's email account has been hacked and an email then sent to you stating that s/he is in trouble on vacation and could you send them a couple of thousand to help him/her out? If you get any emails like this, check that they have actually gone on holiday first!

If this has happened, tell your friend that his/her account might have been hacked. The hacker may have deleted all sent emails so it may not be obvious to them that there was a problem. They will need to change their password straight away and maybe enable 2 step verification.

A stranger sob story

A stranger is dying/ill/in trouble. Please send money quickly. I would ignore these emails. How did they get your address?

An email sent to yourself

In the past I have sent emails to myself to remind me to do things. If there is one person I trust it is me! If I am very distracted it is not beyond the bounds of possibility that I could click on one of these emails by mistake. There is a scam where people have faked the email address so it looks like you have sent an email to yourself. Think before clicking on any links!

Bad grammar and spelling

A tell-tale sign of a malicious email is bad grammar and poor spelling. If you get an email with these features, handle with care.

Bank emails

Your banks will never ask you for personal information by email. They will also never give you a link to click on to log in. If you receive emails that ask for this, use a direct link you already have. These are usually on letters and statements from your bank.

Some of these emails will say your account has been hacked, some money has gone missing or something along these lines. They will encourage you to click on a link in their email which will take you to a special website which will look like your bank's website but will be owned by the scammers. These emails are known as phishing emails. They will ask you to put in your username and password which they will then record. You will be redirected to your actual bank and you will probably not know what has happened until your real bank contacts you by phone or letter.

The way to avoid this is to never click on any link in an email that appears to be from your bank but to go and have a look at your bank's website directly.

The unsubscribe link

Most of the time you will receive emails that you have signed up for in the past. You may not want them anymore but they are not spam as you originally asked for them. To stop receiving these, click on the unsubscribe link which is usually at the bottom of emails that have them.

Occasionally you will receive offers, promotions and other emails that you don't remember signing up for. If this happens to you, don't use the unsubscribe link. This is because these are spam messages used to try and get your details. Sometimes it is just to see if your email address is genuine. A good give-away for this is if your name is in the CC of the email (for example John Smith) but you can also see John A Smith, John B Smith, Jonnie smith etc. in there. They are trying every combination they can think of to get a hit. Other times it is to get other information such as a username or password. If you have different passwords for every website this is not a problem but a lot of people keep the same password for a lot of sites. Once they get hold of *that* password, they have access to those websites which could be banks or stores.

Chapter 5 Sending and Receiving Emails

What to expect in this Chapter:

- What are discussion threads
- How to reply and forward an email
- Composing and formatting emails
- Spell checking
- Deleting emails

Emails are dealt with a little differently in Gmail from some other email services. As long as the subject is the same, everything in one conversation is held in one place. No more searching through your Sent folder to find what you said! This section talks about how to send email but also how the discussion threads work.

Discussions

Discussion threads are conversations. Please see Figure 48 below for an example. If I have sent the email from this Gmail account then it will appear as *me*. Once read, it will go gray as illustrated below.

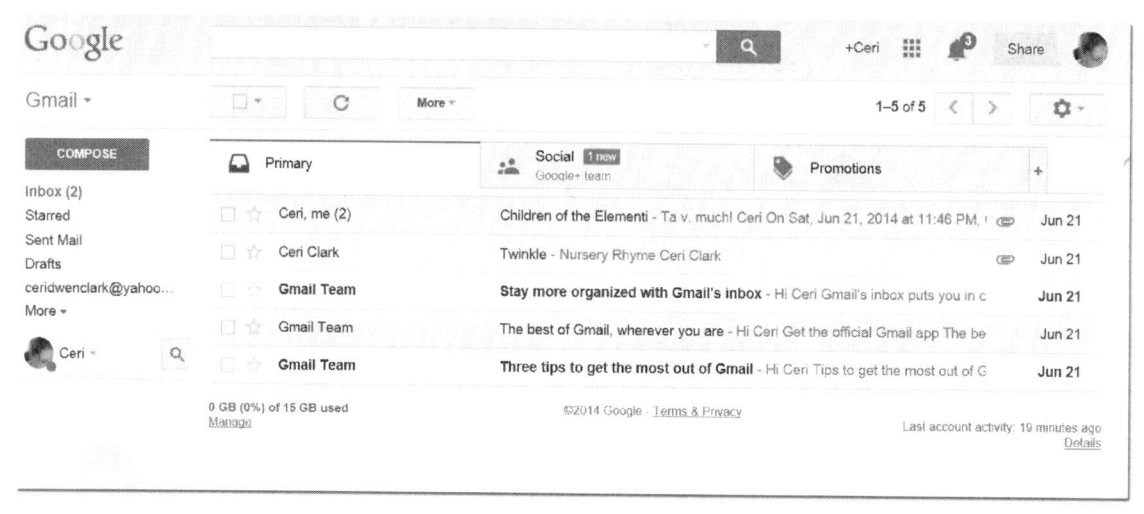

Figure 48 Example of a discussion thread

Notice next to *Ceri*, the number lets me know how many emails are in the discussion. If anyone sends me an email later, it will revert to white (until I click on it) and the two will become a three. Next to the subject Google has also put some of the first line of the email visible, so I can decide if I want to read it or not.

Click anywhere on the row and it will take you to the conversation.

A thread will look like this:

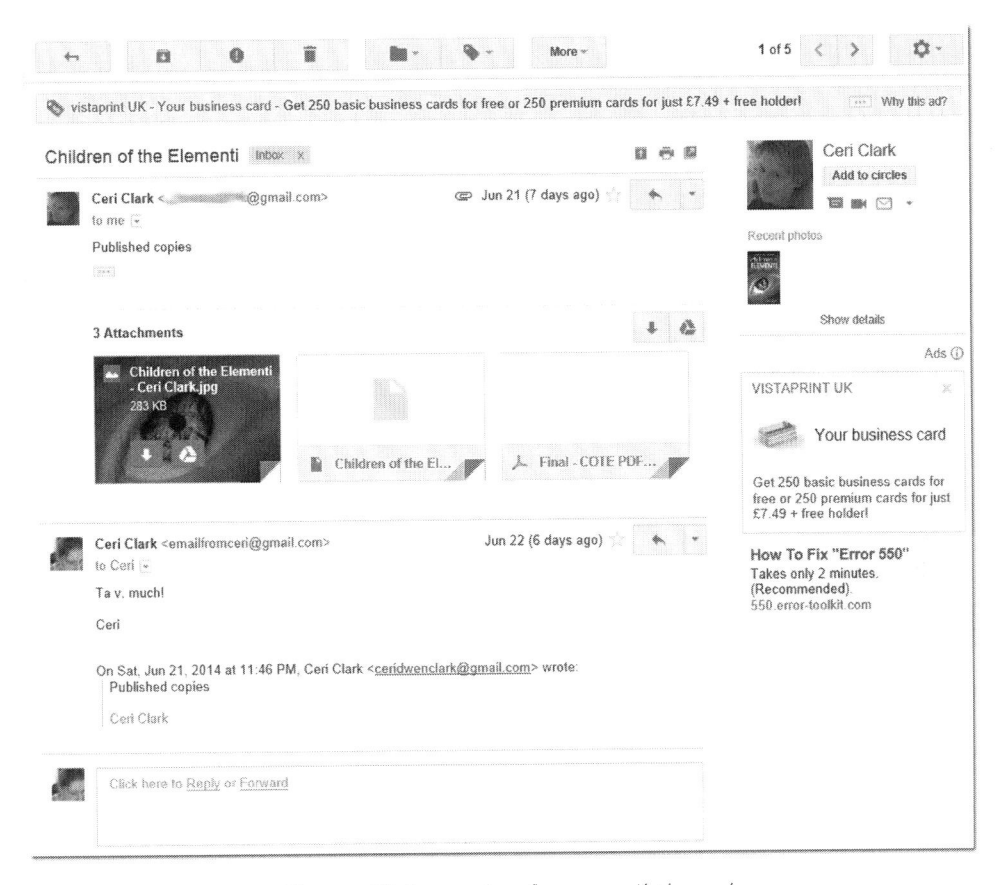

Figure 49 Example of an email thread

If you are not sure which email is the latest, look at the date at the top right of each email, which also tells you how long ago the email was sent. In the example above, the first one arrived on June 21 and the next one was sent on June 22.

In the right pane, information is held on your contact, including other ways to contact them. You can add them to your Google+ circles by clicking on *Add to circles* or by clicking on the symbols below *Add to circles*, you can:

- start a hangout
- start a video call and
- email your contact, as well as
- edit contact details and
- view recent mail from your contact.

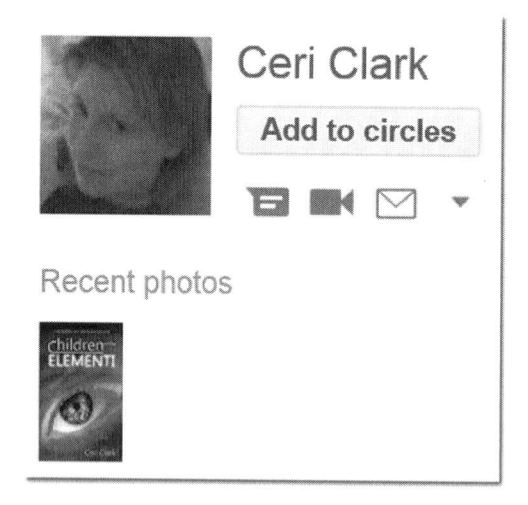

Figure 50 Other ways to contact your friends and acquaintances

These options are a quick way of getting in touch with your contact or editing their details straight from the email you are looking at.

Replying and forwarding an email

Replying to an email is as simple as clicking on *Reply*! Google has made this extra easy by giving us two places to use this. At the top of the email on the right hand corner there is a grey box with an arrow in it as seen in figure 50. Clicking on this will bring up a drop-down list. The top option will be *Reply*. Of course there is always the *Reply* at the foot of each email beside *Forward*.

Sending and Receiving Emails

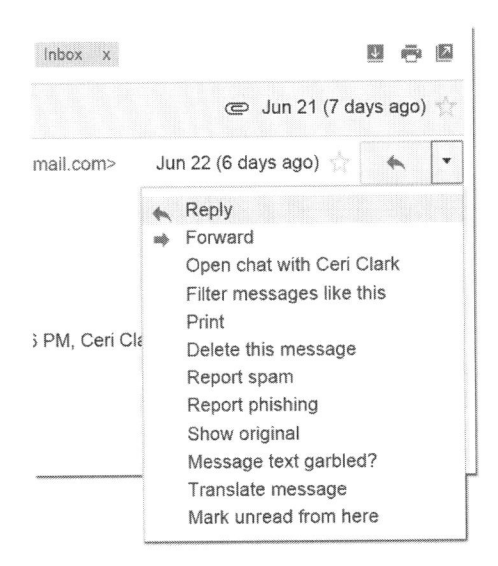

Figure 51 Email options from Reply button

The reply box looks as below. Type in the white spaces and then click *Send*. Your email will automatically get saved by Google. You will then be able to find it again in *Drafts* later, at the left of the screen.

The box where you reply looks very simple but it is deceptive and once you delve into the buttons, there are a lot of options.

Figure 52 Initial reply screen

The convention is to write your reply above the message you are replying to. This means that your correspondent does not have to go looking for your answer. If you are replying to a friend then this does not matter as they will love you enough to go looking for your reply, but if you are using your email for business you do not want to annoy your customers/contacts before they have even read your message.

Google has made this easy by automatically putting your reply first. If you click on the three little arrows under your message but above the button marked *Send*, then the rest of the email thread will appear below your message.

If you clicked on *Reply* but you actually wanted *Forward*. You can rectify this easily by clicking on the little downwards pointing arrow by the bigger arrow (pointing left) next to the profile picture as seen in figure 53. You can also edit the subject here but bear in mind that when you change the subject, your message will appear as a new thread to your recipient and in your sent emails (which might be confusing if you are looking for it later).

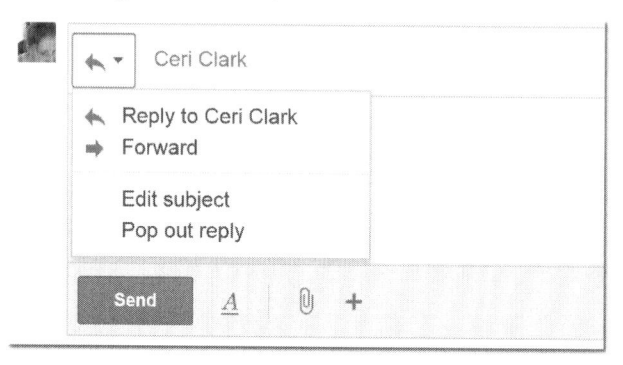

Figure 53 Reply options

If you click on *Pop out reply*, you will be able to type in your message above your main browser emails. This will mean you can refer to other emails while writing your message.

Sending and Receiving Emails

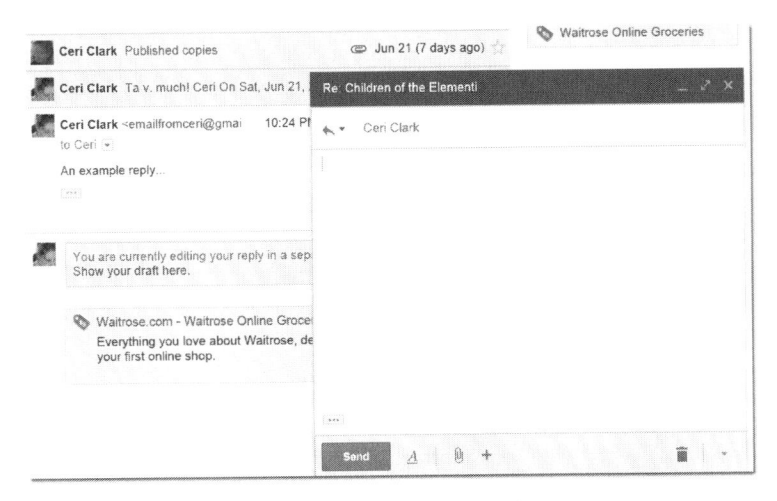

Figure 54 Pop out reply

Once you have clicked on *Send*, you will get a message highlighted in yellow to tell you it has been sent.

Figure 55 Your message has been sent

Forwarding uses the same method but you will have to put in the email address of the person you want it to go to.

The options for formatting an email will appear in the *Composing an email* section below.

Tip

If you want to reply or forward to a particular message rather than the whole thread, choose the box the message is in from the thread and click the Reply button on that particular message. You can choose not to include quoted text.

Replying to a group

If an email has been sent to more than one person in the *To* or *CC* part of an email, then you will have the option to *Reply to all*. Don't do this unless you really want everyone to see your message. The only way to stop the email going to everyone is if you just click on *Reply* and manually add people's email address or when you click on *Reply to all*, you have to delete the people you don't want to see your message manually from the email. You can do this by pressing on the x to the right of each person's name.

Composing an email

Composing an email is a simple process, in the first column of the page, click on the box labelled *Compose*. See below for what it looks like.

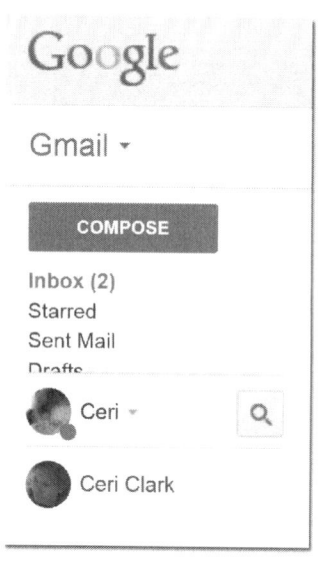

Figure 56 Where to find Compose (mail)

The compose page will load as a pop up on top of your other messages, ready for you to fill in.

Sending and Receiving Emails

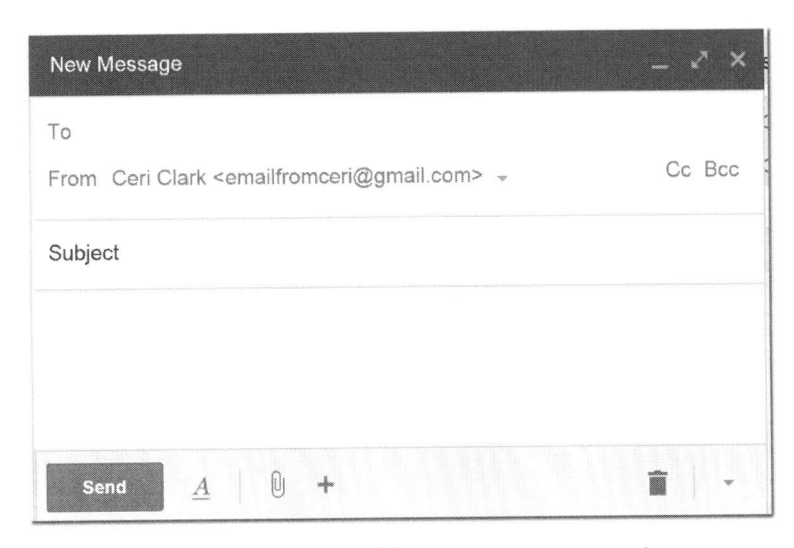

Figure 57 Example of the Compose pop up box

Clicking on the *To* will bring up your address book but I am assuming you don't have one yet. If you know the email address, just type it into the white box. Then type in a descriptive subject and what you want to say in the large box. If you are ready click *Send*.

Formatting your email

You might think your email is a little boring without formatting. As in a lot of word processors you can change the way an email looks and feels by highlighted what you want changed and clicking the B for Bold button, I for italics etc. These used to be lined up above the text box but now you have to click on the *A* with a red arrow underneath to see the formatting options.

Ceri Clark | A Simpler Guide to Gmail

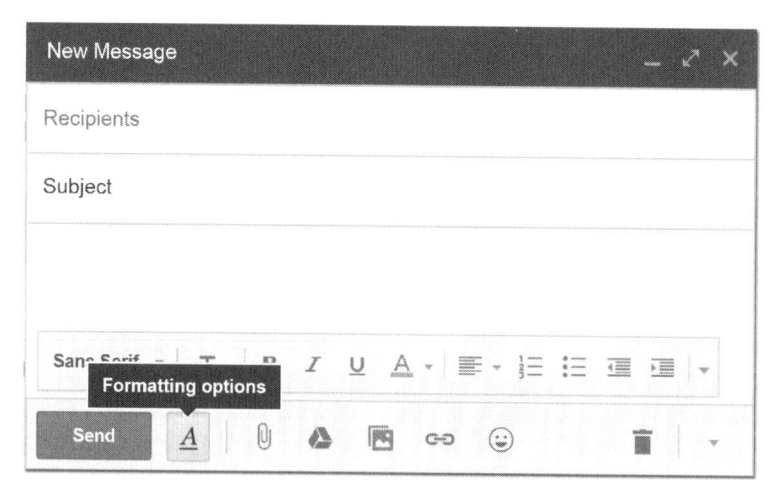

Figure 58 Location of formatting options

The formatting options are very like those in any standard word processor. If you are familiar with one of these then you will know how to use this.

Figure 59 Formatting options

The above image shows what the buttons look like:

- *Sans Serif* – clicking on this will allow you to change font (Sans Serif is the name of a font)
- *Two* Ts – Clicking on this button will make your text bigger or smaller.
- *B* – Bold your text
- *I* – Italicize your text
- *U underlined* – Underline your text
- *A underlined* – Change the color of your text
- *Six horizontal lines* – How do you want your paragraphs aligned/justified?
- *Horizontal lines with numbers* – Bullet your text with numbers
- *Horizontal lines with dots* – Bullet your text with circles (like this list).

Sending and Receiving Emails

- *Horizontal lines with an arrow pointing left* – Indent your text to the left
- *Horizontal lines with arrow pointing* right – Indent your text to the right
- *Quotation mark* – Quote the text
- *Underlined T with cross* – Remove formatting

Adding a link to your email

You may find you want to link to an item at your favorite store such as Amazon for a present or to an article you think your friend mind find particularly interesting.

To add a link to the main body of text click on the little picture that looks like a chain in the row beginning with the *Send* button (as seen in figure 58 above). Fill in the *Text to display and To what URL should this link go?* box and click on *OK*.

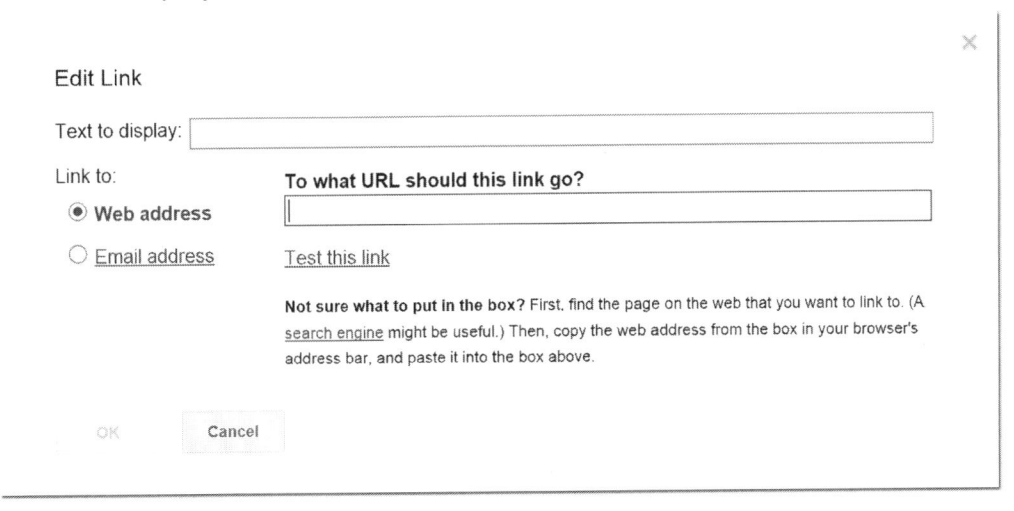

Figure 60 Adding a link to your email

Spell Check

Spell Check is an amazing tool which Google provides for free. To take advantage of this feature click on the little arrow located in the bottom right corner or the pop up box (as seen circled in figure 61).

61

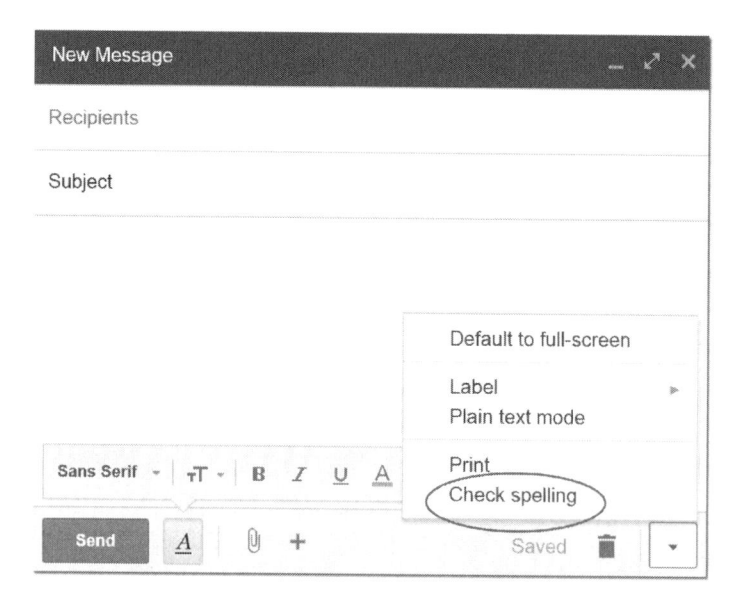

Figure 61 Location of spell check

Once clicked, the spelling mistakes will be highlighted in yellow as shown in figure 61 below.

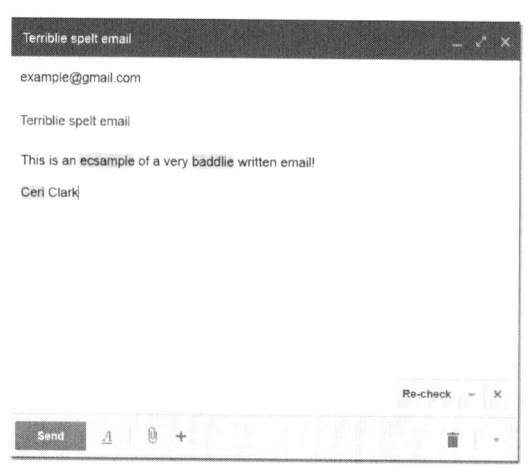

Figure 62 Spell checking

To see Google's suggestions and correct the spelling mistakes, click on the highlighted text.

Sending and Receiving Emails

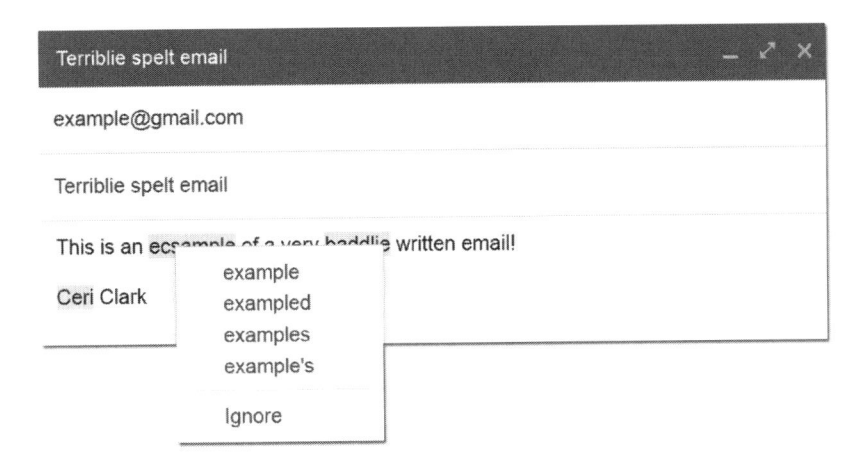

Figure 63 Example of a spell check list

Once a misspelt word is clicked, a list of options appears. Select which one you think is right and click on it. The word will be replaced and the yellow highlighting will disappear. You can click on *Re-check* by clicking on the little arrow at the bottom right of the compose box.

Deleting an email

To delete messages before they are sent click on the little trash symbol at the bottom right of the window. To delete emails that are sent to you, first go to the homepage of your email by clicking on the Gmail logo, then click on the little box to the left of each email that you want to delete. This adds a tick to the box, and then click on the trashcan icon which will appear above your emails list.

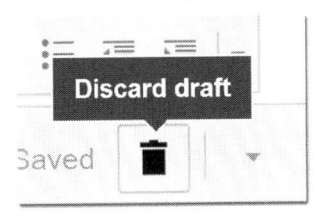

Figure 64 Discard draft button in the compose window

Chapter 6 Address Book (Google Contacts)

What to expect in this Chapter:

- How to add contacts to your address book
- Adding pictures
- Editing contacts

Keeping all your contacts online is a great idea. As well as saving on paper, it also means that you can update your contacts wherever you are, whether at home or on a mobile device when travelling. It is all about convenience.

How to add contacts using the Gmail website

First go to the contacts page, this is usually under *Gmail* and above *Compose*. Please see Figure 64 for a visual clue. Google has a habit of moving things around but in the version at the time of writing the Contacts link can be found by clicking on the little arrow next to *Gmail* at the top left of the screen as in figure 64.

Ceri Clark | A Simpler Guide to Gmail

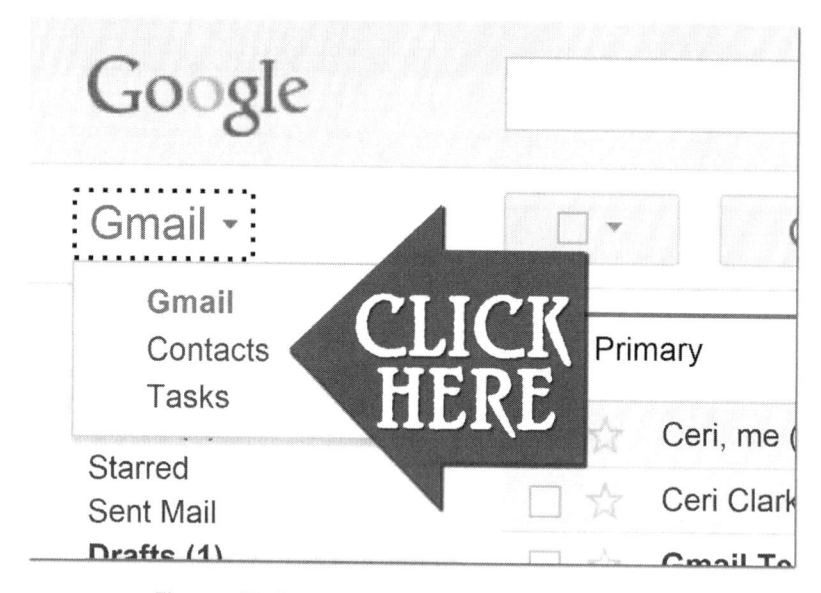

Figure 65 Contacts location on home screen

Once the page has loaded click on *New Contact* on the left of the screen (as shown in Figure 65). This is usually the first option under Contacts on the left of the page.

Figure 66 New Contact button

Address Book (Google Contacts)

Adding a contact using an email address

If you know the email address of your contact and they have a public profile with Google, you can automatically fill in the fields just by clicking into the email field and adding the email address.

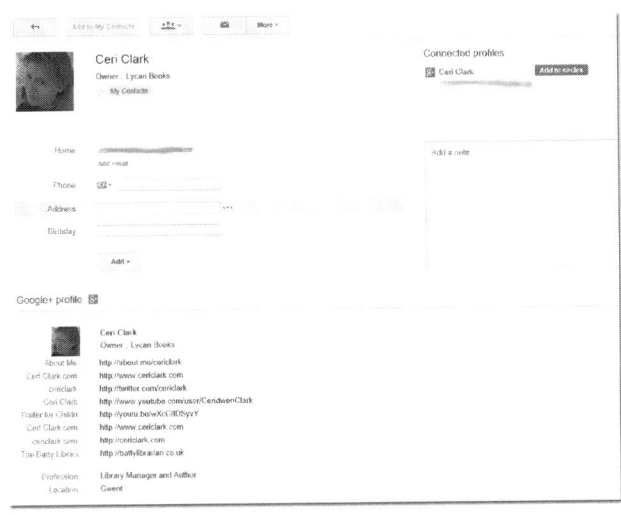

Figure 67 Adding your contact by inputting their email address

The above figure shows my details filled into a contact just by adding my email address. If you look to the top right of the screenshot (or the screen if you have a contact's page on Gmail open) you can see that you can add your contact to your Google+ Circles by clicking on the red button labelled *Add to circles*.

You will still need to fill in details like address and phone number for example as most people will keep these details private. Simply type in the boxes and click out of them (or into the next one) to put in the details. Google will automatically save the information you type in.

Manually Adding a Contact

The first thing you should do is click on *Add name*, once you do this you just need to start typing the name and click out of the box when you are done.

Figure 68 Adding your contact's name

If you are not happy with what you have written or want to add more detail you can hover your mouse over the name and click on the three dots which appear. Click on those three dots and a window will load as in figure 68 with more lovely fields to fill in. You can of course just press the trash/rubbish bin symbol to delete what you have written. If you are of a pedantic disposition, this is wonderful as you can specify a prefix like Mrs, Ms, Mr etc or even a suffix like PhD. In my example, I've awarded my fictional character an OBE from the Queen. I have a high class of fictional friends. Ahem, once the fields are filled in, click *Save*.

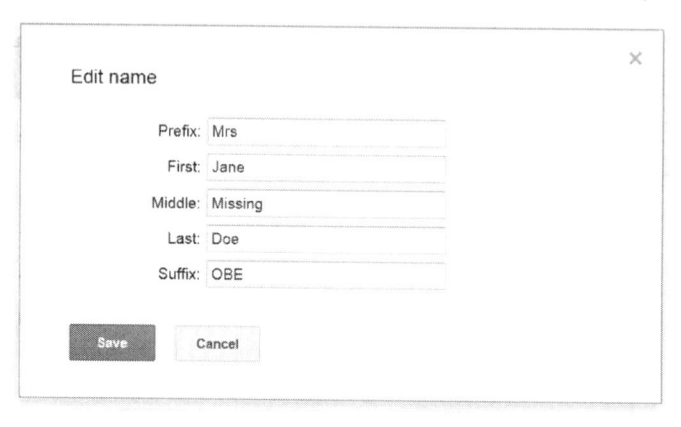

Figure 69 Editing a contacts name

Address Book (Google Contacts)

Adding Pictures to Contacts

If you are syncing your Google Contacts with your phone, then it is always nice to have your friend's picture on your contacts. Even if you are just browsing, a picture can more quickly find your friend than browsing names down a list.

By clicking on *Add a picture*, a pop up will appear asking you to browse your computer for a suitable picture. Remember to click *Save* when you are done.

Figure 70 Adding a picture to your contact

You may notice from figure 70 that you have a few options for adding pictures. You can click on *Upload* to get pictures from your computer, obtain photos already in your Google account, profile photos or no photo at all. You can also drag and drop a photo from your computer directly on to your browser window to upload it.

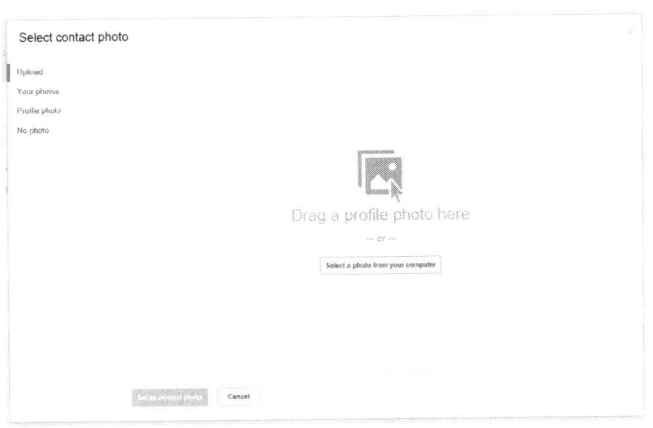

Figure 71 Adding a picture to a contact

If you want to change the picture later, hover your mouse over the existing image and click. You will get the option to change it.

Filling in the fields

Email, *Phone* and *Address* can all be customized. Once you add in your friend's email address, click out of the box and it will automatically save the address. (If you know the email address of your contact and they have a public Google profile all their public details will be filled in by default).

Google will assign the email address as the *Home* address of the contact you are adding. To change this hover your mouse over *Home* and click on the drop down arrow that appears. You have a choice of *home*, *work* or *custom*. If you choose *custom* then when you have clicked on a blank piece of screen, a message to say *Type here* will show. Click on here and type in what the email is for. Home and work are the usual email address types but your friend could have two jobs or she could just have several email addresses. You can keep on adding email addresses by choosing *Add email* which appears under the email address you have entered.

Phone and address is similar, follow the same steps as above to customize these fields.

Under *Address*, Google gives you the option of adding birthdays. This can be changed to anniversary or any other special date by clicking custom.

If your contact has a website, put the address under *URL*. If this contact relates to work, this could your contact's company website.

Last but not least, there is a big box with *Add a note* to the right. This is invaluable for work or acquaintances. Add as much or as little information you want here. This could be particularly useful if you can't remember when or where you met someone!

Editing Contacts

To change the details on your contacts, simply click on the information you want to change and it becomes editable. Change it and click on *Save now*.

Groups

With *Groups* you can organize all your contacts. Why should you add groups? If you have hundreds of contacts in a long list, it can be time consuming to find the name you need. Of course you can search for them, but what if you can't remember how to spell their name or even what their name is?

You may for example have a group for Anycompany PLC. You know you want to talk to the director's PA but can't remember her name. With two thousand contacts (you are very popular), it would be impossible to find him/her just from browsing.

This is where Groups comes into its own. When you were putting your contacts from Anycompany PLC into your contacts you created a group of the same name. Now when you go in to your contacts, your groups will appear under My Contacts on the left hand side (under *NEW CONTACT*). You just click on Anycompany PLC and a list of contacts at that company will appear in the main window.

Of course you could also search for PA in the search window as long as you put his/her job title in their details.

How to add a group

First either click on *New Group* in the left navigation bar if you are in the main contacts window or click on the groups symbol/icon and click on *Create new* as illustrated in the next graphic if you are already on your contact's page. If the latter is the case then your contact will be assigned that group automatically.

Figure 72 Where to add a new group

Next type in the group name you want into the box. This can be anything from a generic category such as family to a company or social group name.

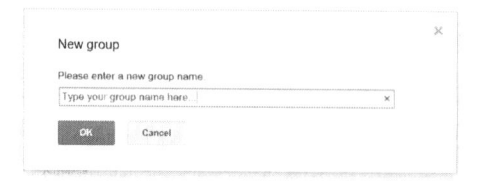

Figure 73 Creating a new Group

Once your groups are created, all you have to do to put your contacts in the right groups is to tick the box to the left of their name on the contacts homepage, then tick the boxes next to the groups you want to put them in before clicking on *Apply*.

Address Book (Google Contacts)

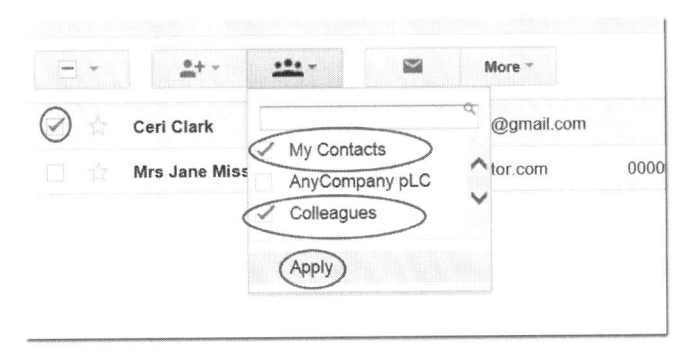

Figure 74 Creating a new Group

If you want to check that the right groups have been assigned, simply look to the right of the rows in the list of your contacts and the groups will be listed there as shown by the circled groups in figure 75.

Figure 75 New groups added

Tip

You can have your contacts in more than one Group. For example your best friend may work for a certain company and you would want your friend in your Friends Group but also for example Anycompany PLC.

Importing and exporting contacts

You may want to either import contacts from another source or export them to share them with colleagues, friends or family. Google makes this easy, please follow the next steps to add or share your contacts.

Exporting Contacts

If you would like to export your contacts you can do this with a vCard or via CSV which is a spreadsheet that can be read by different spreadsheet programs.

Ceri Clark | A Simpler Guide to Gmail

1. Click on *More* in the navigation bar.
2. Then click on *Export*.

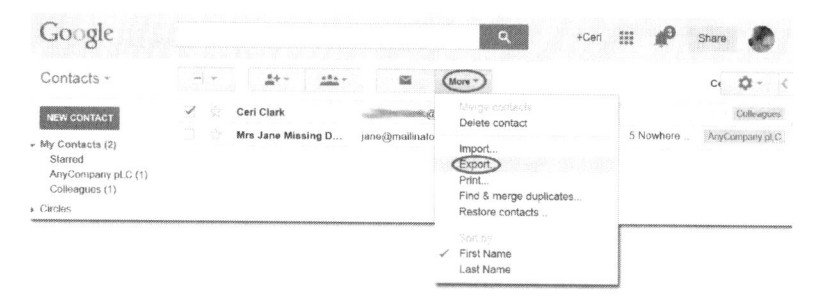

Figure 76 Export option location

A popup will load with three options for which contacts you want to export and three options for what type of file you want to import it as.

If you had preselected one of your contacts the first option (as illustrated in the next figure) allows you to just export that contact. The second choice asks if you want to export all your contacts in a group and the third will export all your contacts. You can obviously only select one of these options at a time.

The second set of options asks you how you want it to be exported. The type of CSV (a type of spreadsheet) that will work with another Google account will be different from a Microsoft Outlook or another application, so you must choose the option for where you want to export to. The third option is a vCard which can be imported into Apple Address books as well as some other applications.

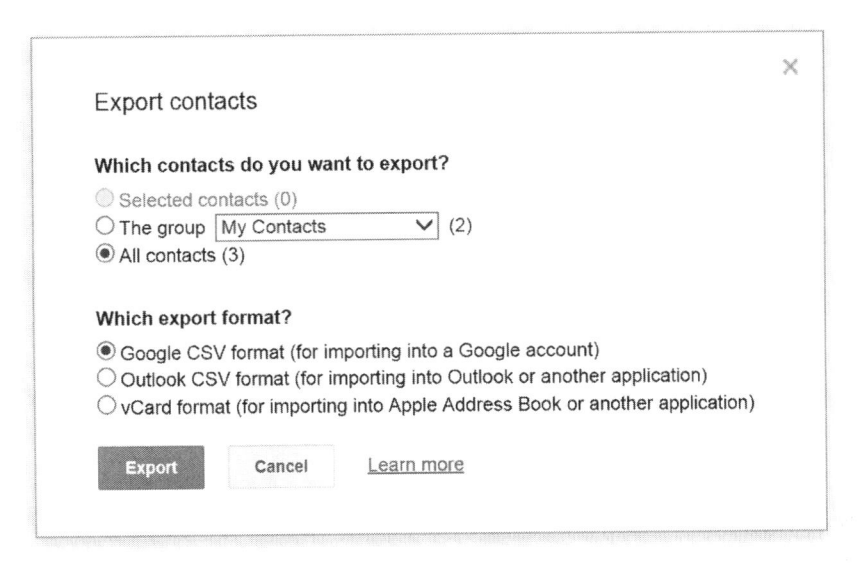

Figure 77 Export options

Click on *Export* and save the file to your computer. The suggested File name is google.csv but you can change this if you want to.

Tip

Back up your contacts by exporting them all to a *CSV* file and saving them on your computer. If you have any problems with your Google Contacts in the future, just delete what is in there and import them again!

Importing Contacts

If someone has sent you a vCard or a spreadsheet with contacts and you want to import it, Google has made this really easy to do. Here are some quick instructions on how to do it.

1. From the main contacts page, click on *More*.
2. Next click on *Import*.

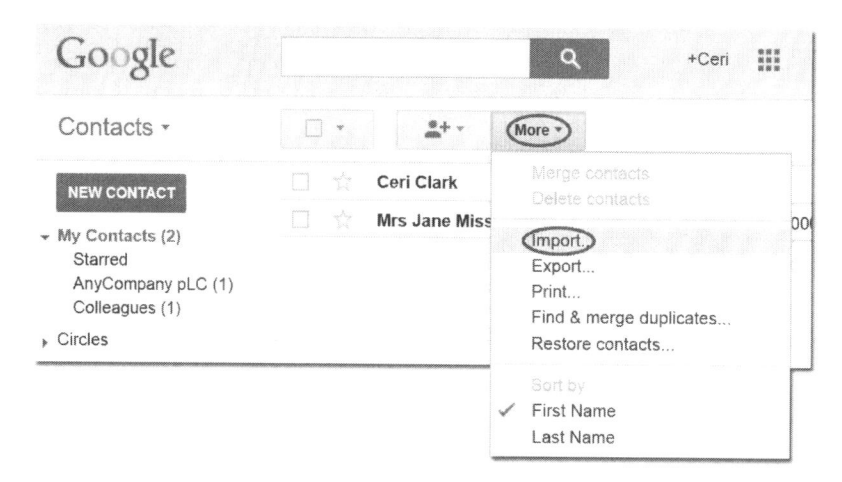

Figure 78 Import location

A pop up will appear.

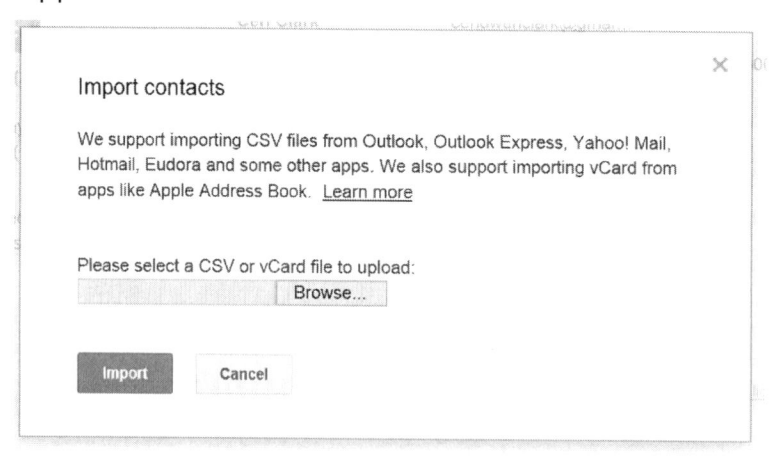

Figure 79 Import your new contacts

3. Click on *Browse* and search for the file in your computer.
4. Lastly, click on *Import* and Google will add the contacts in the CSV or vCard file into your contacts.

Chapter 7 Sorting Emails – No More Folders with Labels

What to expect in this Chapter:

- What are Labels
- How to create them
- How to stop your inbox filling with spam

Google is second to none as a tool for organizing emails. There are four big guns in the Google arsenal. These are discussions (mentioned in detail in Chapter 5), Filters (find out more in chapter 8), Labels and Spam protection. This chapter will look in depth at labels and spam protection.

Labels

Labels are what folders were in other programs and that antiquated filing cabinet gathering dust in the corner of your garage (because of course you have a paperless home office now). I used to have folders for everything including folders within folders. I had folders for holidays, work, friends, shopping, advice and many more. The old way *was* organized but there was always a point where you had to make a choice of where something went in your folder structure. For example if I planned a holiday with my friend to go shopping. Which folder would it go under? I would have chosen holidays in the past. Probably narrowing it down to Holidays > New York or something to that effect.

With Google Mail (Gmail) you don't have to make that choice, create the labels and add them all to the one email. If I look in any of the Holidays, New York, Friends or Shopping labels I can now find it easily and quickly. Simply put, you can label your emails with as many 'labels' as you want. Whatever makes it easier to find the information you need.

Labels

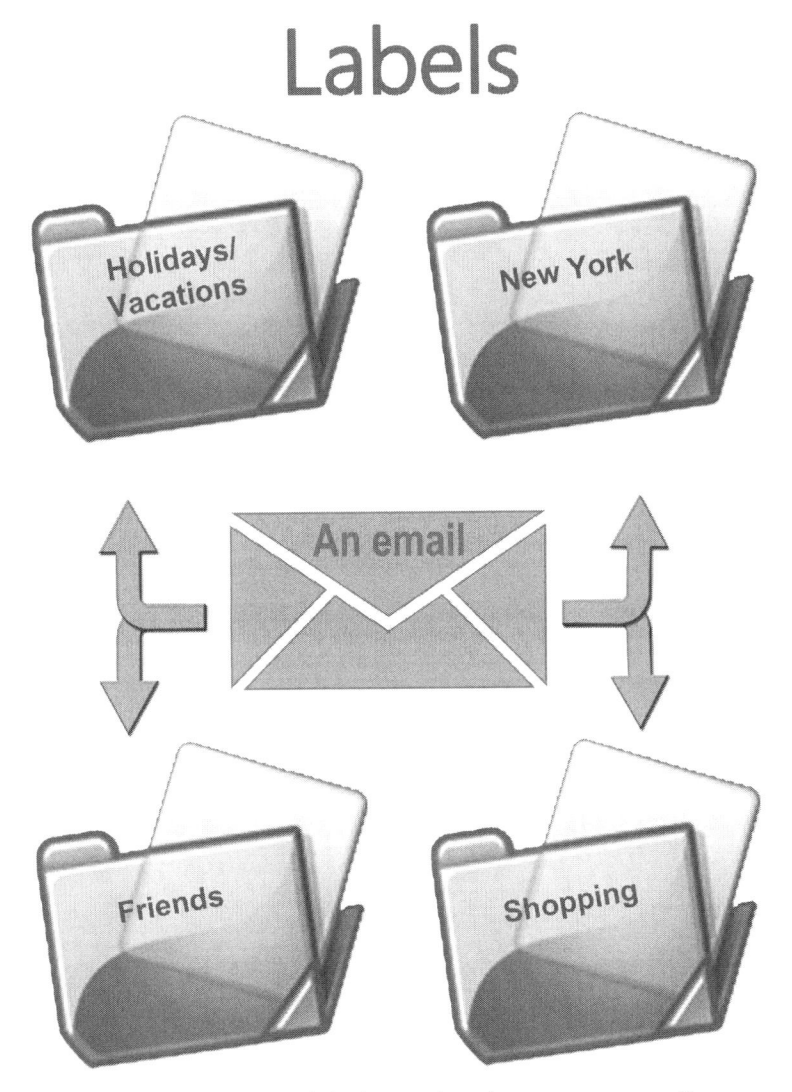

Figure 80 Many labels can be given to one email

Creating a Label

Making a label is simple. Click on the gear symbol at the top right of the webpage (when you hover your mouse over the gear wheel it should confirm that it is the settings function). A drop down menu will appear - you will need to select *Settings*. The reason you have to select it twice is that Google has put a few extra cosmetic options which they feel you might need to see first, such as how compact you would like the webpage to appear. Click on *Labels* as in number 1 in figure 81. Scroll down the page, past *System Labels, Categories and Circles* until you will see just *Labels* as in the section labelled number 2 in figure 81:

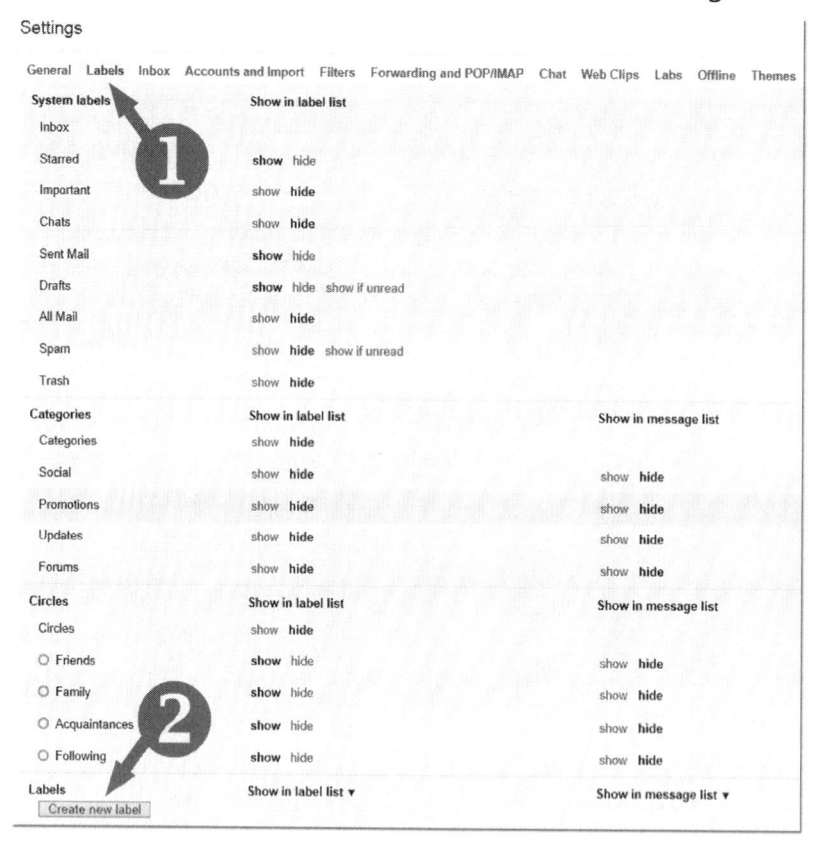

Figure 81 Labels screen

Click on *Create new label* as seen above (the arrow marked 2). Type in the box the label name you want, for example *Shopping* and think about if you want it to be a nested label.

Sorting Emails – No More Folders with Labels

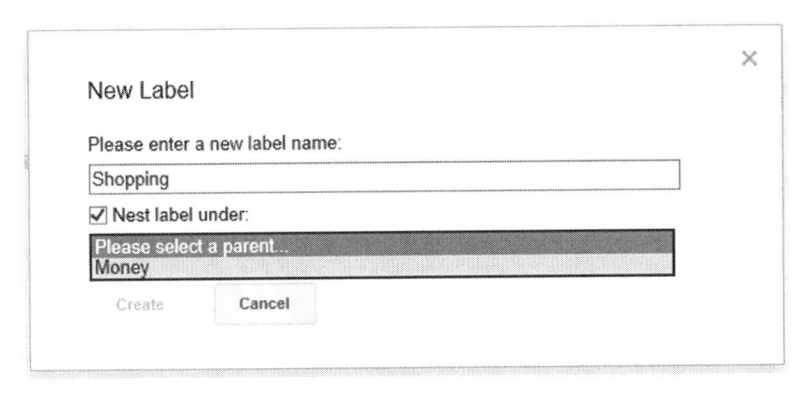

Figure 82 Creating a new label

A nested label means that a label will appear under another in the label list as in the following image:

Figure 83 Labels in navigation bar

Shopping now appears under *Money*. If you click on the little arrow to the left of the *Money* label, you can hide the *Shopping* label and any other label you have 'nested' under *Money*.

81

I would like to sound a note of warning about the use of nested labels. If you label an email with *Shopping*, even though it will be under *Money* in the list, the email will not appear if you just click on *Money*. Therefore if you want it to be available under the two labels then you must make sure that both labels are selected on an email. This way the email will appear when you look under each label.

Click *Create* once you have chosen if you want the label to be nested or not.

Your new Label will then appear in the list of Labels below the box.

All the labels can be customized further. There is a little arrow to the right of each label in the navigation section. Once you click on this a menu will appear with these options. See figure 84.

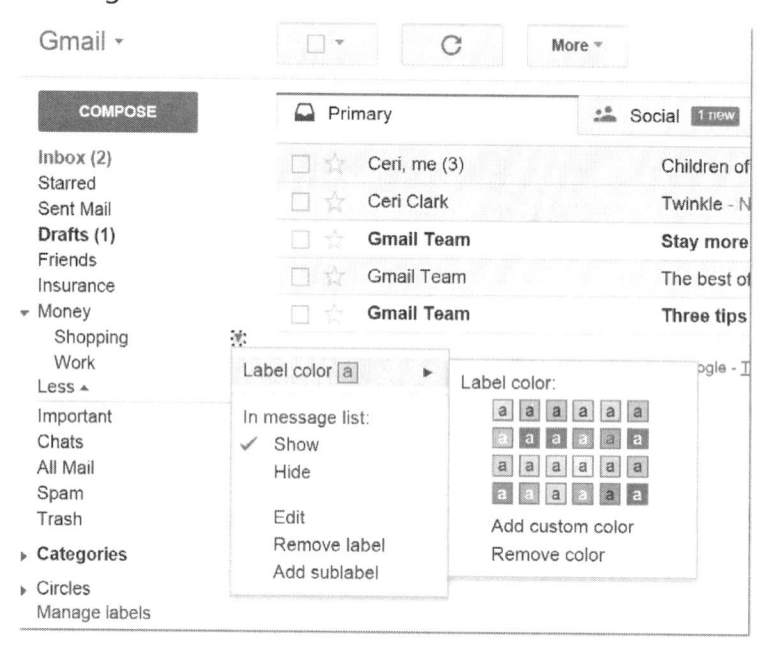

Figure 84 Labels options available in navigation bar

A particularly useful feature is that you can change the color of the labels. For example if you have an urgent label, you could color it red. If your favorite color is blue why not make your Friends label blue?

Circles

This is an option within the Labels settings page. I personally like to keep my Google+ Circles separate from my Gmail. I have made many friends on Google+ but they are not close friends which I would necessarily want to email. That is what I think Google+ is for – to communicate with friends and acquaintances across the world. If I was particularly close with someone in my circles I would move them over into my main contacts.

Therefore my recommendation is to hide Circles from your Gmail account. As illustrated in figure 85, click on *hide* next to each Circle you want to remove from view. The Circles should then disappear from your Gmail homepage.

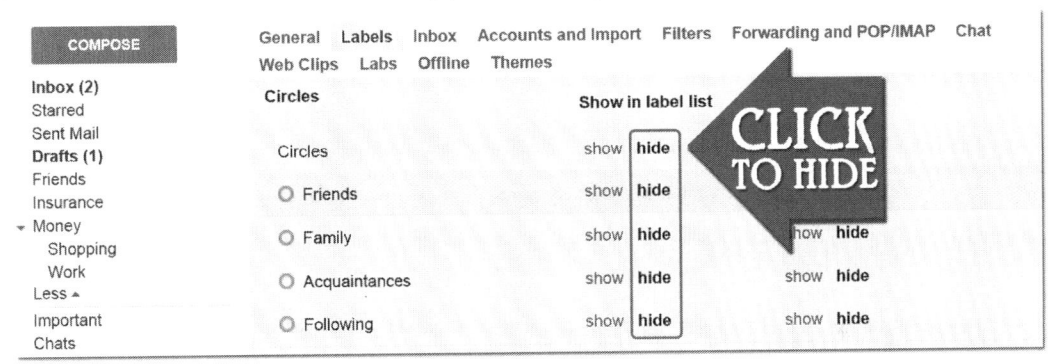

Figure 85 Click on hide to remove Circles from your left navigation bar

If you do want to incorporate Circles into your Gmail, then you need to do nothing but add people to your Google+ account as normal and they will automatically appear in Gmail. For more information on how to do this, please see *Chapter 14 Introduction to Google+*.

Applying a Label

Now that you have created a Label you will want to add it to your email.

From the email list

Check the box on the left of the email that you would like to label. Once you have done this, options for organizing your emails will appear above the email list. Choose the icon (picture) that looks like a luggage label as illustrated in figure 86 by clicking on the little arrow to the right of the icon.

Ceri Clark | A Simpler Guide to Gmail

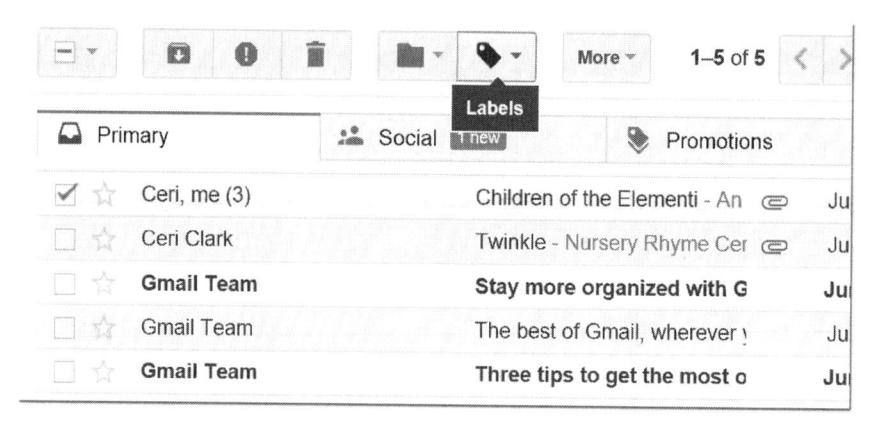

Figure 86 Labels position from the emails list

A dropdown list will appear.

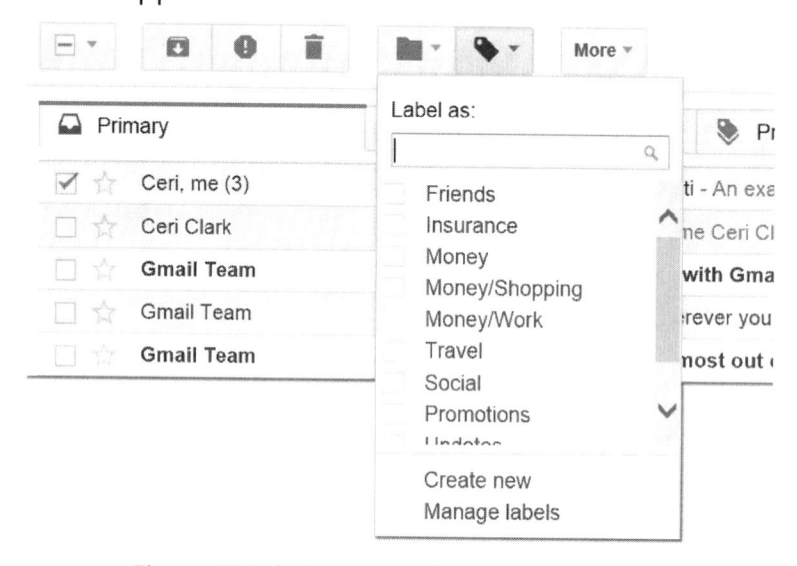

Figure 87 Label options when applying labels

Tick the box next to the label you want, you can choose as many as you like. If you have too many labels to appear in the list without scrolling you can save time by searching for the labels by typing a few characters in the search box. You don't need to search for the whole word. *Create new* at the bottom of the list will do exactly as the name suggests and will allow you to create a new label. By clicking on *Manage labels* you will be taken to the Labels page in the settings area of Gmail.

From an opened email

The options are similar to applying labels from the list of emails in the Gmail homepage. Choose the luggage tag icon to the right of the options as in figure 88.

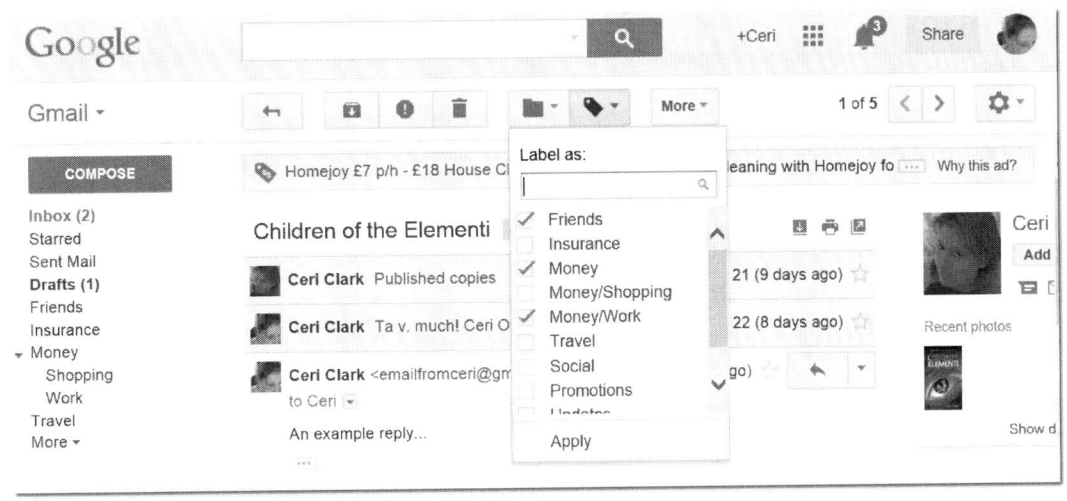

Figure 88 Applying labels from an opened email

At this point you can assign as many Labels as you want to it. Once you click *Apply*, the email will be assigned or 'moved' to the Label 'folder'. Notice that the labels you create are at the top of the list and Google's are at the bottom, e.g. Social, Promotions and Updates.

To remove a Label, click on the X next to the Label. This can be seen in figure 89 below the subject in your email.

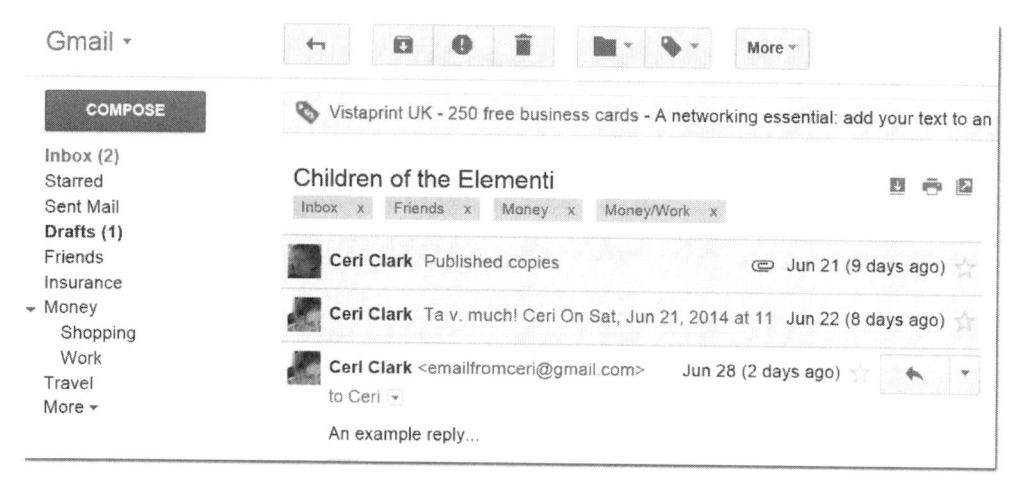

Figure 89 Click the X to remove the labels from emails

You can see what else is labelled by looking at the top of the opened email.

Spam

Spam is the bane of all email users everywhere. Unwanted emails about medical aids, Nigerian princes needing help to take money from you or fake bank emails bring misery to billions. Fortunately Google has one of the best spam filters on the web.

To find emails which may have been erroneously labelled spam, click on *Spam* on the left of the screen in the navigation bar and then re-label it.

One of the reasons that Google is so good with Spam is that there is a community effort to reduce it.

To mark an email as spam, click on the exclamation mark in the octagon symbol:

Figure 90 Spam icon

It is always above your emails so you can let Google know the current email you are reading is spam. Spam is unsolicited bulk email, it may or may not be malicious. It can just be annoying.

There is another type of email which is sent with the sole intent to cause either harm or take money from you. If you receive an email which you think is trying to trick you to going to a fake bank website that has 'slipped through the net', click on *Report phishing* in the menu that appears when you click on the arrow at the top right of each opened email (figure 91 shows the location).

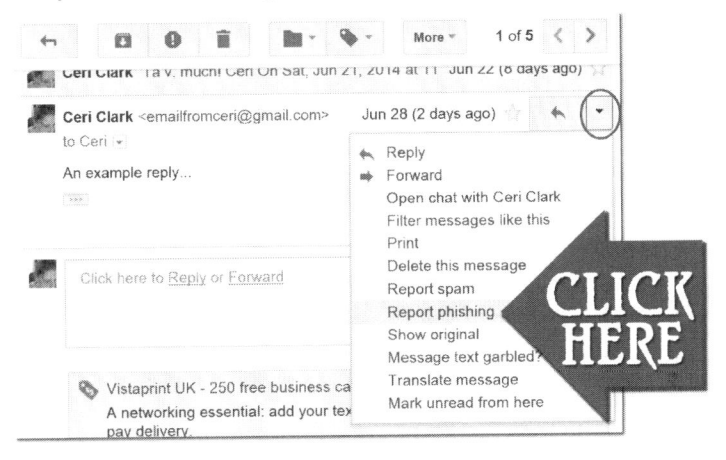

Figure 91 Report phishing

Tip

If you archive emails, you can always find them later in *All Mail*

Chapter 8 Filters

What to expect in this Chapter:

- What are filters
- Making filters
- The settings page - importing, exporting, editing and deleting filters

Applying Labels to everything can be a bit of a chore; however Google has come up with an elegant solution with *Filters* to save you time.

Filters can allow you to automate the process of adding Labels. With this system, if you always want to put all emails from Auntie Flo in a Label called Auntie Flo, then you can get Filters to do this, you can also ask it to treat her emails as very important. It might not mean that you answer her emails any faster but it will mean that you won't lose them amongst the hundreds of other emails you get, or in the spam folder.

Filters also allow you to immediately delete emails from people or companies without ever seeing them or just archive them for later viewing. You can make sure that certain emails never go into spam and that they are marked important or are starred so they are easy to find in the mix of emails you will get daily. Filters are an essential resource for email organization.

Creating a Filter

Go to *Settings* on the top right of the screen (the gear symbol) and choose settings from the dropdown then select *Filters*. Please see steps 1-3 in figure 93.

Click on *Create a new filter, (Step 4 in the image below).*

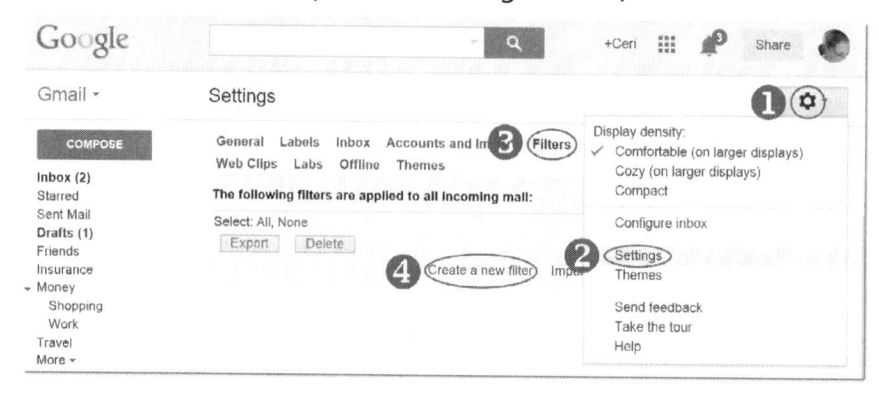

Figure 92 Creating a filter

Options will appear as shown in figure 93

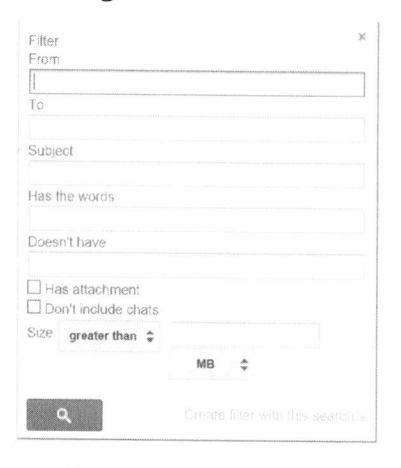

Figure 93 Filter options

Examples of how to filter:

- To label all emails from a person or mailing list, type the email address into the *From* box. For example, auntieflo@gmail.com.

- If there are specific words in the subject you want to pay attention to, for example if you receive a newsletter from horse riding weekly and you want to make sure they all appear together in one place then put horse riding weekly into the *Subject* box.
- *Has the words* are for general keywords, for example any emails containing your family's names.
- The *Doesn't have* is a powerful tool. If you want to label all emails with a word but you are getting too many results and all the wrong results have the same word in them, pop that word into this box and it will ignore those emails with the wrong word in them.
- *Has attachment*. If you want all emails with attachments from a certain person to go in the *Bin* then, type in the person's name in the *From* box and click the box by *Has attachment* and you will never receive the emails again.

Remember you can use one of the filter options or all. You are only limited by your imagination. Once you have put the words you want to put in the filter, click on *Search* to see if there are any emails already in your account with these options. Once you are happy with your selections click on *Create filter with this search*.

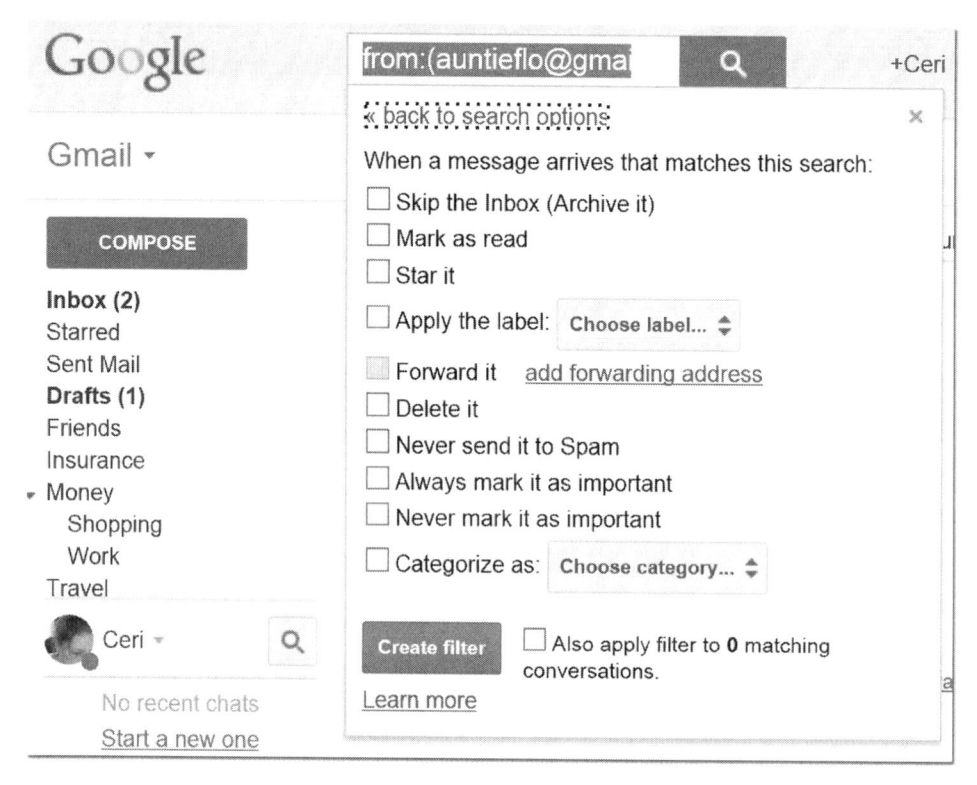

Figure 94 The next step in creating a filter

Figure 94 shows the next options available to you. You can archive it, mark it as read, star it, apply the label, and forward those particular emails to an email address and so on.

The most important options are *Apply the Label* and *Always/Never mark it as important*.

After clicking on *Create Filter*, you will get a confirmation screen to say it has been set up. The downside is that you will have to go through the process for each label as it doesn't allow you to choose more than one label at this stage.

If you are tidying up your emails and want to apply the label to all your previous emails then check the box next to *Create filter* which says *Also apply filter to X matching conversations*. If you are deleting all emails from a certain email address then all of the emails will be deleted not just future arrivals.

Filters in Settings

As can be seen above, you can do so much with filters, but what if you want to edit or delete a filter? Better yet, what if you have spent lots of time creating the best filters and you want to share them with a friend or vice-versa? Google has enabled them so that you can share with your friend (export filters) or have your friend share their filters with you (import filters). This section aims to show how to do this.

How to get to Filters in the settings

To get the settings page, click on the gear wheel at the top right of the screen, then choose *Settings*, then *Filters*. The following page will load:

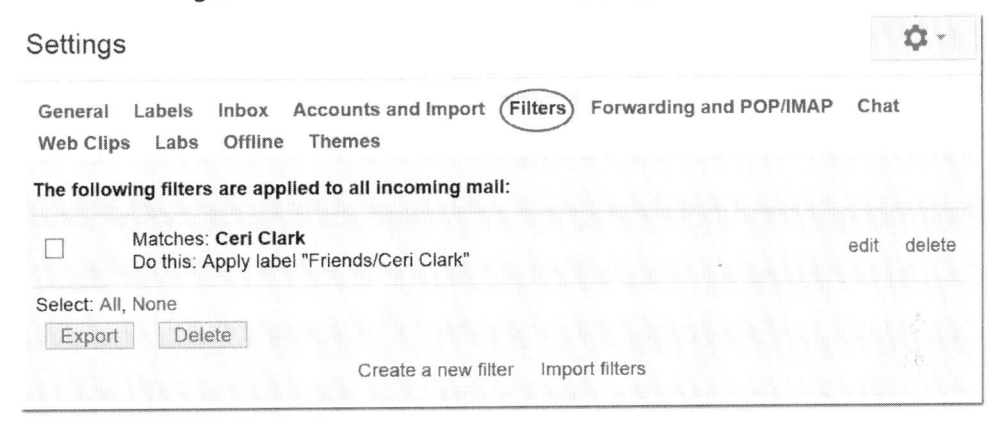

Figure 95 Filters location in settings

Editing/changing a filter

If you think a filter is not appropriate any more you can change the filter by going into *Gear Wheel, Settings > Filters* and clicking on edit next to the filter you want to tweak.

A word of warning, even if you change the filter and apply to all your emails, changes made by the previous filter will have to be dealt with on an email to email basis.

For example I had a filter in my test account which had everything from Ceri Clark go into a *Friends/Ceri Clark* label. All emails which had this label applied, had these words in it. I then realized that the emails from Gmail which stated at the beginning '*Hi Ceri*', were all labelled *Friends/Ceri Clark*. Clearly inaccurate! I edited the label to have all emails sent from my email address to go to that label and all the right emails were now labelled correctly but of course the Gmail emails were still marked as from myself so I had to manually delete the labels from each email. The moral of this story is to think carefully about what labels to apply!

Deleting a filter

Deleting a filter could not be simpler, either, go to *Gear Wheel > Settings > Filters* then click on *delete* on the far right of the filter you want to remove or check the box to the right of the filter and then click on the *Delete* button at the bottom of the Filters page in settings.

Sharing filters with friends (exporting filters)

In order to export your filters, go to the filters section in settings (*Gear Wheel > Settings > Filters*) and click on *Export* at the bottom of the page. Please see figure 96 above to see its location.

Once you have clicked on *Export* you will be asked to save the file on to your computer. The file will be downloaded with the extension of .xml. You can now email this filter to your friend.

Adding filters given by friends (importing filters)

First go to *Gear Wheel > Settings > Filters* and click on *Import*. A new section will load at the bottom of the page which will look like this:

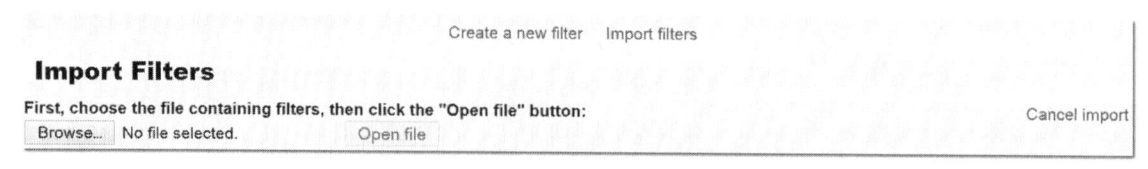

Figure 96 The Import Filters screen

Filters

Click on *Browse* and find the file named *MailFilters.xml* you were given. Once you have clicked *Open* you will return to Google and you will need to click on *Open File*.

The screen will reload with the filters that were in the file. You can stop at this point or you can choose which filters you want to import. Simply click on the little checkboxes next to the filters you want added to your account and click on *Create filters*. If you want the filters to apply to all the emails that are already in your account, click on the little box next to *Apply new filters to existing email*.

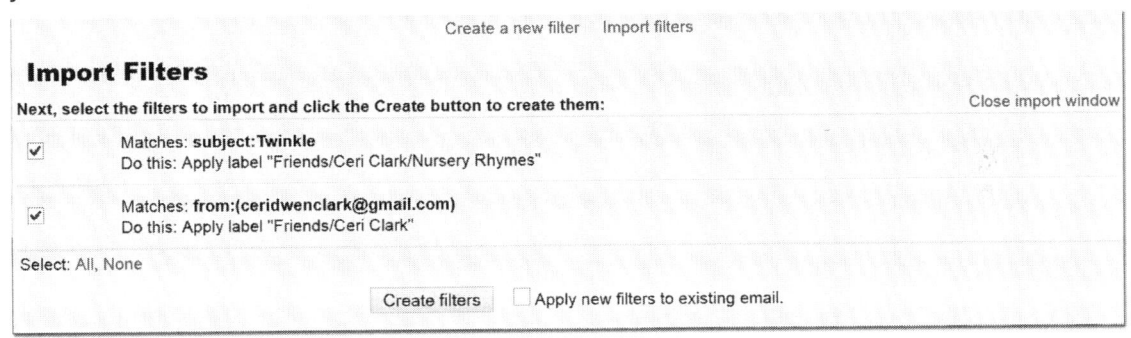

Figure 97 Choose which filters you want imported to your account

Google will automatically create the labels that are needed by the new filters.

Chapter 9 Searching For, and In Emails

What to expect in this Chapter:

- Searching within your labels
- How to search for emails using an email address
- Searching your Sent emails
- Keyword searching
- Searching for emails with attachments
- Searching by size and date.

Searching for your emails is a breeze with Gmail. In the basic sense all you need to do is type in your search term and then click on the magnifying glass, the Google search engine will then search all your email for you.

Ceri Clark | A Simpler Guide to Gmail

Figure 98 Search Google mail

Google does accept Boolean searching, for example using AND & OR, and quotes, but for a simpler way of powerful searching click on the little arrow inside the search box. If you hover your mouse over the arrow, you will get a little message stating *Show search options*. The following screen will appear:

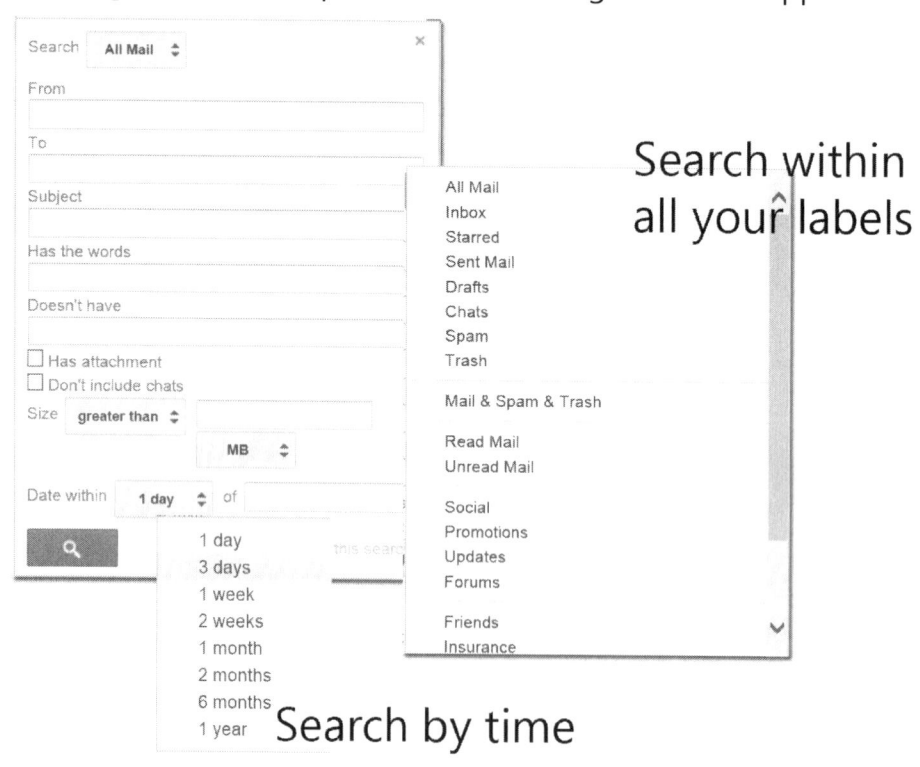

Figure 99 Advanced search options

The beauty of these options is that you can not only search from a particular email address but from emails which have certain words in them. Here are some tips for searching:

Searching in your labels

You can search only within a label by clicking the arrows next to All Mail in the search options. Gmail will automatically search all your mail but you can search in just the email you sent or if you are organized and assigned all your emails labels then you can search within them. A possible scenario is that you may have a label for work related emails and another for personal. If this is the case you could just search in your personal emails if you needed to.

Searching for emails from a certain person

This can be done two ways, you can just put the email address into the search bar or the way I recommend is to go into the advanced search and type it into the *From* field.

Searching emails you have sent to people

As above, you can type their email address straight into the search box or this time I recommend typing the email addresses into the *To* box.

Subject Searching

When you type in this box, it will only search the subject of your emails. If you want to search for say, Washington but you don't want all those emails with Washington in the body of the email, this is the way to go.

This is great if you are getting a lot of emails with the same subject and you want to delete them. For example, you can search for *Annoying Company Newsletter* in the subject box and all their emails will be found. You can delete them at your leisure.

Tip

When you send emails try and make sure that the subject that you write is as descriptive of the content of your email as possible. Not only is this helpful for people receiving your email but when you want to find it again, Google will be able to find it easier if it has the right words in the subject

Searching for emails using keywords (Has the words...)

Whatever you are searching for, the *Has the words* field can be indispensable and with the help of the other boxes you can really narrow down your search.

An example would be if you were searching for the holiday company that you had a holiday with last year because you want to book with them again but you have forgotten what they are called.

You can remember you went to Orlando but the holiday company just eludes you. Type in the box *Orlando* and (if you kept it) Google will find your receipt email which would have the name of the company on it.

Removing emails from the search

The box labelled *Doesn't have* is one of the most useful options in Gmail search. You may be getting lots of emails in your search which are irrelevant but the search brings them up with the words you have put in. Finding words in the email which tells you they *aren't* relevant and putting them in this box will remove them from your search.

Finding emails with an attachment

Ticking the box *Has attachment* will bring up results with only attachments. Gmail will also search in your attachments.

As an experiment I sent myself a document called *Twinkle.docx*. The email subject had *Twinkle* in the name and the content of the email simply stated *Nursery Rhyme*. The document itself had the full nursery rhyme, Twinkle, Twinkle, Little Star, typed out. I searched for *star* in my Gmail and although star was only mentioned in the actual document, Gmail put the email in the search results.

Searching through your Chats

Gmail will automatically search through your chats. If you tick the box labelled *Don't include chats*, Gmail will only search through your emails.

Searching by Size

You can search for your emails by choosing greater than or less than a certain size of email. If you regularly send emails to a friend or colleague and they have sent you an attachment but you've lost the email, you can search for emails of a larger size to narrow your list.

Also if you feel you are using too much space in your Gmail account, you can search for all emails over a certain size to find all emails with attachments. You can then delete emails which you think you no longer need to good effect. One email with an attachment can be worth hundreds of emails without them.

Searching emails by date

The last option is to search within a time period. The options are within 1 day, 3 days, 1 week, 2 weeks, 1 month, 2 months, 6 months, and 1 year of a date you can select by clicking into the box next to this option. For example 1 year of 1 April 2013.

Alternatively, if you want a longer time period, you can type into the main search bar in the format:

after:2012/4/1 before:2014/4/2

Chapter 10 Changing the Look and Feel

What to expect in this Chapter:

- What is display density and what each option looks like
- How to change your background with themes

You've sent a couple of emails, told a few of your best mates about how great Gmail is but you're getting a bit bored with how it looks and you want one of those cool signatures! This is the chapter to help you with this.

All of these changes can be made from *Settings*. This link can be found at the top right of the screen when you click on the gear wheel as illustrated in figure 100.

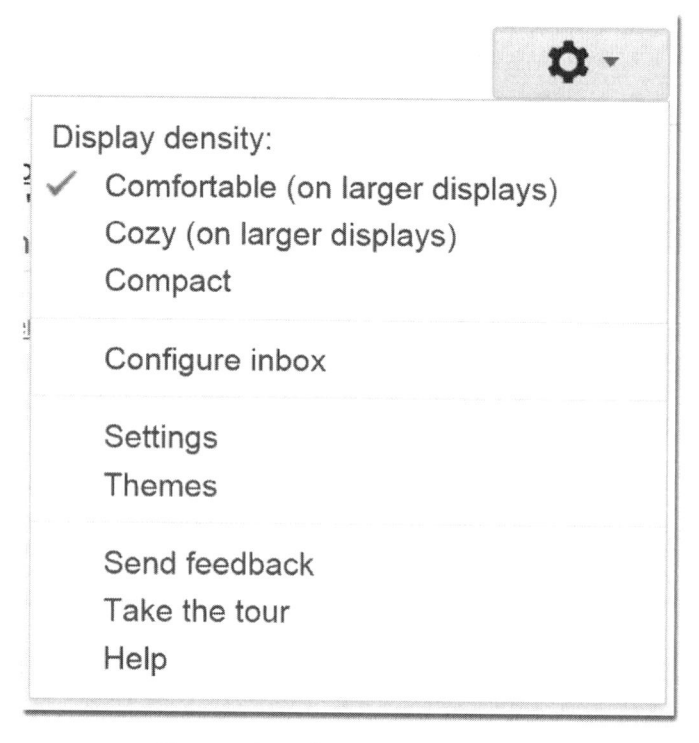

Figure 100 Where to find settings

Display Density

There are three options under Display Density. These are *Comfortable* (for larger displays), *Cozy* (again for larger displays) and *Compact*. Please see figure 102 to see how each view compares side-by-side. They are designed to fit more or fewer emails depending on the size of the screen you are viewing your email on. The space between each email is larger with Comfortable, less in Cozy and in Compact view there is the least amount of space between emails.

Changing the Look and Feel

Figure 101 Density views

Themes

To change the theme, choose the themes option under *Settings* under the gear wheel at the top right of the page. The themes can also be found as a tab at the top of the main settings page.

There are lots of themes to choose from and quite a few change throughout the day, my particular favorite is the planets theme.

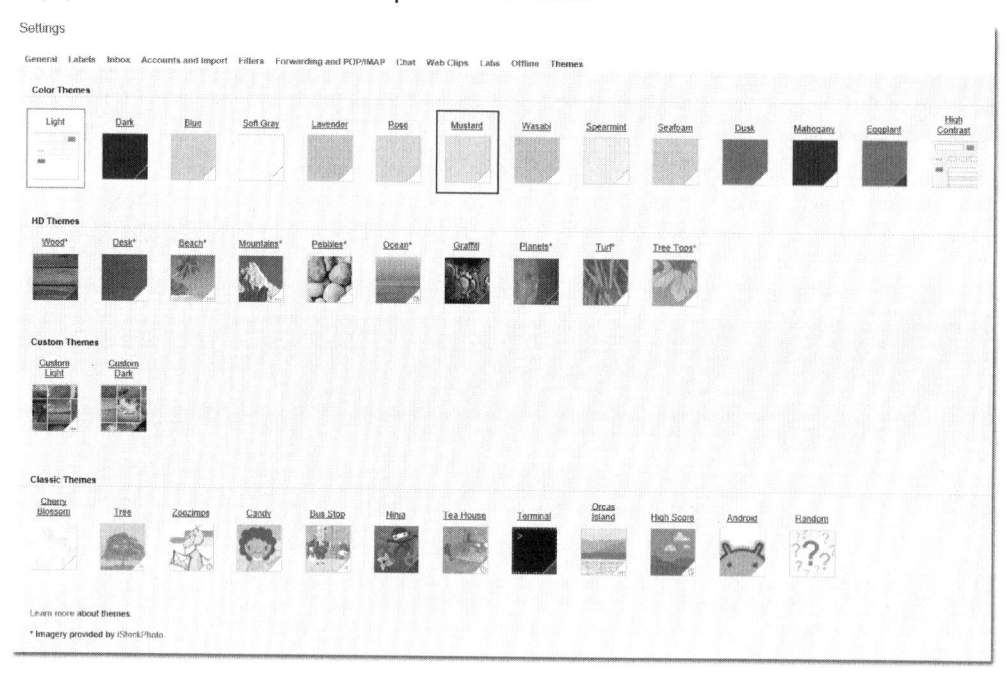

Figure 102 Themes available

If you would like to install any of these themes, all you need to do is click on the square or text that represents them and they should be applied. There are a couple of themes that require you to let them know what country you are in but this is simply because the background picture changes according to the time of day (Mountains for example). It can be nice if you are stuck indoors with the curtains closed to know that it is sunset because your Gmail background changes! If you want the original theme because you don't like the alternatives, choose the original (and first in the list) *Light* theme.

Changing the Look and Feel

Figure 103 Themes available

If you would like a picture with a gentle moving background, then there are moving gifs that can be found on the internet. The moving images can be anything from some grass moving on a mountain landscape, something shooting across your screen or a cat being stroked.

If you would like to add one of these types of pictures to your background, choose *Custom Light* or *Custom Dark* depending on if the picture you choose is light or dark. You can then browse your computer or search for the words *relaxing gif* or *perfectly looped* in the search box. You will then see some moving images you can add as your background.

If you want to change your background to a different moving image you can do this by clicking on the gear when then *Select a background image*.

If you want to go back to the standard themes, go to: *Gear wheel > Themes* and choose one of the options available.

Chapter 11 Under the Hood - Settings

What to expect in this Chapter:

- What else is available in settings and how to use them
- Setting up your inbox view
- Accounts and Import, forwarding and POP/IMAP
- Chat, web clips and offline

This chapter covers all the settings under the general tab in the first instance but then goes into detail about inbox, importing and exporting to other email accounts, forwarding and POP/IMAP, chat, web clips and offline. Lab, labels and themes have their own chapters.

General Settings

The number of general settings can seem quite daunting when you first see them. This section aims to dispel the apprehension of seeing all those settings in one page. To get to these settings click on the gear wheel at the right of the screen and click on *Settings*.

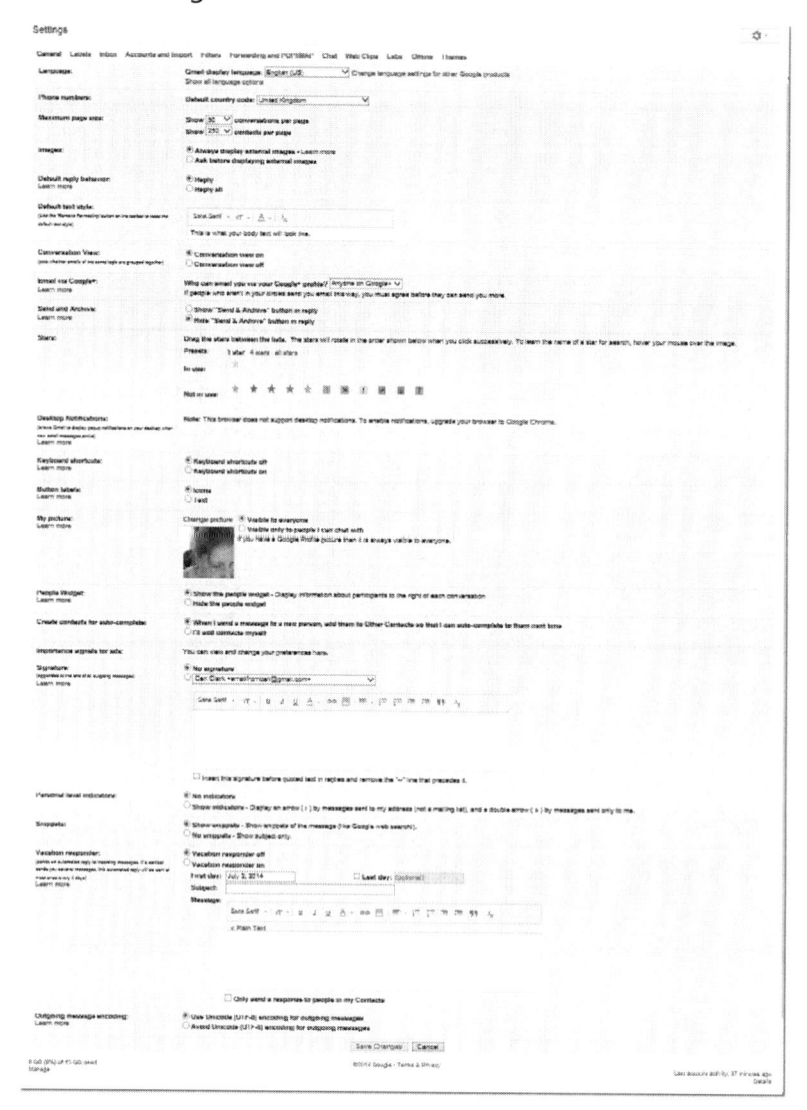

Figure 104 General settings

Remember that if you make any changes you will need to scroll to the bottom of the page and click on *Save Changes* or the new setting will not apply.

Language

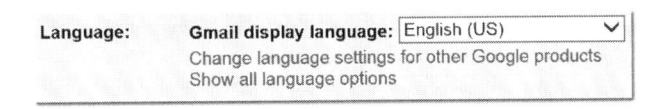

Figure 105 Language settings

Choose the language appropriate to your region, for the US, this is the default, while UK users will have to choose the English (UK) option.

Phone numbers

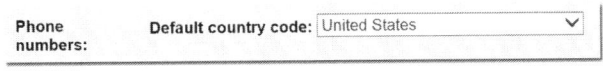

Figure 106 Phone number setting

This option is to allow you to use Google Voice. While it is only available in limited places at the moment the option to choose so many countries suggests that Google are planning to roll out Google Voice to more places in the future.

Maximum Page Size

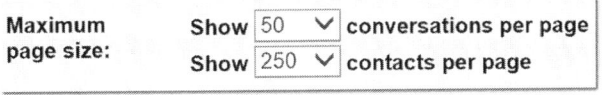

Figure 107 Page size settings

This option depends on how much you want to scroll, the more conversations and contacts you allow on each page the fewer pages you will have to click through but it also means you will have to scroll more.

Images

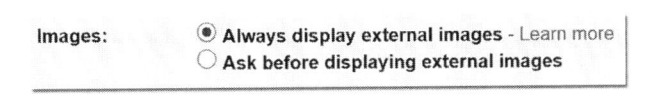

Figure 108 Image settings

This refers to displaying images within emails. While it is nice to see adverts in all their glory, if an email slips through which has harmful code in it, it could damage your computer. It is best to click on *Ask before displaying external content*. If this drives you up the wall, you can always change to the other option again later.

Default reply behavior:

Figure 109 Automatic reply settings

This option asks if you want to automatically reply to one person or all people in your email. I would strenuously suggest that you choose *Reply*. You can always choose *Reply to all* when you are typing the email but Gmail will automatically reply to the sender email address if you click on just Reply.

I would not recommend *Reply to all* as an automatic setting in any circumstances. It is easier to send an email again to people you have missed but very hard to make someone un-see an email!

It can seem very convenient to have a reply to all automatically done for you for every email. It means that no one would miss out on your emails if you are replying back but if you are using your Gmail account for business purposes take the lessons learnt from big business that this may not be the best idea. The news has been full in the past of emails sent to the wrong people by accident and then forwarded on to strangers. The type of email that you shouldn't reply to all will usually find their way half-way across the world before you can say Jiminy Cricket! It is best to think before replying and think twice before replying to all.

Default text style:

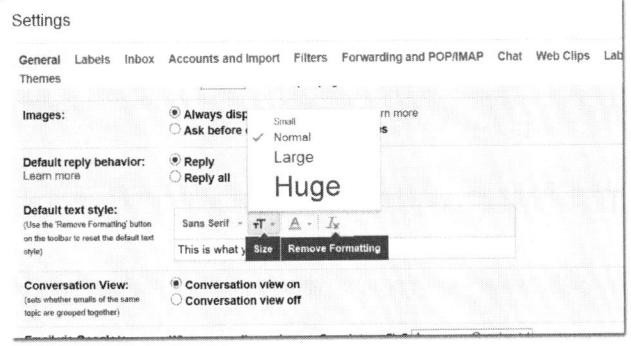

Figure 110 Text formatting settings

If you always want to send emails with the Arial font or larger text size then you can make this happen automatically from here. There are four main options: there is the font (e.g. Arial, Time New Roman etc.), the size of the text, (Small, Normal, Large and Huge), the color of your text and finally you can remove all formatting to bring the text in all your emails to the basic Gmail offering. Set the text to how you want it and all your emails including replies will use this automatically.

Conversation view

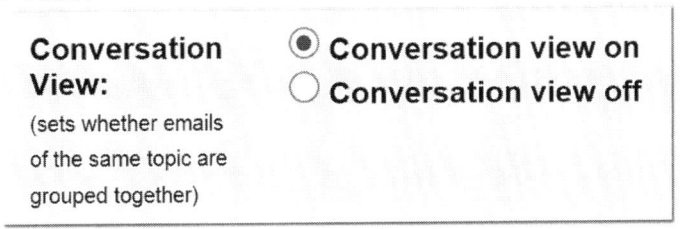

Figure 111 Conversation View settings

You can turn this off or on here. I would recommend you keep this on as it means you keep all your email about one 'subject' in one place but if you like all your emails separated so you can see everyone's replies on individual rows on your email homepage then you can turn it off here as well.

Email via Google+

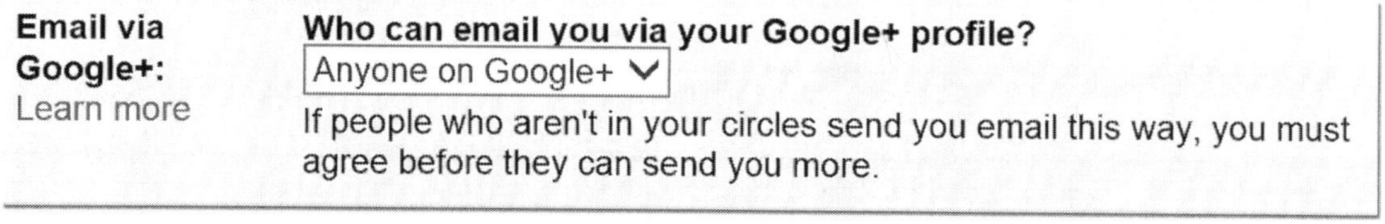

Figure 112 Google+ email settings

This is relevant even if you have a Google+ profile but don't use the service that much. Anyone can email you as long as they have your profile in their circles (groups) and anyone can add anyone to their circles in Google+.

This setting has 4 options, anyone on Google+, extended circles, circles and no one. How you want to use this service is dependent on your personal circumstances. You may want anyone to be able to contact you if you are selling a service or product. It may be the case that you have been highly selective about who is in your circles and you need to be able to contact them (and they you) but you don't want to give out your email address. I personally like to compartmentalize my life and prefer that my social networking stays on social networking sites and I chose no one in my personal account. This however is up to you how you want to use it.

It should be noted here that you can also email others in Google+ without knowing their email address. If you have put someone in your profile in Google+ and you want to send them an email, type their name in the *To:* box while you are composing your email and Gmail will search your Google+ circles for that person and show their name and photo when it is found. Select that person and your email will get to them.

Send and Archive

Figure 113 Send and Archive button setting

Enabling this function will save you a lot of time! With one click you can send a reply to an email while archiving at the same time. Without this, you can reply as normal but the email will stay in your inbox until you archive it manually. I highly recommend this button!

Stars

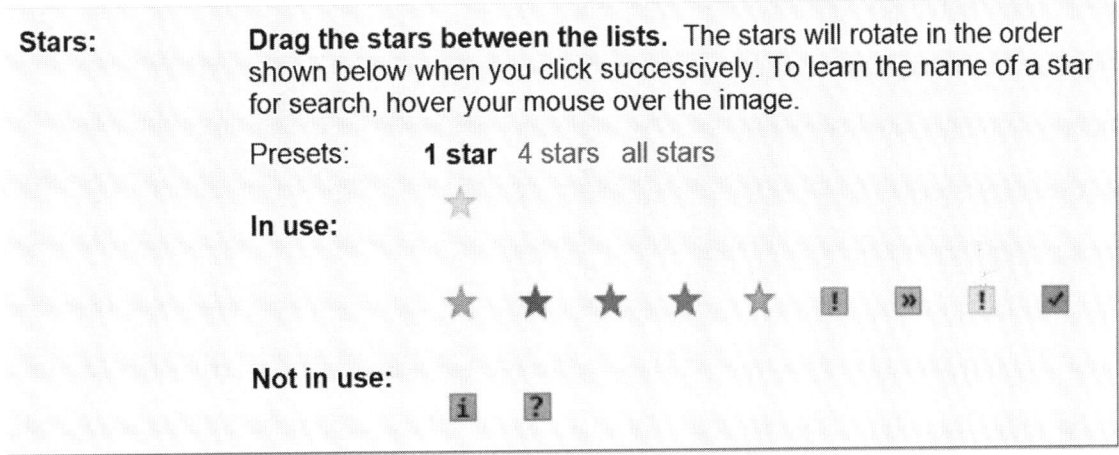

Figure 114 Drag the stars and symbols from the Not in use row to the In use row to use

Stars are used to help organize your email. For example if you star an important email that you need to deal with by next week, then you can search for just starred email. Use this section to choose what stars will be available. Drag the stars and symbols from the *Not in use* row to the *In use* row and click *Save changes* at the bottom of the page. To choose a different star, in your inbox click on the star symbol next to the email in the inbox. Keep clicking to get the different star and symbol options.

Desktop Notifications

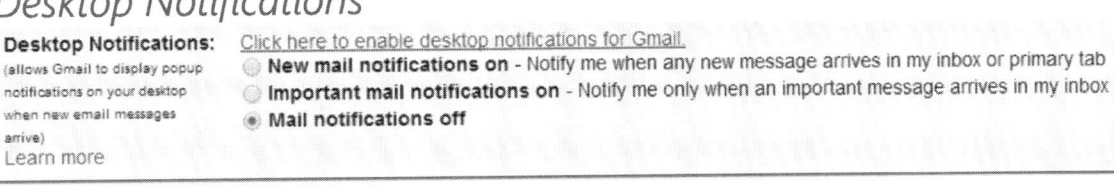

Figure 115 Desktop notifications setting

115

If you are using Google's Chrome browser, then you can get notifications as popups to let you know when you have got new email. It doesn't work on other browsers at the time of writing and the options won't show up in others.

Keyboard Shortcuts

Figure 116 Keyboard shortcut setting

Turn these on or off depending on how much you want to use your mouse. I would recommend this is turned on so that you have the option to use shortcuts if you want to. A selection of shortcuts taken from the Google help pages are:

To compose a message, type c or Shift + c if you want it in a new window

To return to the inbox type "u"

To archive a message, type "e"

To report spam, type "!"

To bring up the label menu, type "l" (lowercase L)

Add a Cc address to your email, type Ctrl + Shift + c (Mac: ⌘ + Shift + c)

Add a Bcc address to your email, type Ctrl + Shift + b (Mac: ⌘ + Shift + b)

To undo an action (it might not *always* work), type "z"

For all Google Gmail shortcuts, visit the Google help page at:
http://support.google.com/mail/bin/answer.py?answer=6594

Button labels

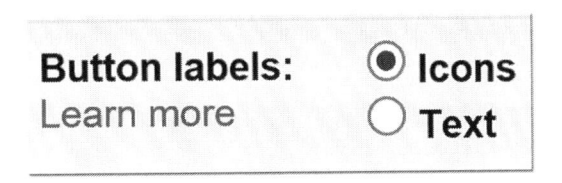

Figure 117 Button labels setting

If you find the icons too small or confusing, it is possible to change the navigation bar above emails to have words instead of pictures. The next graphic illustrates how the two views compare.

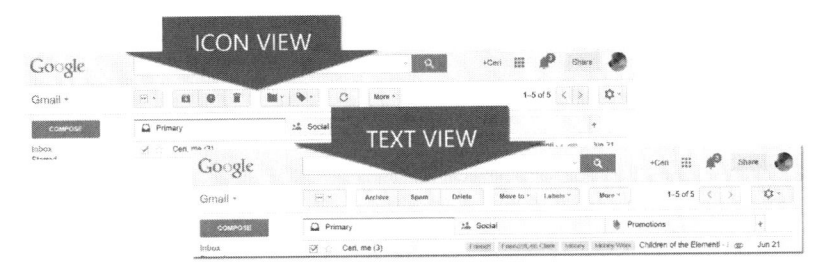

Figure 118 Icon and text views

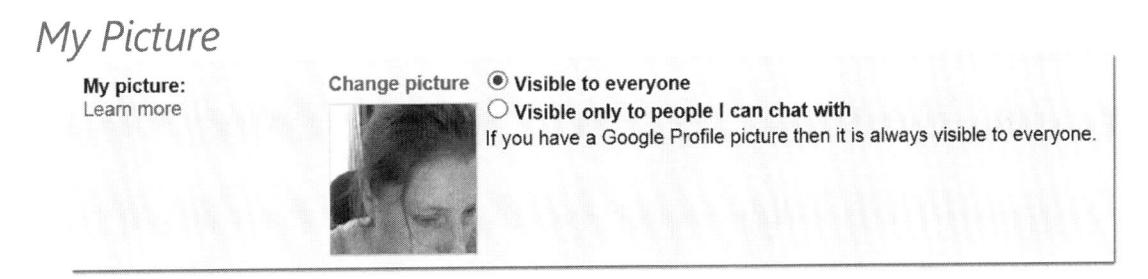

My Picture

Figure 119 Changing your picture and its visibility

In this section you can change the picture you selected during setup. Clicking on *Change Picture* (above your photo) brings up a window where you can search your computer for your favorite pic of yourself. You can always use your cat's picture if you prefer!

Remember you can control who can see your picture, whether just people who chat with you or who email you once you have uploaded the picture. Google+ profile pictures are always visible to everyone.

For more in-depth guidance on adding/changing your picture, please refer to the *Adding your profile picture* in Chapter 2.

People Widget

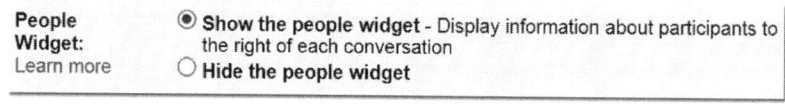

Figure 120 See your contact's people while reading or sending emails

This shows information about your contacts next to your emails, usually at the top right when you are in an open email.

Create contacts for auto-complete

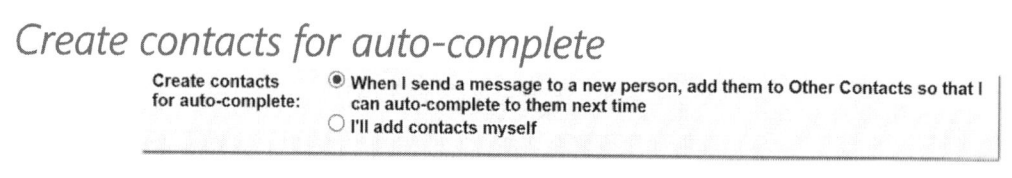

Figure 121 Auto-complete options for contacts

This is a great time saver. Instead of adding contacts manually, Gmail will add them automatically when you send an email to someone. Of course if you send a lot of emails to people you are sure that you never want to contact again then using the *I'll add contacts myself* option would be better.

Important signals for ads

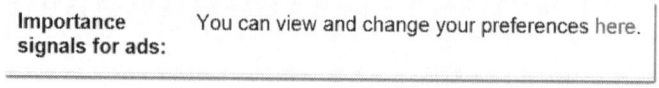

Figure 122 Advert settings

This setting is to show you what Google is using to target your adverts. When you click on the link you will be directed to a page which will show you what information Google is using and from where. At the bottom of the page you can also opt-out of interest based adverts. What this means is that you will still receive adverts but they won't be targeted and you can get anything!

Figure 123 Advert settings information

Blocking adverts from individual advertisers

Above the opt-out for targeted advertising (as seen in figure 124) is where they show you advertisers that you have blocked. The adverts appear to the right of emails you are viewing. If you would like to block offensive or irrelevant adverts from an advertiser you must first click on the little (i) next to *Ads* as seen circled in the graphic below.

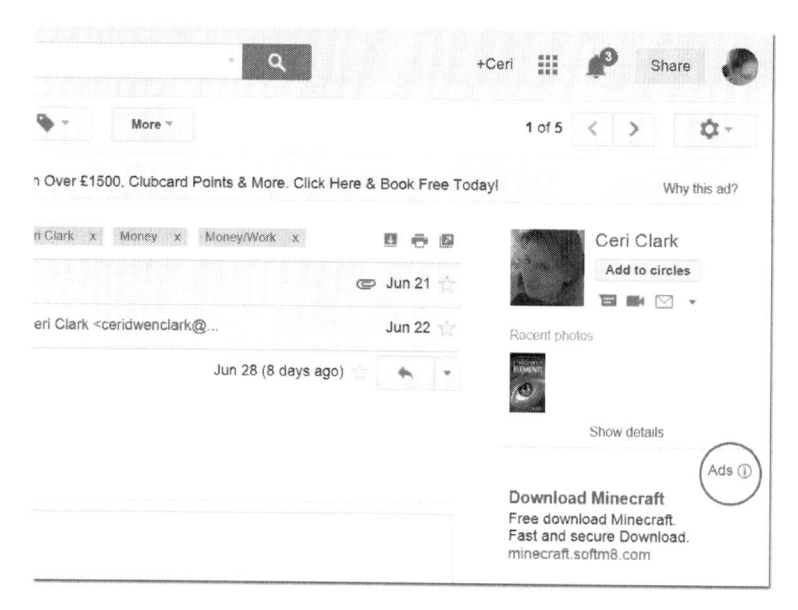

Figure 124 Blocking advertisers

A pop up will load which will allow you to click on Ads Settings.

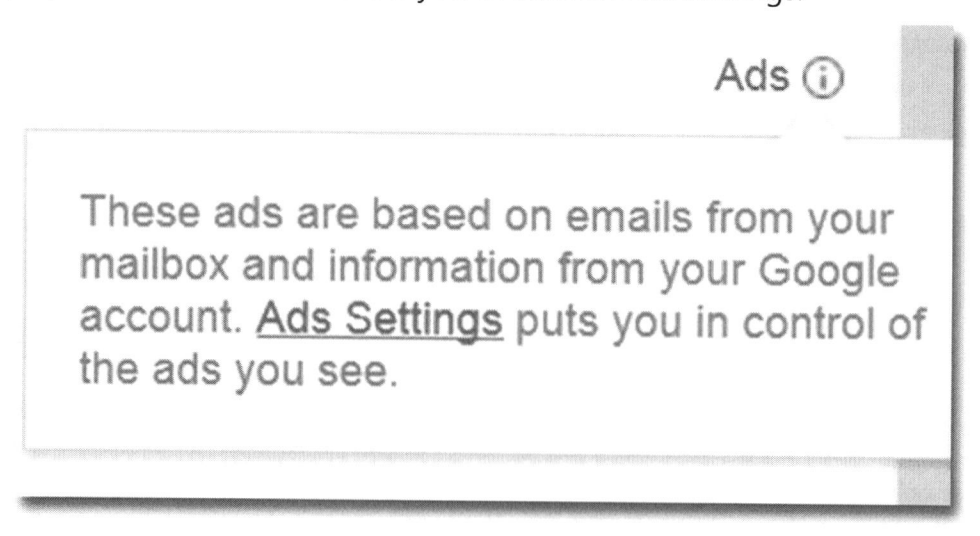

Figure 125 Ads Settings

This will bring up yet another page which will give you the option of blocking adverts. The URL if you want to go here directly was: https://www.google.com/settings/ads/preferences. This will affect all of Google for that account.

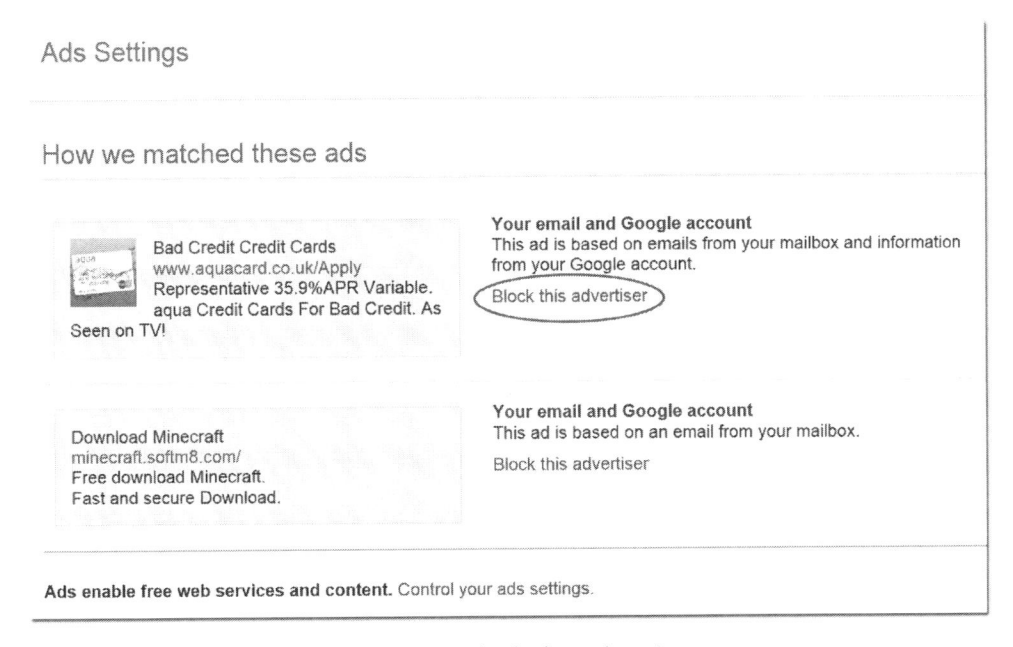

Figure 126 Block the advertiser

Click on *Block this advertiser* as seen circled above. A message, replacing *Block this advertiser* will let you know it is blocked and will also give you the option to *Manage ads settings*. This will bring you back to the initial ads setting page you went to when you clicked on important signals for ads. This time however it will show you that the advertiser has been blocked as seen below.

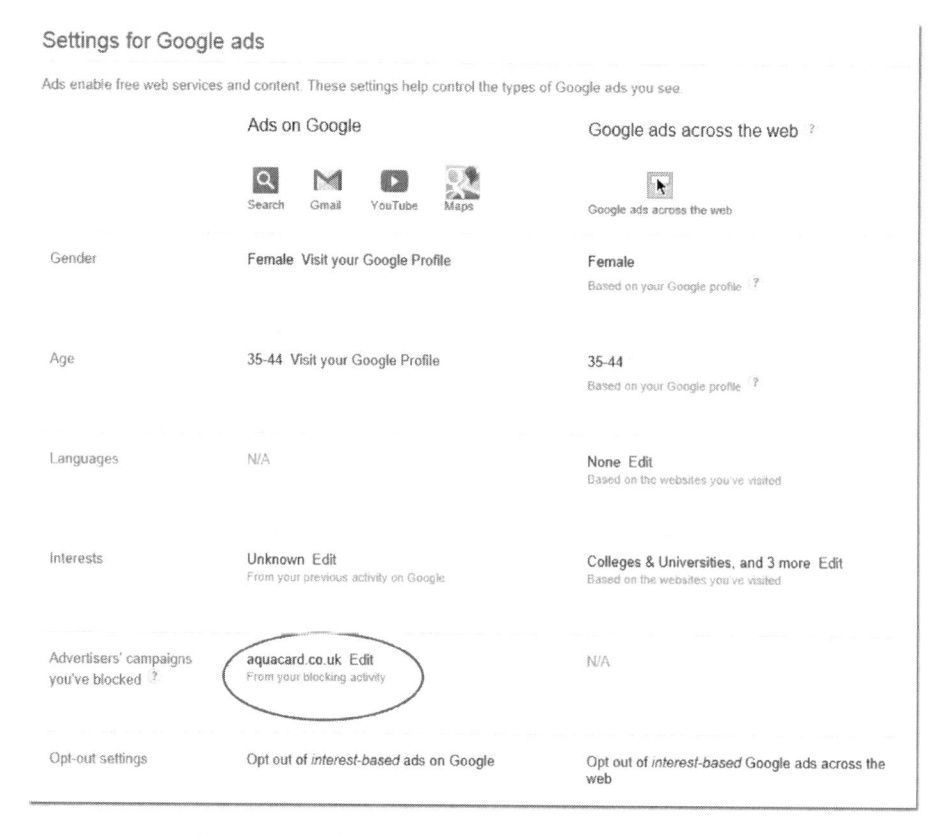

Figure 127 Advertisers' campaigns you've blocked

Signature

Figure 128 Example of a signature

Your signature is how you end your email, it saves you having to type the same information time and time again. You can just add text, your name, address, phone number etc., or you can even add images. The formatting options are above the typing window as it is in composing emails or in your standard word processor.

Tip

You can have different signatures for the different email addresses you have in Gmail, If you set up the *Send mail as* option in *Accounts and Import* then you can choose an option in the dropdown box (under *No signature*) to set up a different signature for each email address you can send from.

Adding an image to your signature from Google Drive

You can add an image from any publicly available online storage simply by typing the location of the image in the box provided. However, Google's Drive is the logical choice if you do not already have storage, after all by opening any Google account you will automatically have a Drive account.

What is Drive? Drive is free online storage of files and photos. It is also the place where you can create free spreadsheets and documents, however for the purposes of the email signature the online uploading feature is the one you need.

In your email, click on the picture of 9 squares and choose *Drive* as seen circled in figure 129 below.

Figure 129 How to get to Drive from your email

Next, create a folder where you can keep your signature images. You may want to have a different one for different email addresses. Click on *Create* under *Drive* and choose *Folder*.

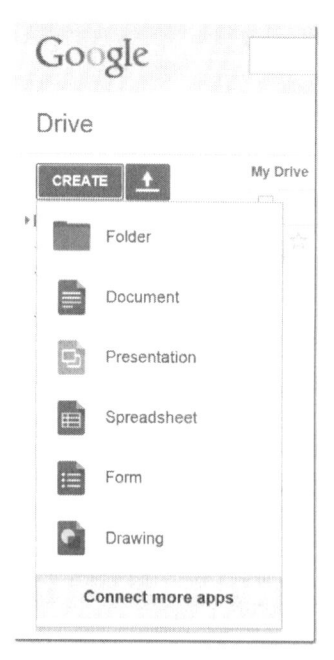

Figure 130 Create a folder

Type in a name into the box that pops up, I chose *Signature* as I think that best reflects its purpose and click on *Create*.

Tick the box next to the new folder name that loads and click on *Share* where you can make it publicly viewable.

Next to *Private – only you can access* and click on *Change*. On this page you can also see the link for sharing. You will need this later. Open a new document in a program such as notepad or a word processor and copy the link from the webpage (Ctrl + C) and then paste into the new document (Ctrl + V).

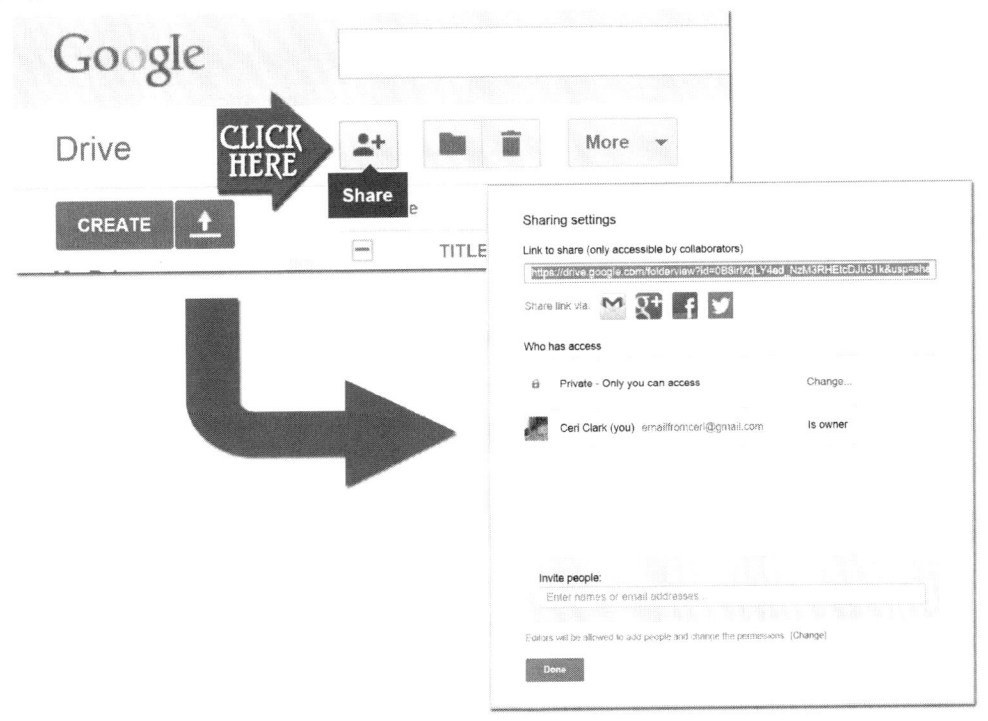

Figure 131 Sharing settings

Click on the circle next to *Public on the web* and then click on *Save*.

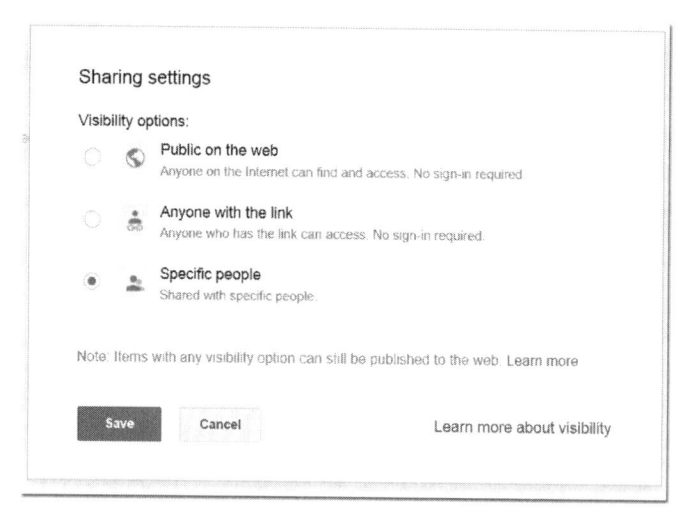

Figure 132 Make your folder Public

Anyone can now view anything in this folder as long as they have the link.

Click on your folder name in the list and then either drag your folder on to the page or click on the upload icon next to *Create*. The upload icon looks like a horizontal line with an arrow pointing up. Click on *Files*.

Figure 133 Upload your file

You will then be able to choose your image file then click open for it to upload. Your file will inherit the public view status from the folder but you can check this by clicking to the left of the file name and then clicking on *Share*. You will see its visibility status there.

You will now need to know the file name. Click on the file in the list and the screen will darken. You will be able to see the file name at the top left of the screen (it will usually end in jpg or tiff). Copy and paste the name into the document you opened earlier in this section or just type it.

Figure 134 Upload your file

Next, you will have to make the URL to put in your signature. The beginning of the URL should read https://googledrive.com/host/. After this you should put the folder id and the filename.

In my example the URL would be constructed like this:

Beginning of the URL

https://googledrive.com/host/

Folder ID

Look for the numbers and letters after *id=* in the URL and finish before the *&* sign.

URL of folder:

https://drive.google.com/folderview?id=**0B8irMqLY4ed_NzM3RHEtcDJuS1k**&usp=sharing

Id:

0B8irMqLY4ed_NzM3RHEtcDJuS1k

Filename

mysignature.jpg

Finished URL:

This would make the image URL:

https://googledrive.com/host/0B8irMqLY4ed_NzM3RHEtcDJuS1k/mysignature.jpg

Now that you have the Image link to add to your signature, go back to the signature settings (*Gear Wheel* >*Settings* > *General* > *Signature*). Click into the signature box where you want the image to appear and then click on the add picture icon.

Figure 135 Add an image to your signature

Copy (Ctrl +C) and paste (Ctrl + V) the URL you constructed earlier into the Image URL box and if the URL is correct the image will appear below as confirmation.

Figure 136 Add the URL to the image box

Finally click *OK* and then *Save Changes* at the bottom of the settings page and your new signature will become active. Every time you compose and email, the signature will appear.

Figure 137 Email with active signature

It has been known for a picture in the signature to not work. It appears that the link may get corrupted somehow. Keep a note of the picture URL that you constructed earlier in this section and save it in your Google Drive beside the picture.

If you have any problems with the picture in your signature, simply remove the original by clicking on the little x where the picture used to be and choose *Remove*. Then paste the URL from the document that you made before into the link box again (click on the picture of the chain) in your signature in settings and you should see instantly that the picture is working again.

Personal level indicators

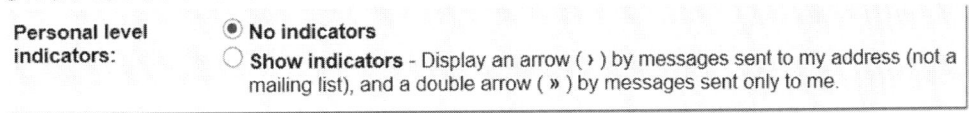

Figure 138 Turn on indicators to show if an email was sent only to you

I would recommend turning these on, but if you don't plan on joining any mailing lists, then this is not important. This could be a good indicator of spam. You would find out if the email was sent directly to you and not to a generic mailing list address before you opened it.

If you are using your account for business purposes then this is useful as an email sent only to you could be an indication of whether you have to action the email.

Snippets

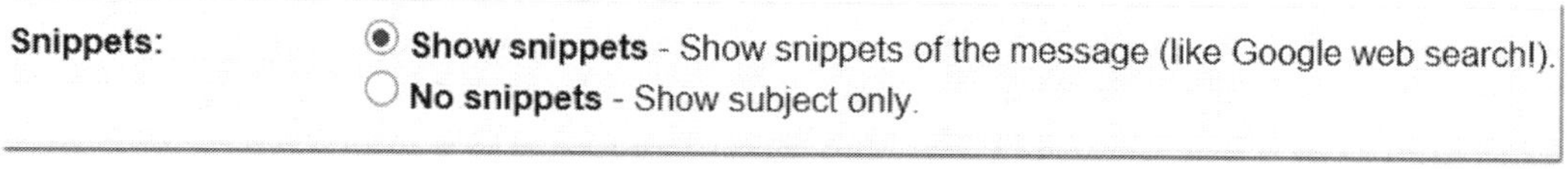

Figure 139 Allow the first line of your emails to be seen in the email homepage

This option is a matter of personal preference. If you check your email in a public place then you may prefer to have this switched off. What it does is put the first line of your email viewable from the inbox. It can be a time saver as it tells you what is new in a conversation at first glance but it can also let other people looking over your shoulder know a little of what has been sent to you. The choice is yours.

Vacation responder/Out of Office AutoReply

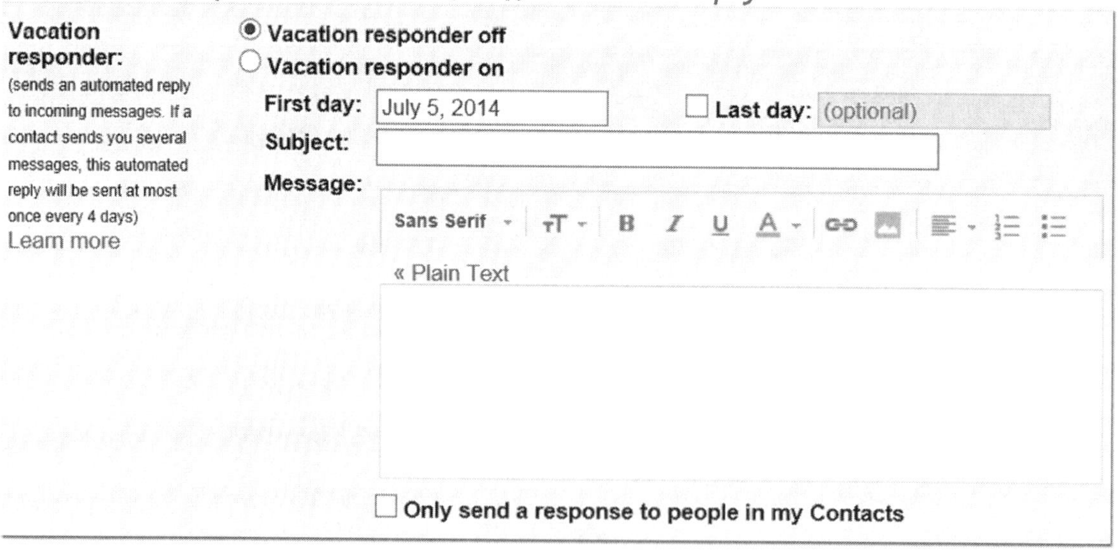

Figure 140 Vacation auto-responder/out of office settings

This section is very useful in a business context. It allows you tell your contacts that you are not available when you are on holiday or if you are indisposed. If you want to use this for your holidays, remember to click on *Only send a response to people in my Contacts*. You don't want potential burglars knowing you are on holiday or spammers/hackers knowing you might not be checking your email!

Under the Hood - Settings

You can schedule the message so it will be sent while you are away and automatically turn off when you are back.

Another possible (business) use is as an auto responder if you were to not include an end date. You can write a message such as "Thank you for your email. Your message is important to us and we will get back to you as soon as possible."

Again you can restrict this message to people in your contacts if you put phone numbers and other contact details you may not want generally known.

Outgoing message encoding

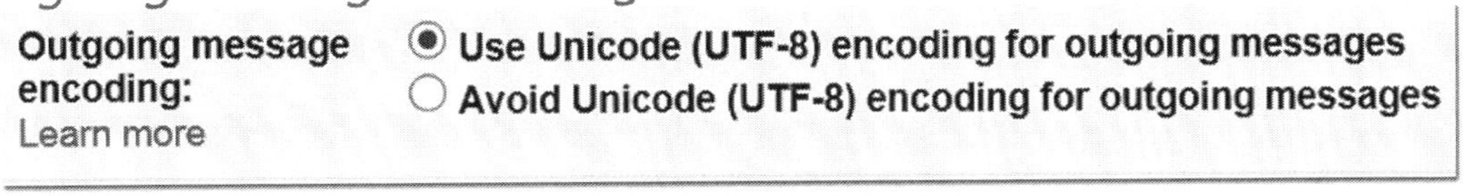

Figure 141 Unicode settings

Keep this as the option already chosen. This will allow you to communicate with other countries where a different script is used.

Remember to click on *Save Changes* after each change to your settings!

Labels

I have gone into more depth in *Chapter 7: Sorting Emails – No More Folders with Labels*, but if you have jumped to this section, basically, think of them as folders but where one email can be in several folders/places at the same time.

This is the place where you can organize your emails by specifying what labels i.e. 'folders' you want to see on the left column. I would suggest you need the Sent Mail, Drafts, All Mail and Bin and add anything else when and as you need it.

Inbox

The inbox settings are Google's way of organizing your emails for you. If don't want to use filters, using Google's Inbox feature can de-clutter your main inbox window without any effort other than choosing which of their categories you want to use.

Figure 142 Inbox settings overview

The first options that you will see are the inbox types. You can customize how your inbox is organized here. These options will change what you will be able to see and do in the settings page:

- Default
- Important first
- Unread first
- Starred first
- Priority inbox

Each option has their own particular look and functionality. Try them all out to see which suits you best. I will talk in more details about each type next.

Default

If you choose default next to inbox type, then you can choose which categories you want to activate (if any). If you do choose default and categories I would strongly suggest that you also check the box next to include starred in Primary, simply for the reason if you have gone out of the way to star it or make a filter to do it then you clearly want to see it as a priority. You wouldn't want your starred email to be buried in social for example.

Under the Hood - Settings

> **Tip**
>
> If you just want one inbox without any tabs, simply choose default and then uncheck all the categories.

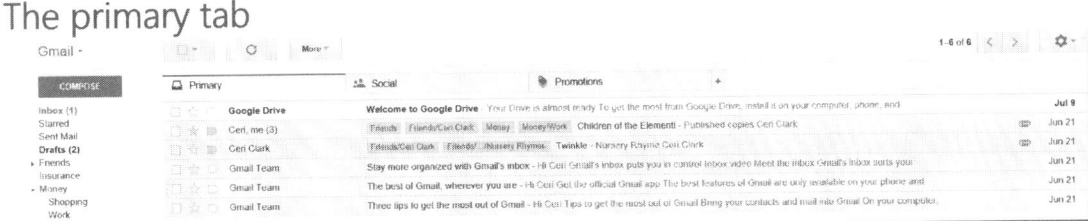

The primary tab

Figure 143 Default inbox example (Primary tab)

Your primary tab, is the first tab you will see when you open your inbox. It should have all the emails that you or Google thinks are important to you. If Google cannot classify emails, then they will go into here.

The social tab

Figure 144 Default inbox example (Social tab)

Google will put any emails from social networks in this tab to stop them cluttering up your primary inbox. These can be from Facebook, Goodreads to Twitter.

133

Ceri Clark | A Simpler Guide to Gmail

The promotions tab

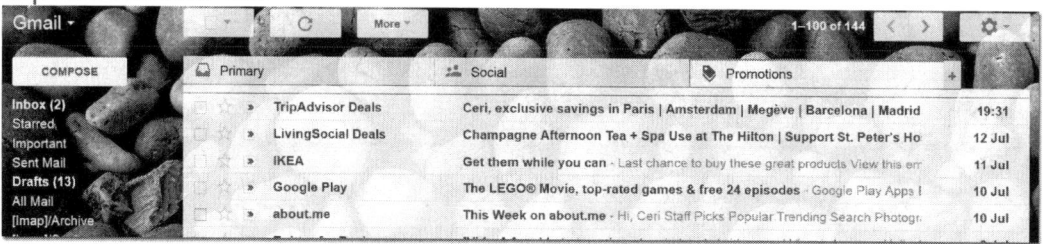

Figure 145 Default inbox example (Promotions tab)

The promotions tab is for all those emails offering you deals on your favorite stores that you signed up for in the past. If you don't want these but you remember signing up in the first place then you can usually unsubscribe by going to the bottom of the open email and locating and clicking on the word *unsubscribe*. If you didn't sign up for the emails then feel free to mark them as spam.

The updates and forums tab

The emails categorized as updates are usually confirmations, receipts, bills, and statements and emails put into the forums category are usually from mailing lists or forums.

Tip

Sometimes emails are put into the wrong category. You can easily tell Google where the correct place to put these emails by the following two methods:

1. Drag the email from its current location and 'dump' it in the tab you want.

2. a) right-click on the offending email

b) then, right-click on *Move to tab* and choosing the correct category as seen below.

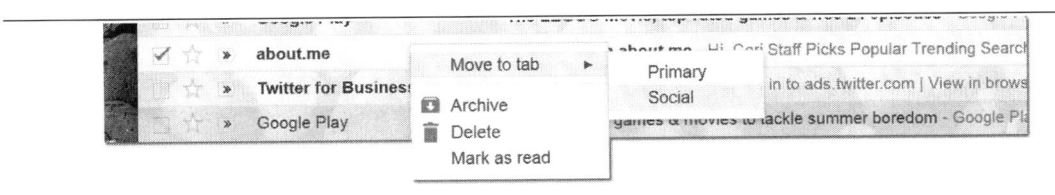

Figure 146 How to change a wrong category

In either method, Gmail will ask you at the top of the page if you want it to remember this categorization for future emails. Click *Yes* if you do, ignore if you don't.

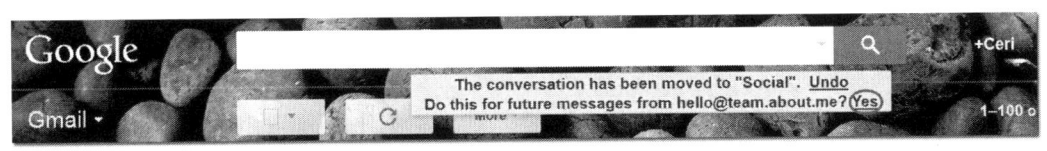

Figure 147 Make change of category apply to future emails

Important first

The *Important first* inbox type puts important emails at the top and everything else below. This has the benefit of only having the one inbox. However you will have to trust what Google considers important mail unless you have created filters for emails you know are coming.

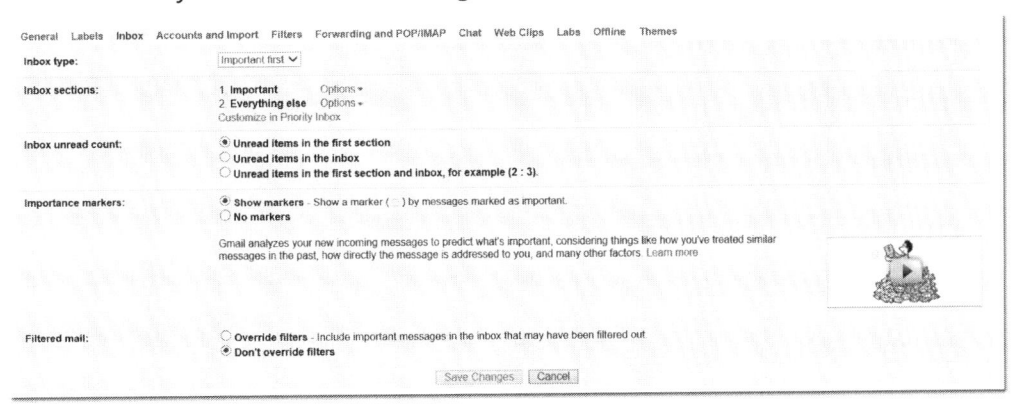

Figure 148 Options for Important first inbox type

If you only have a few emails, then this could be the answer. If you have been using your Gmail account for a while and have consistently organized your email with filters and generally used your account, Google will be able to make more accurate guesses for what is important to you.

If you hover your mouse over the yellow arrow next to your email discussion, Google will explain why it thinks the emails are important. You can click on the arrow to let Gmail know it isn't important.

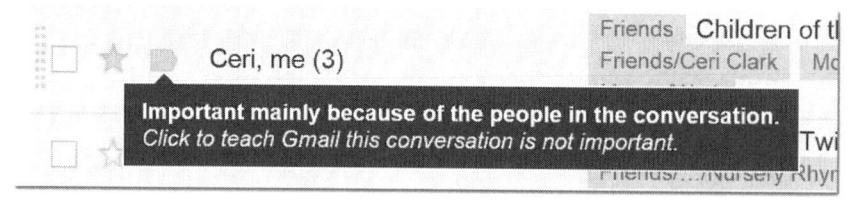

Figure 149 Why emails are marked important

The different options in the *Inbox unread count* didn't change the inboxes in the tests I undertook so I would leave these options as they are when you find them.

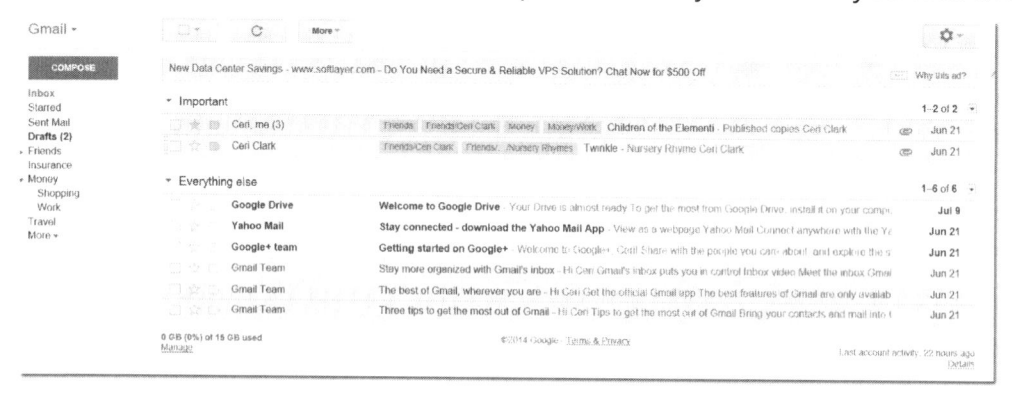

Figure 150 Important first inbox type layout example

Unread first

The Unread first inbox type does what it says. Any email that you have not read yet will appear at the top of your inbox. Again, you will only have the one inbox to look through. If the way you use your email is task based (you assess an email and deal with it immediately or later) then with this option you will see which are the new emails first that you need to sort out when you first open up Gmail. After this you can tuck in to the emails that you have read but didn't immediately need action.

Under the Hood - Settings

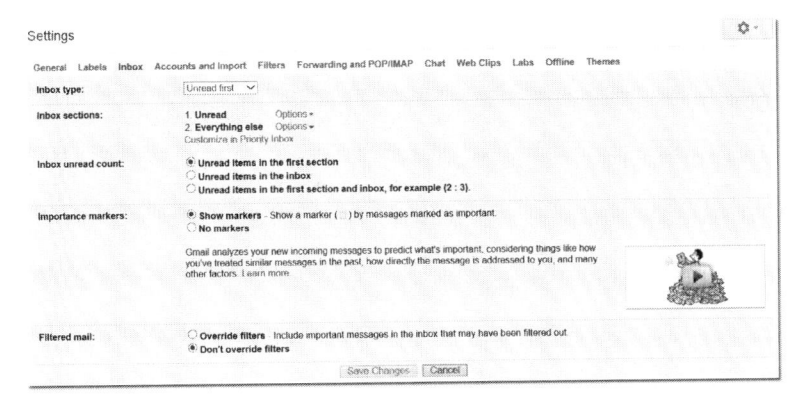

Figure 151 Unread first inbox type settings

The different options in the Inbox unread count didn't change the inboxes in the tests I undertook so I would leave these options as they are when you find them.

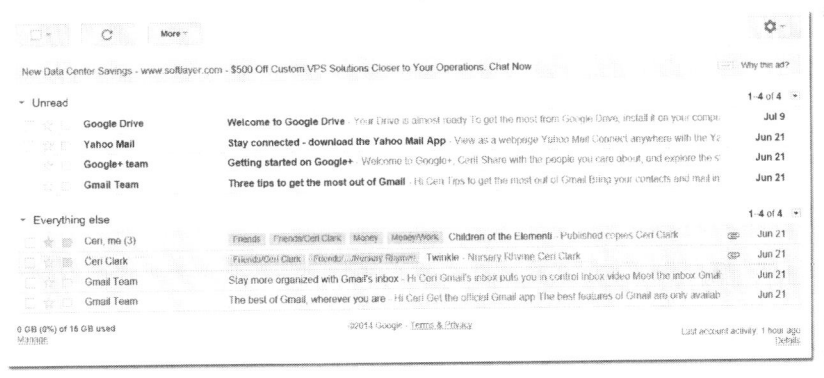

Figure 152 Unread first inbox type layout example

Starred first

All emails that you star or have starred by Gmail using filters will appear at the top of the list and everything else separated underneath. This option also means that you only have the one inbox to look through.

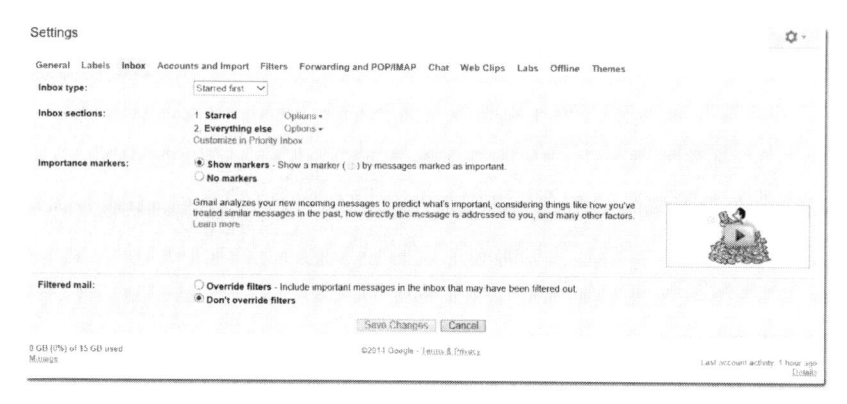

Figure 153 Starred first inbox type settings

If you have a lot of starred emails, it could get a little annoying to scroll through lots of email before you get to new emails. However if you star emails you are working on or only have a few, then this could be a good option for organizing your email.

It is possible to prioritize your starred email by clicking on the star beside the email you want to mark important. By clicking on the star you will scroll through the options you set in the general settings. As you can see below, Gmail will group the stars of the same type together.

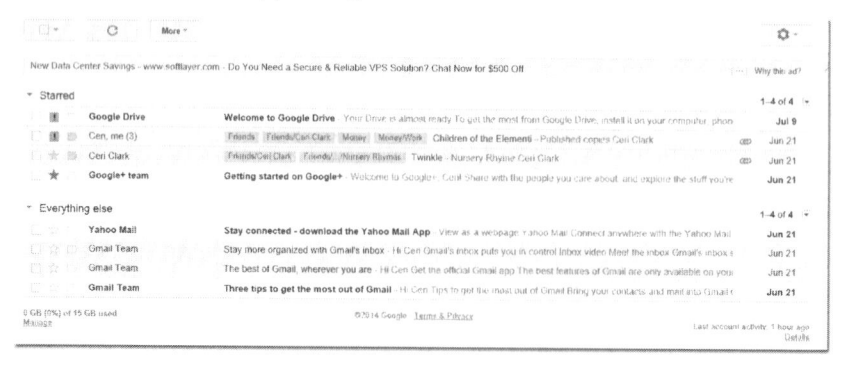

Figure 154 Starred first inbox type layout example

The order that you have the stars in the settings will set the importance in the starred list. The first stars are the least important while the last star you drag and drop will become the most important.

138

Priority inbox

This leaves the Priority inbox. In this view items that Google think are most important will appear at the top. Click on *Priority inbox* next to the inbox type to activate it and then *Save Changes*.

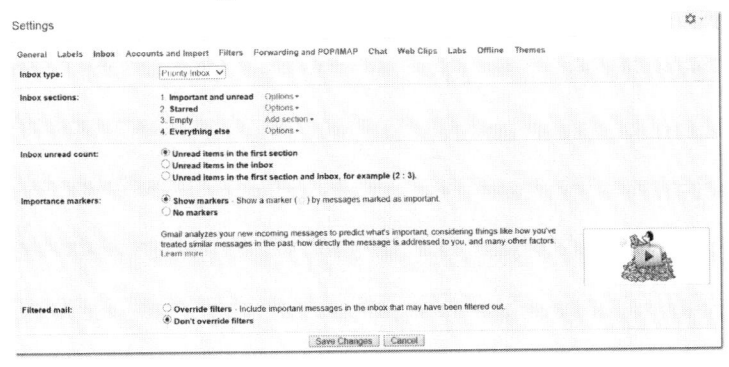

Figure 155 Priority first inbox type settings

Even though Google will try to prioritize for you, you can also dictate inbox sections by clicking on *Options* next to the appropriate section (see the next graphic for more details).

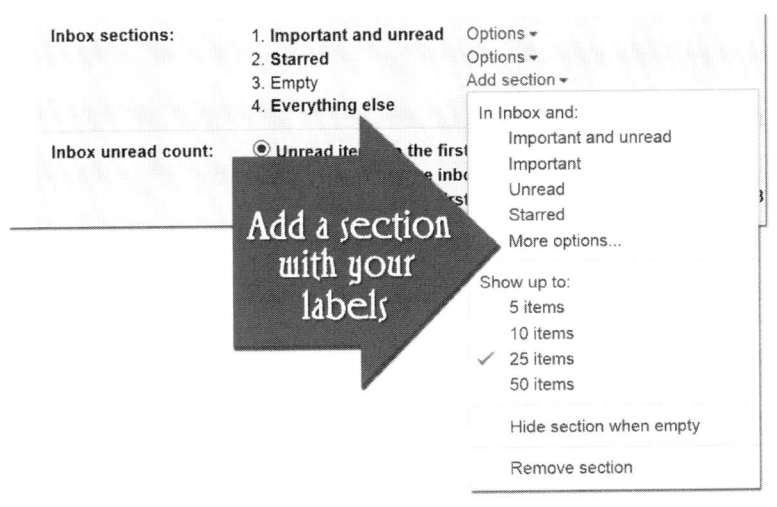

Figure 156 Inbox sections settings

If you click on *Options* or *Add section*, you will have the options above. You can choose the Gmail standard inbox settings or you can add your own section based on labels you have created. You can also choose how many items will be displayed and whether you want to hide or remove a section.

When you click *Save Changes*, your inbox will instantly change as seen here:

Figure 157 Priority inbox enabled

Your inbox can be customized further, once you have chosen the priority inbox you can choose how it is laid out with the following options:

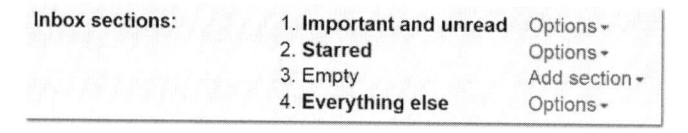

Figure 158 Priority inbox sections

By clicking on *Options* you can change how many emails appear in each section but number three is the most interesting option of these. Click *Add Section* and you can choose a label as a section. This means that you can have all your emails about a certain subject right there in full view in your inbox. If you have set up filters so that your inbox is bypassed, you will see the newest five emails on the subject of your choice.

You can bypass filters by the *Filtered mail* section of the inbox settings. This will include emails that Google feels is important to you even if you have filtered them out.

Under the Hood - Settings

Accounts and Import

This section is for changing your password, importing your old email from another provider, granting access to your account and adding storage.

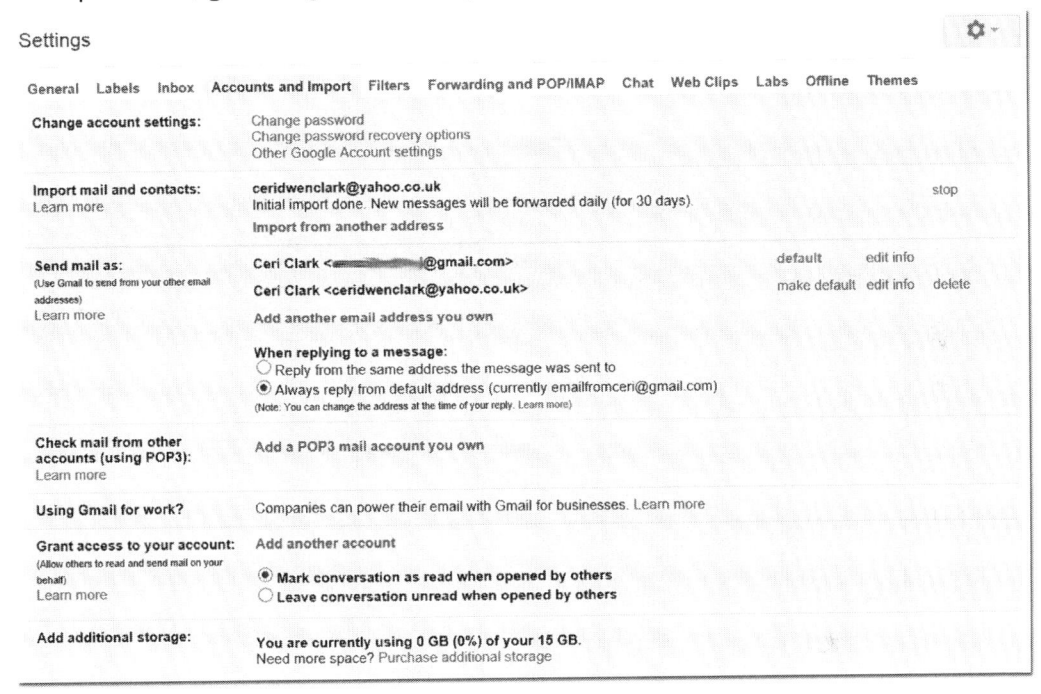

Figure 159 Accounts and Import settings

Change Account Settings

Figure 160 Password and other Google Account settings

You should always have different passwords for different websites. Google allows you to have one password for all of its services. You may need to change this password from time to time. Perhaps it has been used on more than one site and has been compromised, or the password just needs changing. Clicking on *Change password* allows you to do this.

If you forget your password you will need to have made sure that your recovery settings are updated. The second option in this section will give you a page where you tell Google about a phone number or an alternative email address in the rare circumstance that you have forgotten your password.

The *Other Google Account settings* points to a page where you can again put in alternative contact details but it also gives you access to settings for *Other Google services*. For example, the link sends you to a page about your profile but there are tabs along the top where you can look at security, language, data tools and account history. It is worth having a look around these pages even though they are not strictly just Gmail related.

Import mail and contacts

Figure 161 Importing your mail and contacts from your alternative and old email accounts

When you first set up your Gmail address you will have imported mail and contacts during the set up process. You can either stop the importing (if you took the option to import new messages daily for 30 days) by clicking on stop to the right of the email address or you import from another address you may have.

If you would like to Import from another address please click on the link and then see my tutorial *Importing mail and contacts* in *Chapter 3 Getting Started*.

Send Mail As

Figure 162 Sending mail as if from another address

You may have several email addresses which you may want to keep but only wish to send email from one place. This can be done in the *Accounts and Import* section under *Send mail as*. This will mean that you can choose to send from email addresses you already have access to, which will make the recipient think you sent it from somewhere else. It also means that all your sent email will be in the one place for ease of searching.

As you would expect the email address you just created is already there. To add another one, click on *Add another email address* you own. A popup will appear giving you a wizard to follow:

1. Enter your name and email address that you already own or have permission to access.
2. Decide whether to keep the *Treat as alias* ticked or not. Un-tick if you are emailing on someone else's behalf and you want replies to go their inbox and not yours).
3. For ease of setup, choose *Send through Gmail servers*, instead of your other provider's or you can follow the instructions provided to set it up through Yahoo's servers for example. If you send through Gmail's servers and you are pretending to be from say Yahoo then this can cause problems with email systems not trusting your emails. Please bear in mind the ease of use against the possibility of not being trusted in your decision of which servers to use.
4. Verify your email address. Click *Send verification*. Google does not want unauthorized people sending from other accounts. It also ensures that if someone tried to do this for *your* account without you knowing you are

notified that someone is trying to access it. You or the person you are allowing access to your account will receive an email checking to see if they are okay with this. They or you need to click the confirmation link in the email address. If there is a problem with the link, there is a verification code as well. The easiest way by far is to click the link though.
5. Close the window and you will see that your new email address now appears in the settings with *unverified*, *verify* and *delete*. It is of course unverified until the confirmation link is clicked, verify will send you another verification email and by clicking delete you remove the email address from the account.
6. Once you have verified the access, log back in to your account. If you go back to your *Accounts and Import* section in the settings you will see that the previous options of *unverified*, *verify* and *delete* have been replaced with *make default*, *edit info* and *delete*. Only click on *Make default* if you want this to be your primary address, the one that you want to receive and send emails with. Otherwise you will get the option of which email you want to use each time you compose an email.
7. Make sure under the *When replying to a message* that you choose the *Reply from the same address to which the message was sent*. Otherwise, life can get very confusing for you and your recipient. They won't know where they should be emailing and you may give out an email address you wouldn't want a stranger, for example, to know about.

You are now set up. When you next compose a message in the *From* field where your email address appears, you can now select the new address if you so wish simply by selecting the little arrow to the right of the email address.

Check mail from other accounts (using POP3):

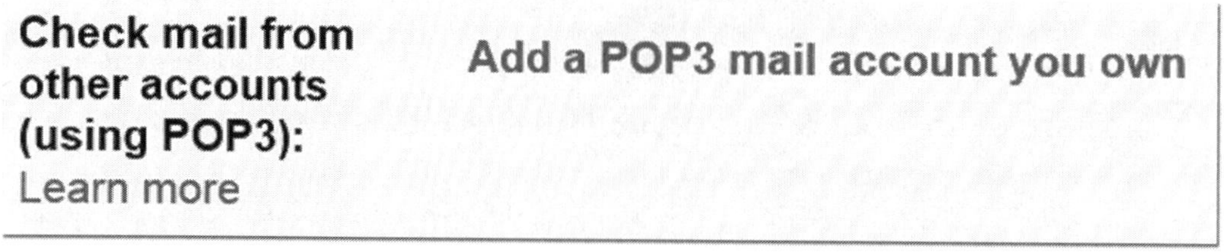

Figure 163 Sending mail as if from another address

Also in this section, you are given the option of using POP3 email. I would not recommend this. I would say import your emails and contacts and either use your new email address as is, or use the *Send mail as* feature through Gmail.

Using POP3 to import email means that you can import the email from the email address you have just created or from another address to this one on a regular basis but all folders won't be the same in every device you use. If you send from a different device then the emails from that device won't be replicated in your webmail account for example.

IMAP is a better solution which means there is a two way communication between the locations. Instead of just having your email 'pushed' to your new address, with IMAP your sent and received emails will be synchronized. This means if you are using IMAP and you are using Outlook to send emails, the emails you send will be on the web version of Gmail and also on your Android/Apple phones (if you use them). This is harder but not difficult to set up but you may as well just use Gmail on the web for convenience if you don't want to use IMAP or POP3.

If you do decide you want to use POP3, then please see the following tutorial. You can add up to five accounts.

Step 1: Type in the email address that you want to import from and click on *Next Step*.

Figure 164 Step 1 to adding a mail account

Step 2: Type in your username and password and select what you want Gmail to do to your emails and click on *Add Account*.

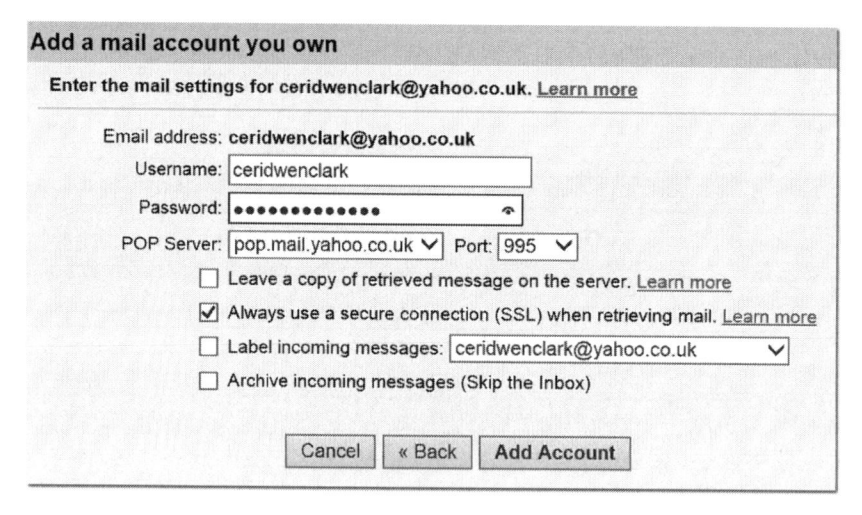

Figure 165 Step 2 to adding a mail account

Please note if you are importing from another Gmail account you will need to make sure that POP email is enabled. This setting can be found in *Forwarding POP/IMAP*. This is an important security feature as this setting could be used by hackers. Google has bypassed this by making sure you are the one to enable the feature.

Using Gmail for work?

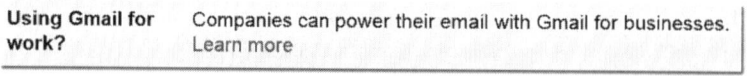

Figure 166 Gmail offers a business level service

Google does ask if you are using Gmail for work and refer you to their apps accounts. They do not guarantee anything with a free account. After all it is free and they are running a business. If you want more 'protection' then a paid apps system may be the way to go. Gmail can be sufficient for sole traders but you would need to read the terms and conditions of use to make a fully informed decision of what service you want to use.

Grant access to your account:

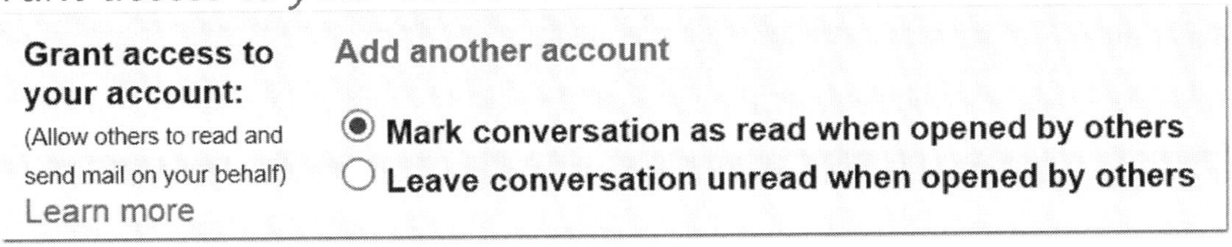

Figure 167 Let someone else use your account

Another interesting and useful feature is the *Grant Access to your Account*. This should only be done where there is the utmost trust involved but if you have a family member who doesn't really use email but they still need an account then this is a great way to help them. Another possible use is if you are a couple and want to use one account for accessing services. Instead of setting up forwarding for the emails sent by your electricity supplier why not have a joint account to which you both have access? You can of course remove access by a click of a button if you need to regain control.

Add additional storage:

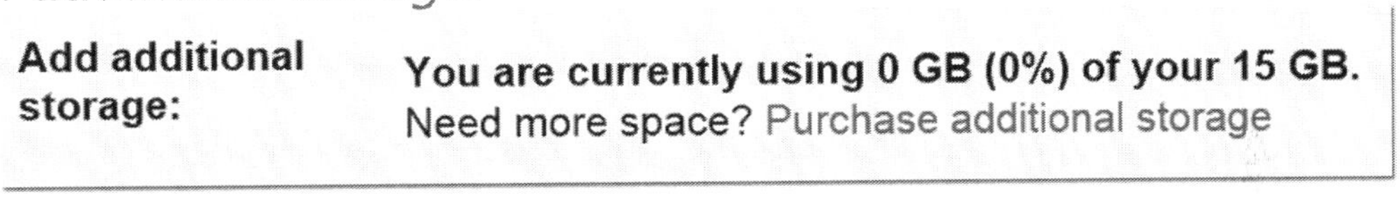

Figure 168 You can buy more storage space

When you have used your account for some time, you may feel you need more space. Click on *Purchase additional storage* in Gmail for the latest prices and limits on offer by Google.

Filters

Please see *Chapter 7 Sorting Emails – No More Folders* for more information on this. If you just need to find them, go to the gear wheel on the top right of the screen >*Settings* > *Filters* as illustrated in the next image.

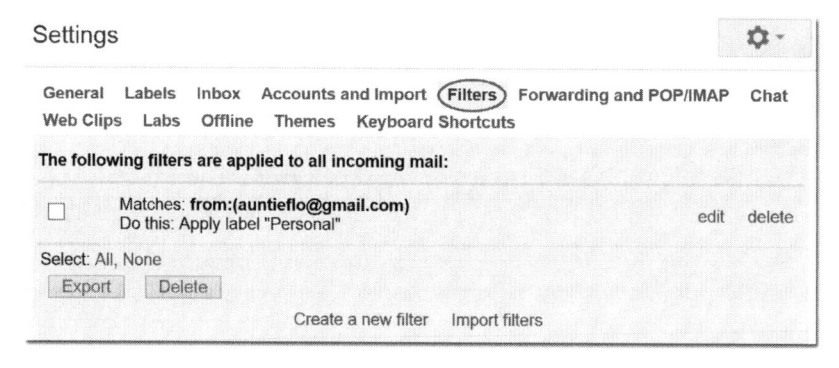

Figure 169 Location of filter settings

Forwarding and POP/IMAP

It is possible to forward all your email to another email address. For example if you would like your email to be forwarded to your work email address, then this is one possible way.

To find the options go to the gear wheel on the top right of the screen >*Settings* > *Forwarding and POP/IMAP* as illustrated in the next image.

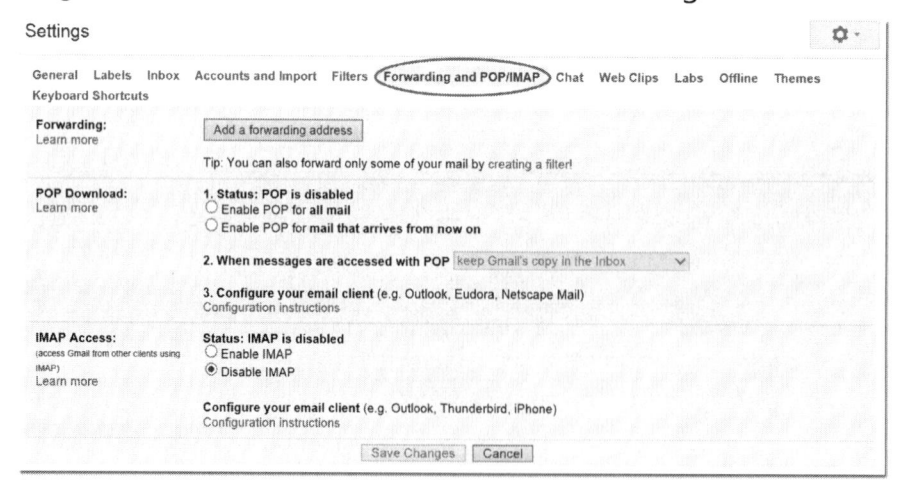

Figure 170 Forwarding and POP/IMAP settings

> **Tip**
>
> You can forward specific emails by using filters instead of forwarding all your emails. For example you might find this useful if you want to forward copies of all emails from a utilities company to your partner/spouse.

Forwarding

To add a forwarding address, click on the gray box with the words *Add a forwarding address*. A pop up will appear asking you to add an address, type it in and then click *Next*.

Figure 171 Adding an address and the Forwarding address confirmation screen

Click on *Proceed* and then *OK* and then go to the email account you specified. Click on the link in the email sent to you from Gmail. A confirmation in a browser window will let you know you have been successful. If the link doesn't work, you will be able to use the code in the same email to confirm that the other email address is happy to receive the emails.

POP Download

POP mail is used for downloading into a desktop email application such as Outlook, Thunderbird, Postbox or MacMail. This is a new email account, enabling POP for all mail if you want to use Outlook or another desktop client can be a good option. I would also recommend Archiving Gmail's copy in the drop down box. This means that when you visit the web version of Gmail you won't be overwhelmed with new email. You will know that if it has been downloaded it won't be in the inbox.

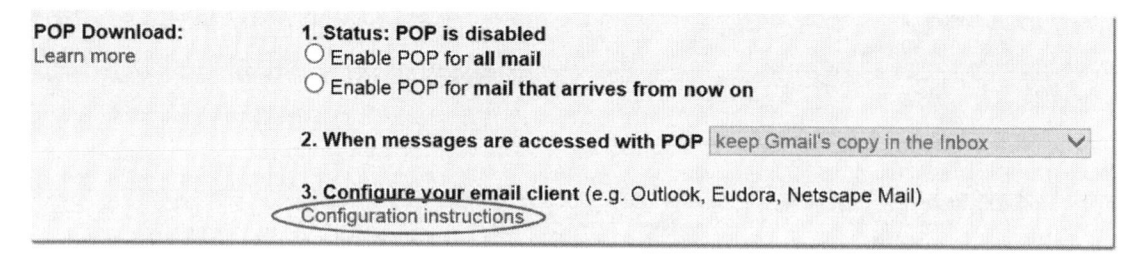

Figure 172 Pop download options

If you want to configure the settings on your particular email software, click on *Configure instructions* as seen circled in number 3 in figure 172 above.

IMAP Access

This is recommended over POP as instead of simply downloading your emails you can interact and sync it with both your email desktop application such as Outlook etc. and the web version of Gmail. This means that if you move an email in Outlook to a folder it will appear labelled in Gmail as well as other ways of accessing your email and vice-versa.

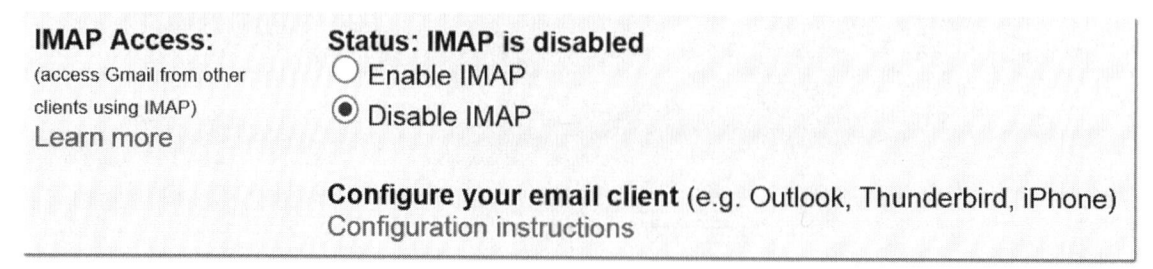

Figure 173 IMAP Access options

Make sure IMAP is enabled by clicking *Enable IMAP* and then remember to save any changes you've made.

The key settings to remember for setting up your IMAP access on your device is *imap.gmail.com* using port *993* (with SSL) for the incoming server and the outgoing server should be *smtp.gmail.com* on port *587* (with SSL).

If you are using an apps account, then you will need the same settings. The device you are using may try to use the domain from your email address but ignore this and put the Gmail information in. For example don't let it put in imap.yourdomain.com, it should be imap.gmail.com.

Chat

If you enable this option then I would recommend keeping the options as they are. The only changes I would recommend would be to change the *Auto-add suggested contacts* to *Only allow people that I've explicitly approved to chat with me and see when I'm online*.

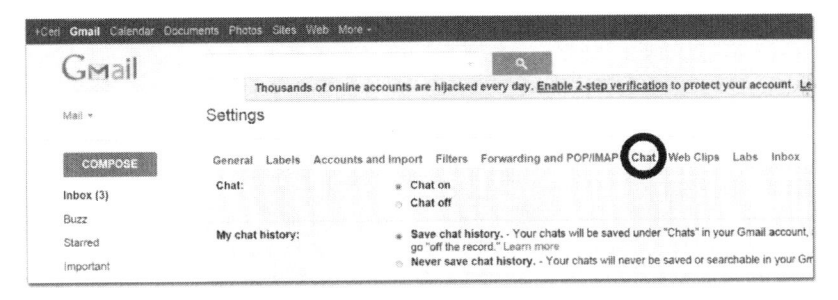

Figure 174 Chat settings

Web Clips

Web Clips are targeted ads, tips and other content Google feels you may be interested in. You have the option of turning them off by *un*ticking the check-box labelled *Show my web clips above the Inbox* at the top of the settings area. There used to be an option to keep webclips but remove certain subjects but this has been removed. I would recommend unchecking this box as there is already advertising in Gmail on the left of viewed emails so if there is an opportunity to minimize advertising I would take it.

Labs

I would ignore this setting until you are completely familiar with the Gmail system. For more information on these, please see *Chapter 19: Advanced Features - Google Labs*.

Offline

Only enable this if you have an unsteady internet connection or none for periods of time. Gmail is designed to be used online and works best this way.

Themes

There is more information on themes in *Chapter 10 Changing the Look and Feel*. However if you have jumped to this section you can changed your theme by clicking on the picture you like in *Gear wheel > Settings > Themes*.

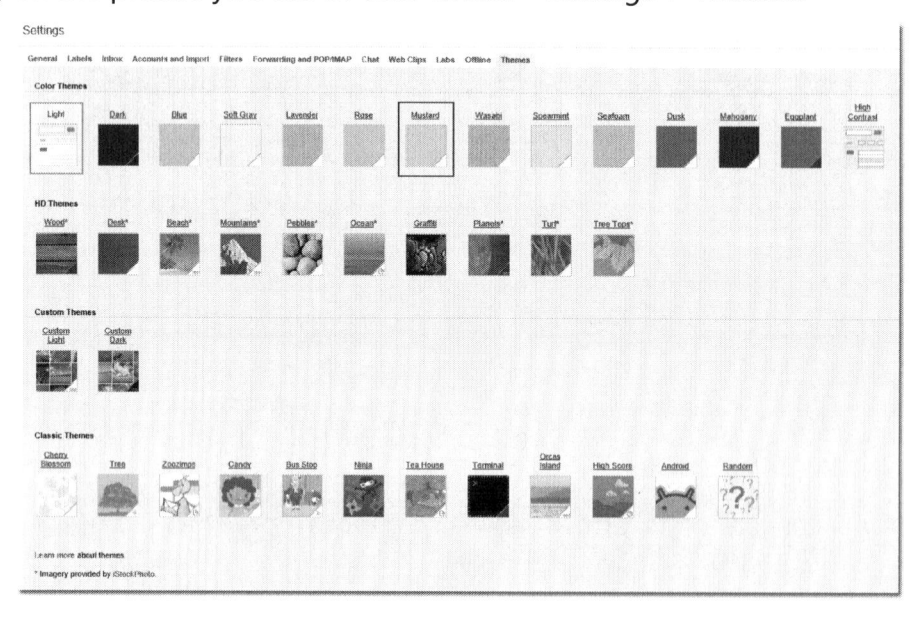

Figure 175 Themes available

Once saved your Gmail account will now always show the theme you have chosen (until you change it again of course). The screenshot below shows the *Planets* theme.

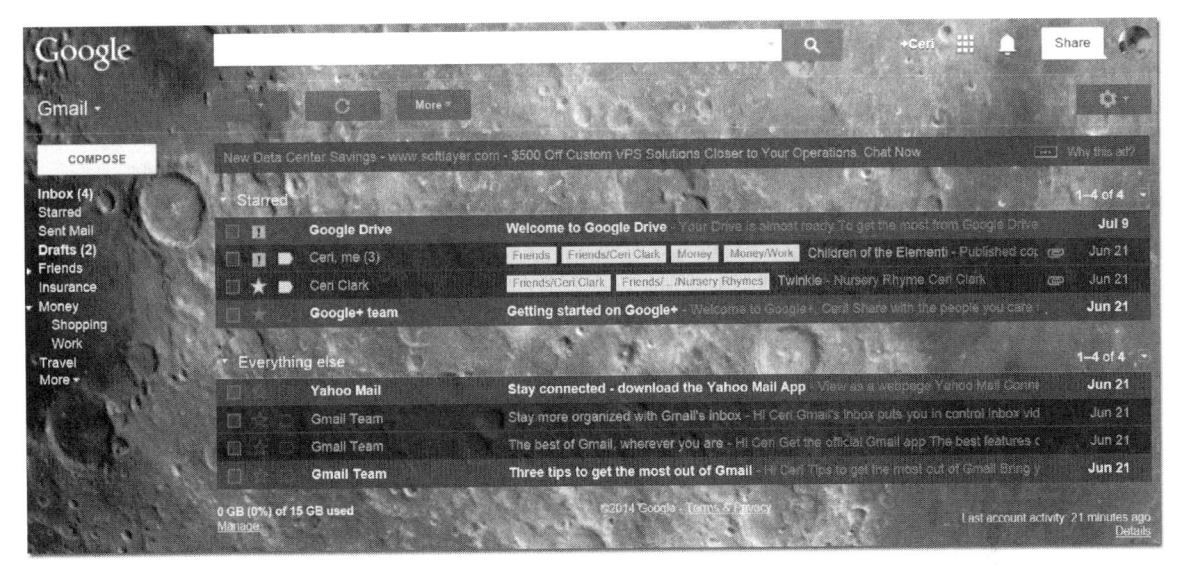

Figure 176 Planets theme

Chapter 12 Google Accounts and Your Profile

What to expect in this Chapter:

- Where to go to edit your account
- Creating your public profile

Gmail is one in a large family of products offered for free by Google. All of these services can be accessed using your Google Account and Profile. The same account for all the products that Google offers means that you only need one username and password to use Gmail, Google Docs, Calendar etc. Who wants to remember hundreds of passwords? Note, you can go direct to these services from the top of Gmail as can be seen in figure 177.

Figure 177 How to get to other Google services from Gmail

You can put as much or as little information into your Google Profile. You only need to have a public profile if you intend to use Google+.

To modify your account or edit your public profile, you need to go to your account settings, click on your picture on the top right of the screen, then click on *Account* and then choose *Edit your Google+ profile* in the Personal info box.

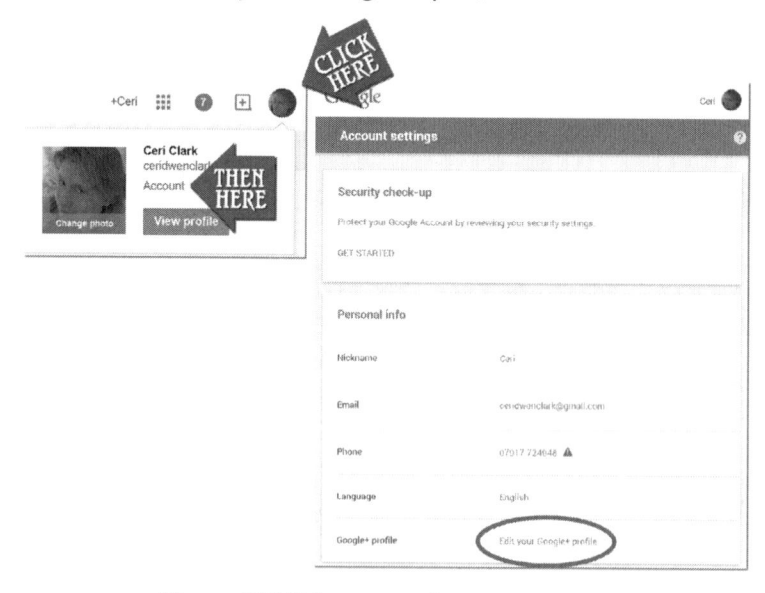

Figure 178 Where to edit your account

Google Accounts and Your Profile

You will be taken to Google+ where you can see and edit your public viewable account.

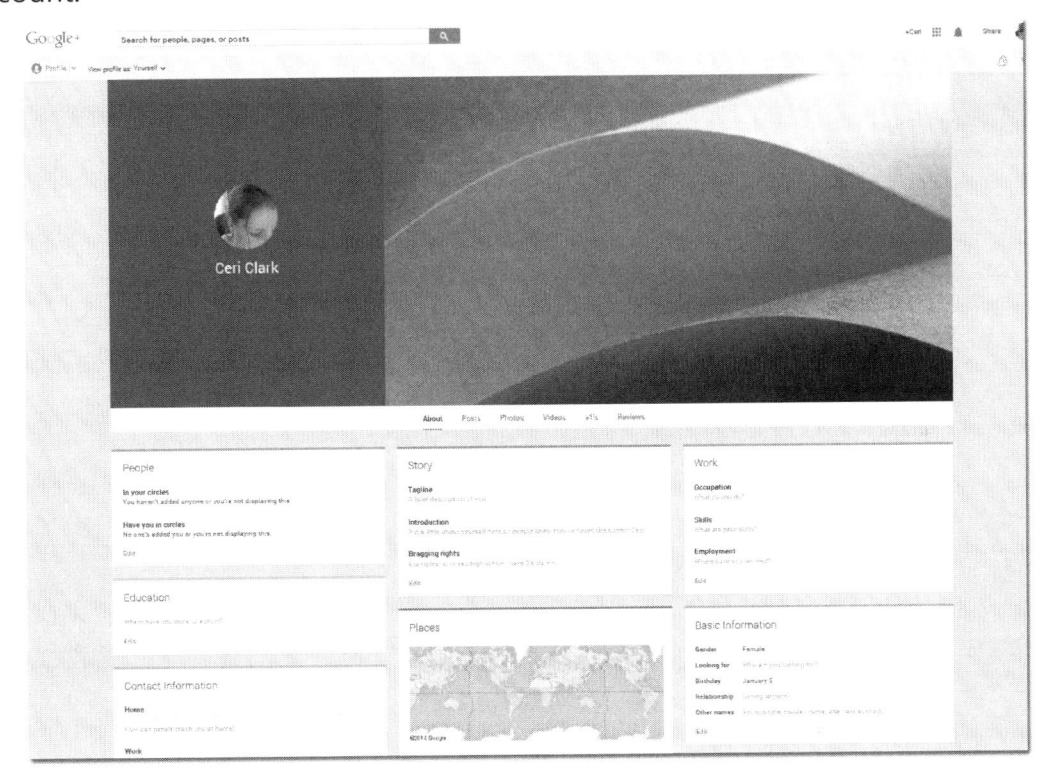

Figure 179 Where to edit your account

Creating a Public Profile

You will need to have a public profile to use Google+. Once you are in your account page (follow the instructions at the beginning of this chapter), click on *Edit* in every card you want to change. Figure 180 shows a typical card.

Figure 180 How to edit your account

Once you click on *Edit*, a page will load allowing you to put in what you want people to see. Click on *Save* when you are finished. Notice that to the right of each entry you can choose who you want to see the information. This can be just you, people in your circles, public or individuals.

Google Accounts and Your Profile

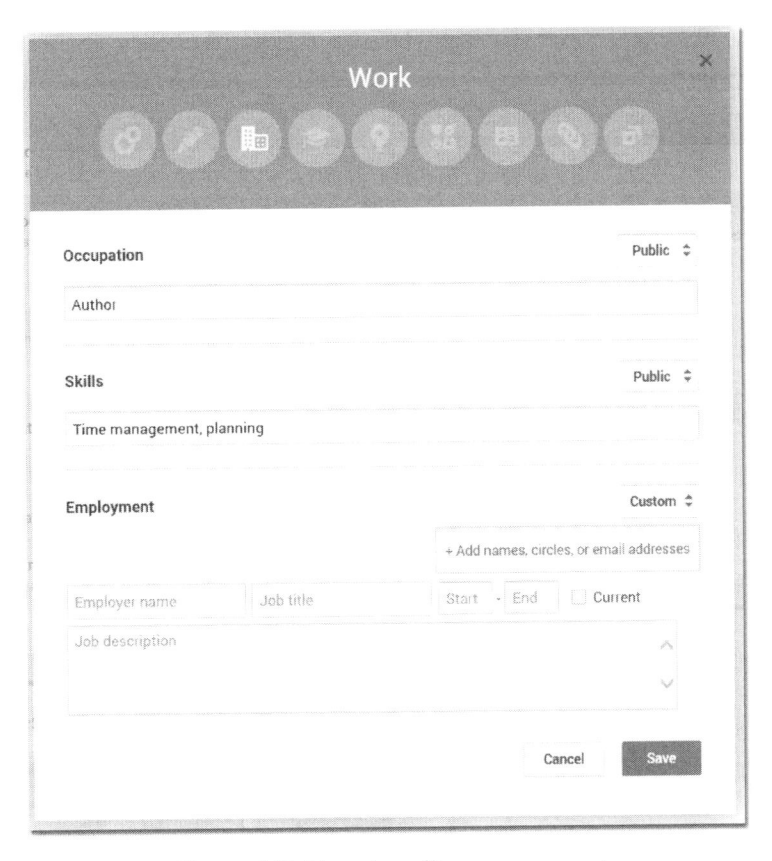

Figure 181 How to edit your account

Instead of going back to the previous page you can flick through the circles under the title of the card you are on, in the example above, *Work*. The circles represent different cards to fill all your information into. Figure 182 shows what cards are available and the symbols highlighted represent the titles of the cards. For example the first card shows two circles which represents People in the Google universe.

Adding as much information as possible can make it easier for your friends to find you but consider how much information you are comfortable sharing with the world.

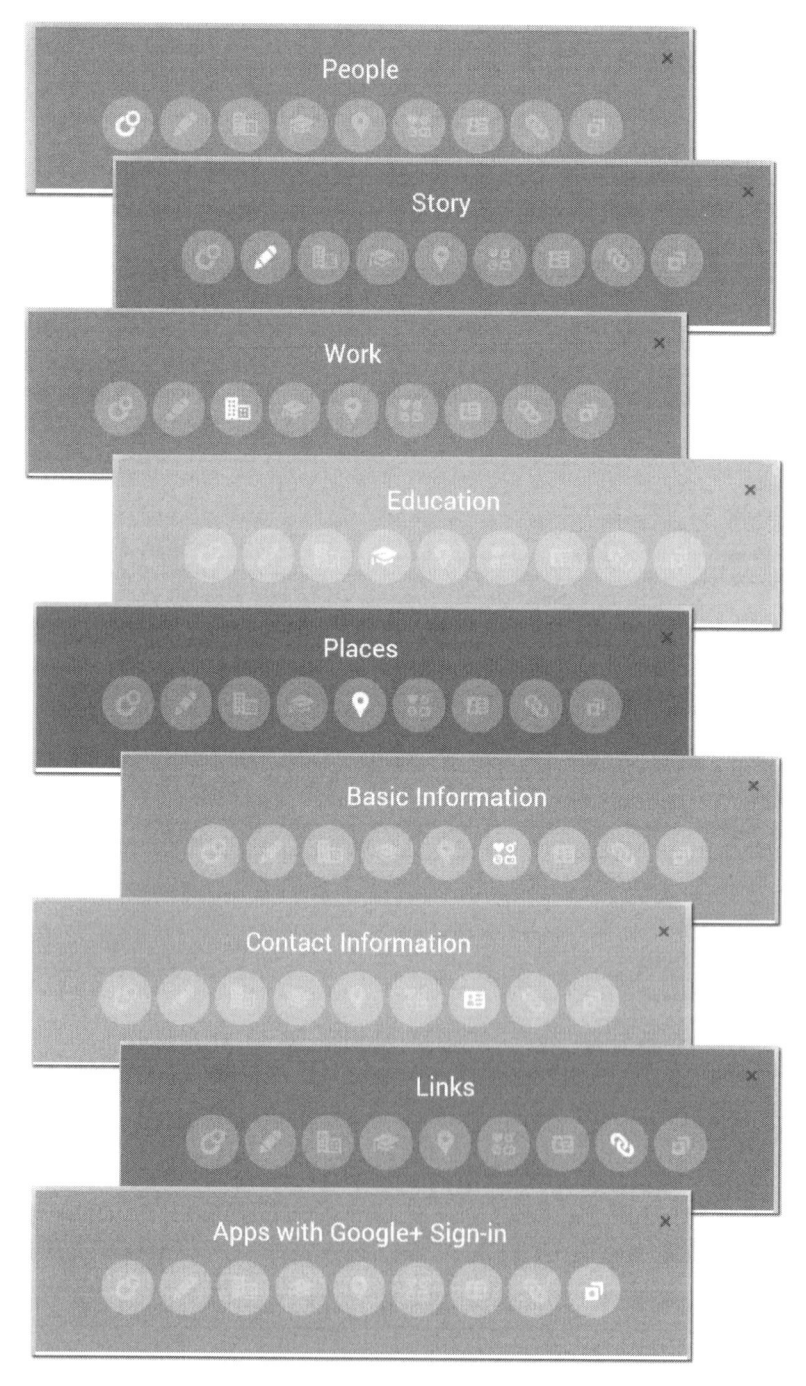

Figure 182 Updating cards

Chapter 13 Keeping Your Email Under Control

What to expect in this Chapter:
- Strategies for time management
- Blending Gmail tools to best organize your emails

Spending time setting up Gmail is only the start to keeping your email under control. If you have set up filters, labels and your settings correctly then you will only need to spend a few minutes each day going through what is important with a few more minutes to deal with non-urgent matters.

Time management

To really get to grips with your emails, I would suggest spending 10 minutes of your time each morning to deal with your emails and an hour on a Monday or Friday morning to attend to new emails and keep them organized.

To make good use of your time, I recommend turning off email notifications. Before you say but *I need to know when they arrive*, do you? If you can schedule a time or times each day to check your mail, then you can give your emails the attention they deserve. You will be able to check when you are ready and not be at the mercy of your email.

Prioritize, prioritize, prioritize

I can't stress enough how important prioritization is for an organized inbox. Google gives you several tools for this, which includes filters but starring emails will prioritize emails within inboxes, whether created by Google or yourself.

Starring emails

Star emails to be actioned. You can have different stars for how urgently the emails need to be dealt with. For example, an exclamation mark (this is still classed as a star), would be emails that need to be actioned within the next couple of days, a red star within the week, a blue star within the month and a yellow star to be dealt with by the end of 6 months. Anything that has to be sorted out immediately should already have been sorted out in your primary inbox.

If you can, set up filters that will automatically star email and sort them into the appropriate inbox. When you have dealt with your really urgent emails you will know that the less urgent emails will be there waiting and you will have a starting point for prioritizing further.

Replying to messages

Knowing which emails you need to reply to can save you time. If you have been sent an email but it wasn't directed at you i.e. you were in the cc: box, the email is probably just for information. The sender will probably be very happy not to receive 200 messages to say that the recipients have received it.

You don't have to reply to every message that needs to be actioned straight away but you can use *Canned messages* to say thank you for your email and that you will be dealing with it soon with a filter to automatically send replies.

Keeping Your Email Under Control

If you want to enable the canned response lab, go to the cog or gear wheel on the top right of your Gmail screen, click on *Settings* then *Labs*. Find *Canned Responses* and select *Enable* before clicking on *Save Changes*.

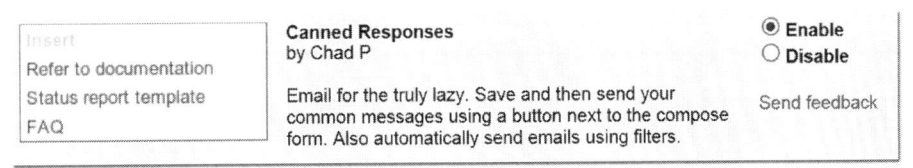

Figure 183 Enable Canned Response

Now that *Canned Responses* is available on your Gmail account, start a new email and type in what you want in your canned reply into the email. You can use the usual formatting options for example, bold, italics as well as including pictures and links.

On the bottom right of the email next to the picture of the trashcan/bin, you will see a little arrow pointing down. Select this and click on *New canned response…*

Figure 184 Creating a new Canned Response

163

A new window will load, prompting you to name your canned response. Choose a name that resonates with you. You might make a lot of these and you will want to be able to find it later.

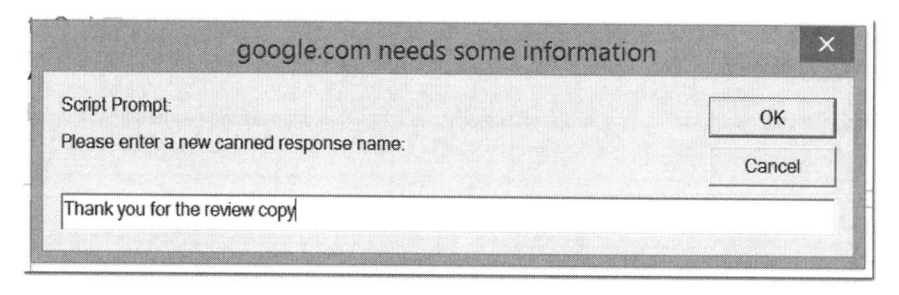

Figure 185 Naming your new Canned Response

If you made the canned message in response to a message, go ahead and click on Send. If you created the message from scratch, delete the message you created. It will now be in your canned responses.

Replying with a Canned Response

Click on *Reply* or start a new message. Go to the bottom right of your message and click on the little arrow next to the trash can/bin. Select *Canned Responses* and then choose a response from the list that you want to reply with.

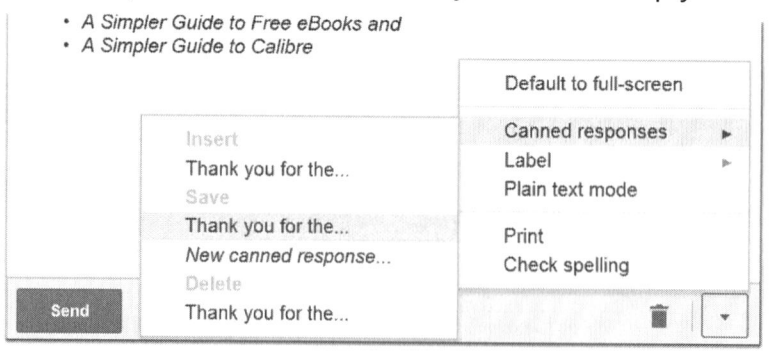

Figure 186 Inserting a Canned Response

Editing/Overwriting a Canned Response

Unfortunately you cannot actually edit a canned response but you can overwrite it. Simply follow the steps to create a canned response as detailed above and then click on the name of the canned response when you save the message.

Keeping Your Email Under Control

Deleting Canned Responses

Deleting a canned response is similar to overwriting one. Go to the little arrow on the bottom right of a new email. Click on *Canned responses* and then choose the canned response you want to delete under the light gray *Delete* as can be seen in figure 186.

Using filters to automatically send Canned Responses

If you have several canned responses, you can filter your emails so that when you get emails that meet certain criteria, they will get a canned response automatically.

In the following example I will walk you through how I would send canned responses to emails that I receive for review copies.

First create your canned response (please see my instructions on how to do this earlier in the chapter).

Go to the cog/gear wheel (top right of Gmail screen) > *Settings* > *Filters* > *Create a new filter* (bottom of screen).

For this example I typed in *Review* and checked the box labelled *Has attachment*. You can just as easily put in email addresses or a subject if the sender knows to put an exact subject in.

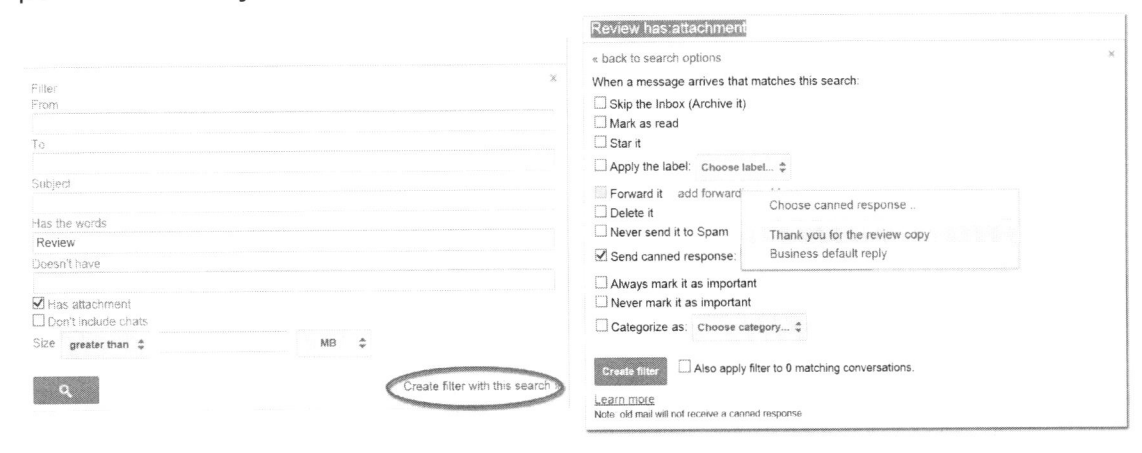

Figure 187 Creating a filter for a Canned Response

Next, click on *Create filter* with this search. On the next screen check the box next to *Send canned response* and click on *Create filter*. Now any email that has review in it and also has an attachment will automatically get the canned response I selected.

Using the inbox tabs

The goal is to have only the important unread emails that you need to deal with in your inbox. Anything else should be in folders (labels) that you deal with when you have time.

Tip

If there are emails in the wrong tabs, then all you need to do is grab the email using your mouse and drag it to the appropriate tab before dropping it in it. You will be asked if you want all future emails from that address put into the new tab. I would recommend you do so unless the email you are dropping into it is a one-off.

Using labels/folders as customized inboxes

Creating folders for your messages which do not have to be dealt with as soon as you open Gmail will mean that you will work on what matters first and then the rest in order of priority. While you can have several folders within folders for example, Newsletters, then Business Week Daily and possibly Reuters Money which could be Newsletters/BusinessWeekDaily and Newsletters/ReutersMoney, the aim is to quickly check these folders daily so you don't want to make work for yourself. I recommend having no more than three extra folders. Simplicity is the key. If you have too many folders and it gets too complicated, you just won't do it anymore. There are always far too many interesting things to do than dealing with your Gmail. Before I streamlined my email, my house received a regular lovely spring clean as a delaying tactic. My house is no longer as tidy but my email is now ultra organized!

The three labels/folders I would suggest are:

1. Pending
2. For Information
3. Newsletters

The Pending folder will contain all the email that you need to deal with that are not important enough to be in the Primary inbox, starred by importance.

The newsletters folder/label would have all your newsletters from different sources. Chances are you will not have time to read all the newsletters anyway as there are always more coming in than there is time to read. Just pick the most recent or that look the most interesting and delete the rest. Be honest with yourself, are you really going to read all those newsletters?

The *For Information* folder is for all email that you have been CC'd in. If you have been cc'd then the email was not sent to you directly. This means you can class it as not urgent because presumably whoever it was directed to is dealing with it. This means they can wait until you have time to look at them.

Your aim is that the above three folders should only have active emails in. If you only want to keep it in case you need it, file it somewhere. These folders are there to organize your mail not as storage. Set aside up to an hour on a Monday or Friday morning to sort emails out each week. If you follow all the advice in this book it could be reduced to as little as ten minutes. It will make you feel a lot better to finish the week or begin the week all organized!

Other Folders

Labelling emails is essential in Gmail. Once emails have been dealt with and archived, you may want to get hold of them again. It will be a lot more efficient to find an email if you can search within a label as your Gmail account fills up.

Another reason to have other folders apart from having the inboxes as described earlier in this chapter is for family emails that you don't want distracting you during your working day.

Using filters with labels

I go into great depth on how to use filters in *Chapter 8 Filters* but if you only use filters with labels then you will go a long way to organizing your mail. If you want to assign the label *Jobs* to all emails from your contact Jenny@WorkCorp.com, then go to the cog/gear wheel at the top right of the screen > *Settings* > *Filters* > *Create a new filter*.

Type @WorkCorp.com (in case your contact from the company changes) into the From box and then click on *Create filter with this search*.

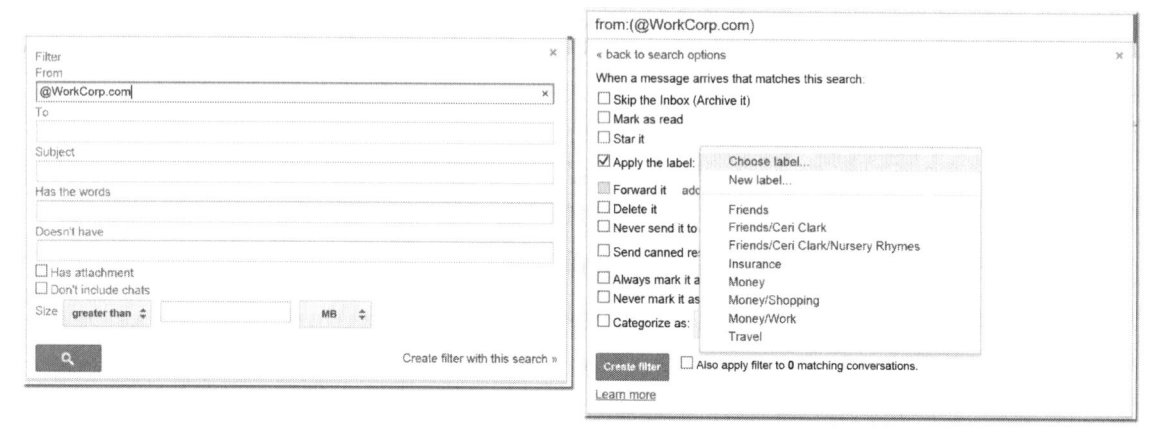

Figure 188 Creating a filter to add labels

On the next screen check the box next to *Apply the label* and if you haven't already created the label, choose *New Label* where you can input the new name. Choose the label you want, *Jobs* in this example, (once it is created) and click on the box next to *Also apply filter to x matching conversations* before clicking on *Create filter*. This will then apply to all old emails already in your account and new email that you will receive in the future.

Setting up filters from related email in your inbox

There is a quick way of creating filters straight from your inbox. This will save you an enormous amount of time.

Check the box next to the emails that you want to filter, then click on *More*, then select *Filter messages like these*:

Keeping Your Email Under Control

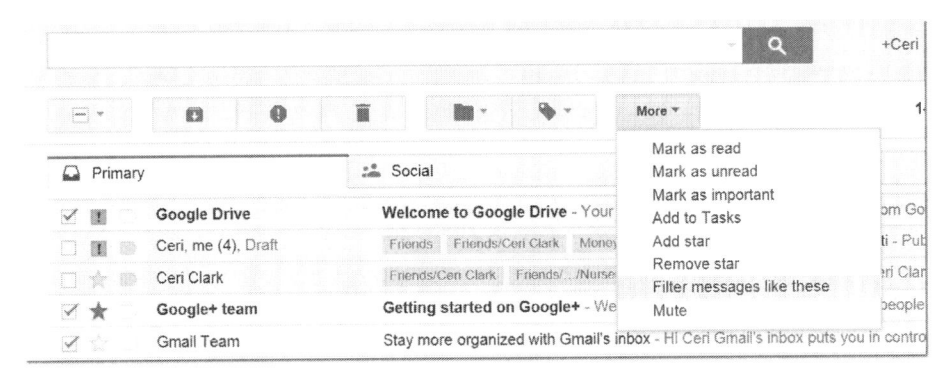

Figure 189 Signing up to Unroll.me

Gmail will populate the *From* field for you so any action you choose on the next screen will apply to any messages sent from the email addresses of the emails you originally selected.

In the example below I have skipped the inbox and chosen the label *Google* for messages from the google addresses I have already received email from.

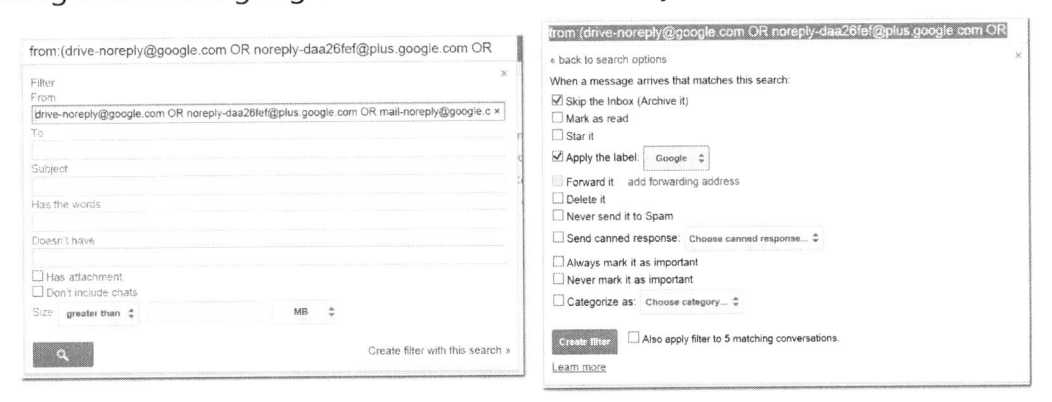

Figure 190 Filter messages like these

Unsubscribe from unwanted Newsletters

You may have signed up to newsletters in the past that you may no longer want. You can unsubscribe manually using the instructions at the bottom of emails. This is not always a reliable method as there are some disreputable companies that don't always unsubscribe you.

I would like to introduce you to a service named Unroll.me. https://unroll.me/

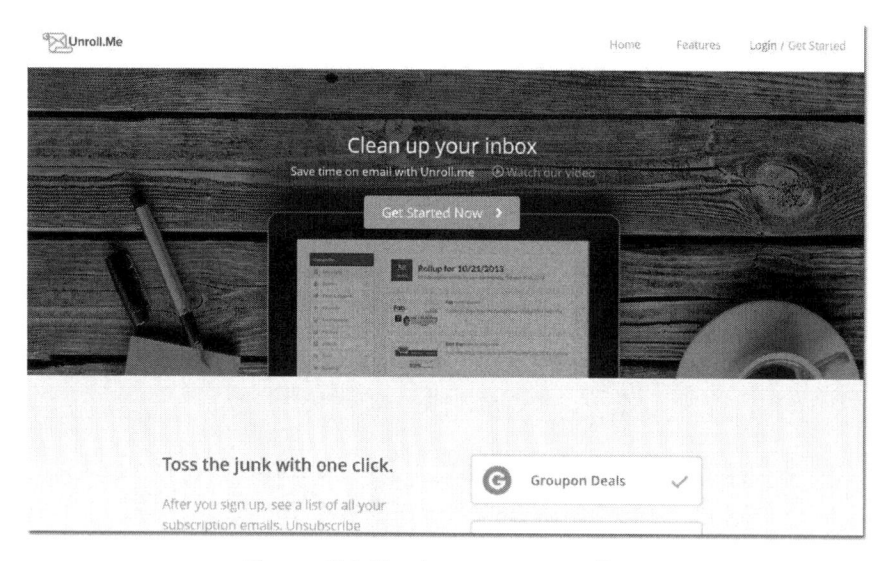

Figure 191 Signing up to Unroll.me

This service will find all the subscriptions that you have signed up to over the years in your email and it will remove them from your email in the future. You can either unsubscribe, ignore or rollup newsletters.

Your emails will be unsubscribed 24 hours after you click the box. Unroll.me follows the sender's rules for unsubscribing but in case the email sender doesn't honor the request they will trash the email for you, so you will never have to see them again. If you ignore the email at the selection stage, then the emails will remain untouched in Gmail.

The rollup newsletters are a really nice benefit to the service. All your newsletters that you want to see will be rolled up into one which you can peruse at your leisure. They are categorized so you can easily find what you want to see quickly.

Keeping Your Email Under Control

Signing up to Roll.me

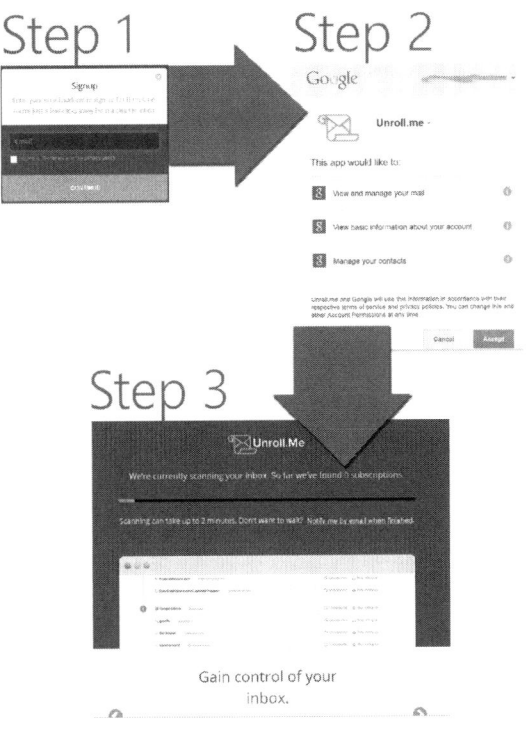

Figure 192 Signing up to Unroll.me

Step 1: Click on *Get started now* as seen in Figure 192 and then add your email address to the box provided before checking the box to agree to the terms and conditions of use.

Step 2: Accept that Unroll.me will have access to Google functions as set out in *Step 2* in figure 192.

Step 3: Watch as Unroll.me finds all your subscriptions then click on *Continue to next step*.

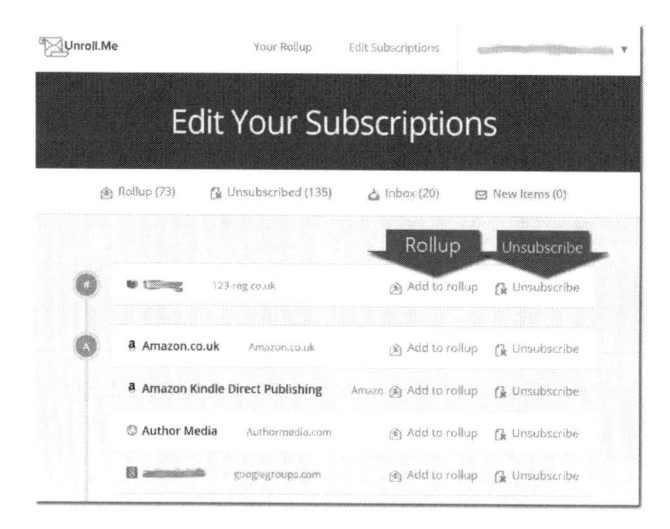

Figure 193 Add to rollup and Unsubscribing

To finish your set up, either click on *Add to rollup* to get a daily digest of all your newsletters in one email or *Unsubscribe*.

If you want to change your subscriptions at any point simply login to Unroll.me and click on *Edit Subscriptions* at the top of the screen.

Lastly find what works for you

People can only ever give you advice on how to do deal with your email. Organizing your email is a highly personal thing. What works for you does not necessarily work for someone else. You may prefer to have all your emails in a subject together as a discussion while another may want to turn this feature off (possible in Gmail) and have each email come in separately so you can see instantly what needs to be done.

It is possible you do not receive many emails at all, in which case I am very jealous, but this does make much of this chapter irrelevant. Maybe all you need is the Google inbox tabs or you are happy to turn them off and deal with emails as they come in. There is no correct way to deal with email only what works for you.

Organising your email is a continual process, using the *Filter messages like these* option will make this easier but there will always be the odd email which doesn't

Keeping Your Email Under Control

fit into any category. Unsubscribing and the spam button are also important tools in your fight to keep your emails under control.

Using all of the tips in this chapter will not only save you time but will make you work more efficiently.

Chapter 14 Introduction to Google+

What to expect in this Chapter:

- What is Google+
- Homepage Overview
- Circles and how to add people to them
- Sharing with Google+
- Hangouts

Google+ is a growing social network. It is a cross between Facebook and Twitter with the advantages of both and has a higher attention to privacy issues. At its most basic level it is a way to communicate locally and globally, with friends, acquaintances and strangers by posting and commenting, pictures, videos, as well as text and video chat.

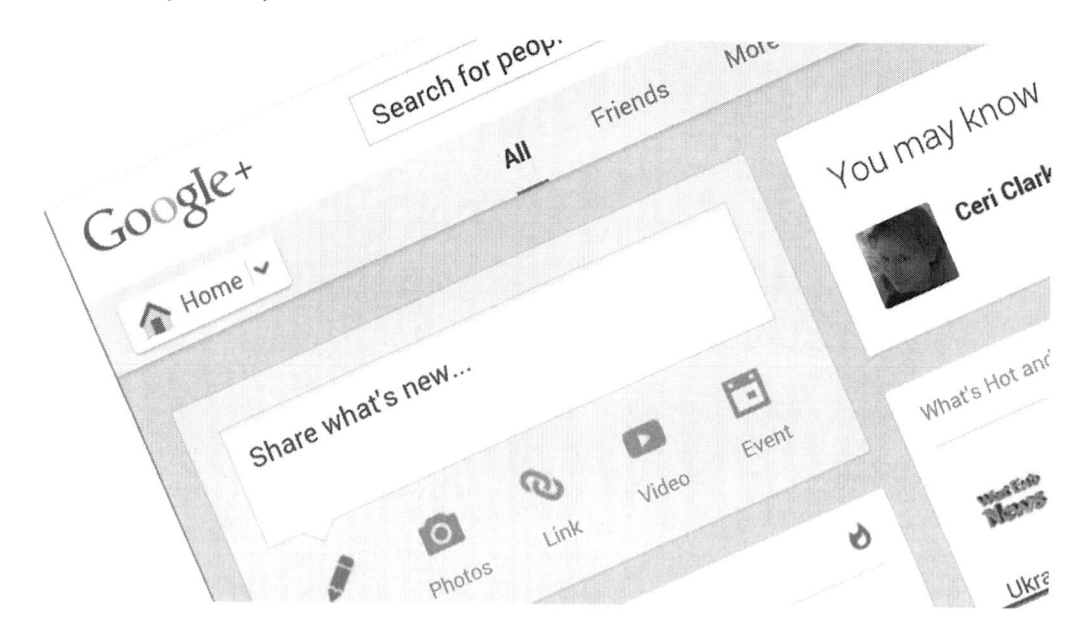

Why use Google+?

Posting on Google+ is as easy as Twitter or Facebook but it is easier to choose who you want to see your posts as you type them. In my personal experience, it is easier to have a conversation with Google+ than with say Twitter because you can say more (with better spelling!) and it is very easy to find people of a similar mind on this platform. Google+ is very content-centric, by this, I mean people are very willing to share advice, knowledge and even friendship.

How to get to Google+

Now that you have a Google Account you will automatically have a Google+ account. To login, simply find your name on the top right of the screen when you are logged in to any Google service and click on your name. There is usually a + before your name. For example, my account says +Ceri. If it says +You, then you are not logged in to Google.

If you want to go directly to Google+ type in https://plus.google.com/ into your browser.

Your Google+ homepage – an overview

Here is a brief explanation of the main elements on your homepage:

Home (the stream)

All posts in your circles will appear in the stream including yours. These can range from text only, to links, photos and videos.

Navigating Google+

The top navigation bar

The top navigation bar contains another which will drop down when you hover your mouse over *Home* or you click on it.

The next elements are where you can limit posts by clicking on your circles. This looks like this.

Figure 194 Limit the posts in your stream by selecting one of your Circles

If you can't find the circle that you created, click on *More* and all your circles will appear in a drop down bar.

Further along the horizontal menu, you will see a people icon. Clicking on this will give you some recommendations for contacts that Google thinks may interest you.

The last symbol is the hangout symbol. If you want to quickly start a hangout click here.

The dropdown navigation menu

This bar will allow you to navigate around Google+ with ease.

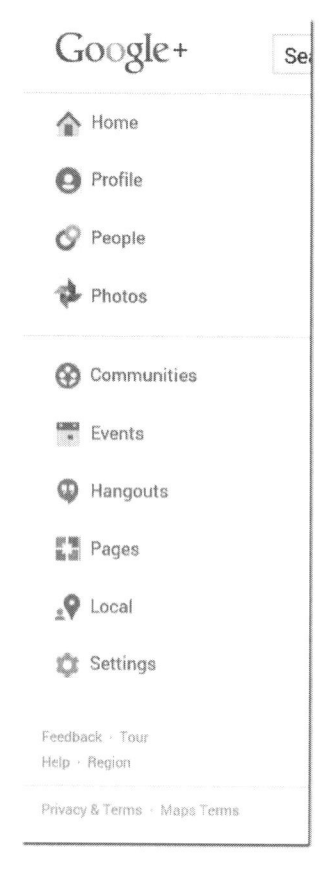

Figure 195 Click on Home to find the dropdown navigation bar

Home
Wherever you are in Google+ if you click on *Home*, it will bring you to your Google+ homepage where you will find your news stream.

Profile
You can find all your own posts here and also edit your public profile viewable from Google+. Please see the *Your Profile* section later in this chapter for more details.

People
This will take you to where Google will suggest people that it thinks you will be interested in.

Photos
This is where all the photos and videos you upload can be seen. You can choose how they are visible on Google+ and who can see them from individuals to Circles (groups of people).

What's hot
This may not appear in the menu until later, but when it does, it suggests posts you may like.

Communities
Find people of a like-mind by searching for subjects you like and join communities of people talking about the subject.

Events
This is a nifty page where you see scheduled events, hangouts or watch videos of events that you missed.

Hangouts
Go to the right of the screen to start a hangout or click on the links to apps for Android and Apple devices

Pages
Do you have a business? Do you want your business to be promoted on Google for free? Then this menu item will take you to the page where you can set up a business page on Google+.

Local
This link will send you to businesses that Google recommends which are local to you.

Settings
As the name suggests, this is where you go to view and edit your Google+ settings. I recommend looking at these every couple of months or so to see if there are any extra options.

Your Profile

If you haven't already set up your Google+ Profile, then this should be your priority. When people search for more contacts or Google recommends someone for you to add to your circles, the recommendations and results are based on what you put in your profile. If someone is looking for librarians or photographers for example, and it is not in your profile but you want to share that great article you found about your job, Google won't know so no-one will be following you to see your great post.

Setting up your profile

The information you put in your profile is important for discoverability in Google+ results. You can not only choose to put as much or as little details as you like but you can control who can see the information that you put in the profile. To get to this section Click on *Profile* in the dropdown navigation bar.

Adding a photo or cover

If you haven't already put in a photo on your Google account yet, then please do so by clicking on the circle with the blue person in it and following the instructions. I have written in more depth about this in *Adding your profile picture* located in *Chapter 2: Opening Your Account > Creating your profile*.

Your cover image (the larger picture to the right of your profile picture on Google+) can say a lot about you. It can be a picture of you at work or leisure or it could just be a picture that you like. To change your cover, hover your mouse over the big picture and the option to *Change cover* will appear on the bottom right of the picture as seen circled below.

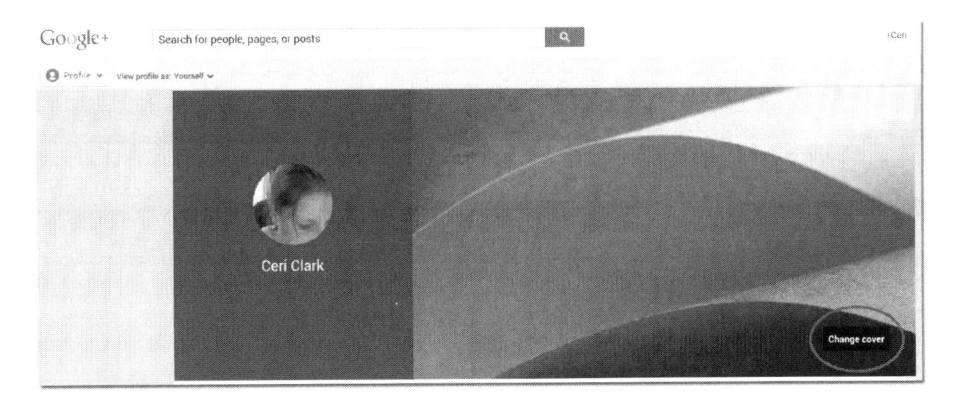

Figure 196 Changing your cover photo

Once clicked on, the link will take you to a page where you can add pictures from three places. There is the Gallery (of which a selection can be seen in the next graphic), you can upload from your computer, search albums (from pictures already uploaded) and finally from cover photos you have previously set.

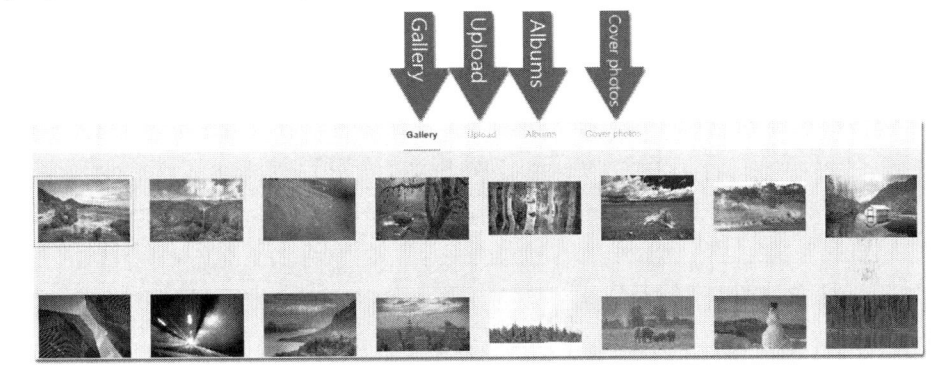

Figure 197 Cover photo options

Select the photo you want via the method you like and the picture will load in a new page with the option of resizing the image to fit the size of the cover. You can control the box by dragging it to the size you want. It will always be the right dimensions, it is just the size that changes. You can also move the box by dragging it with your mouse if you want to focus on a particular element of the picture. Once you are finished click on *Select photo* on the bottom left of the screen and your new cover photo will be applied.

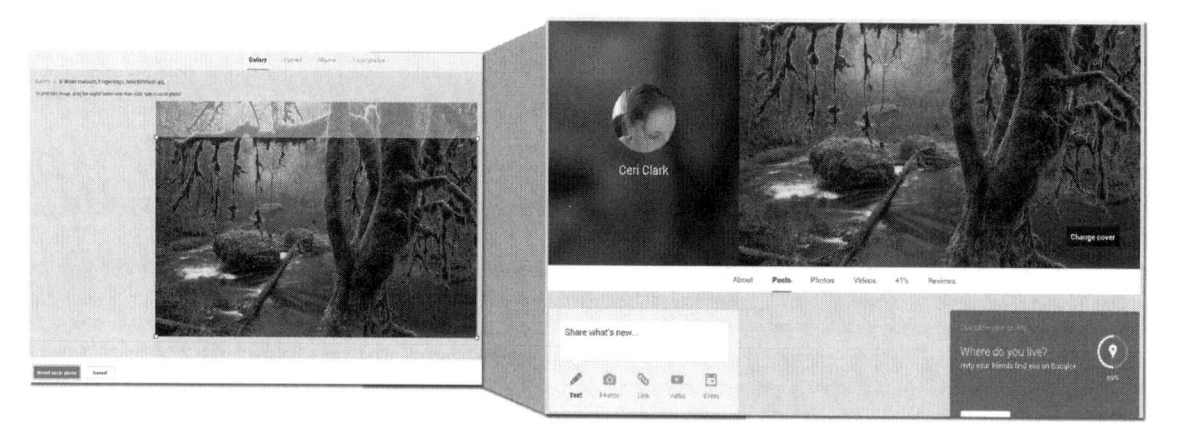

Figure 198 Resizing the cover photo

Adding Profile Information

If you want to add or edit your profile information the easiest way to get to the right page is to click on *Profile* in the dropdown navigation menu and click on *About*. You will then be able to click on *Edit* on any of the cards to update/fill in the information. It doesn't matter which card you choose you will be able to access all the cards by the buttons on the top of any card you choose.

There are 9 cards in your profile which are People, Education, Contact Information, Story, Places, Links, Work, Basic Information and Apps with Google+ sign-in. Each card has the following headings and you can switch between cards by clicking on the other circles.

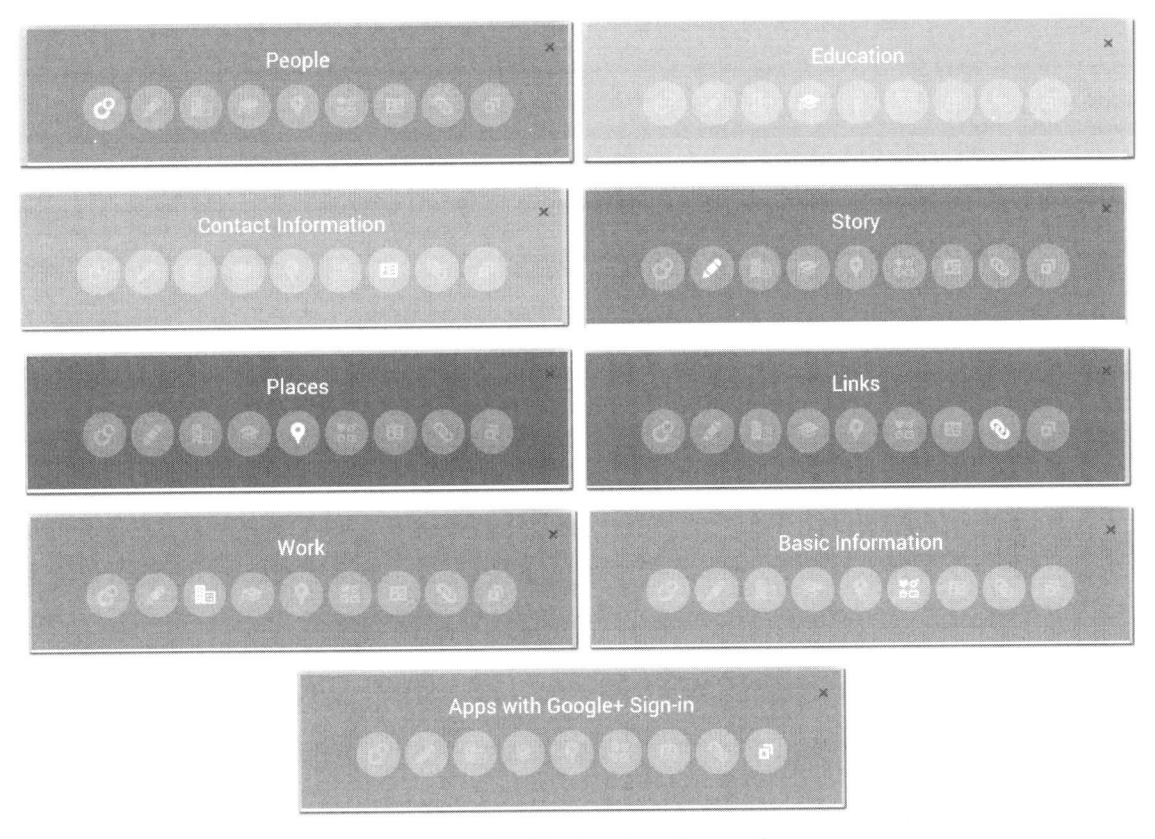

Figure 199 Navigating the cards

Filling out each card is as easy as typing into the boxes but I will illustrate the Story card as an example.

The Story card is all about you. The more information you put in here the better for people finding you.

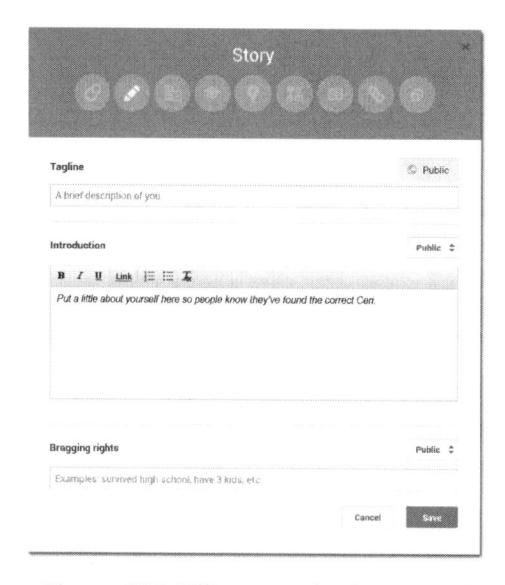

Figure 200 Filling out the Story card

For your tagline choose two or three keywords which really reflect who are and what you want people to know about you. In my personal profile (Ceri Clark), I put Author, Graphic Designer and former corporate and school Librarian.

As can be seen illustrated above, you can format your introduction using the usual options such as bold italics etc. although the tagline and bragging rights will simply be text.

It can be good to mention what you offer rather than your actual job titles for example as these will be covered in the Work card. In mine, I mention briefly what types of jobs I have done, what my mission is and then I list my books with links to them.

I found it difficult filling in the bragging rights but looking at other profiles, it appears that most people put when they graduated, their most impressive job and their family who are invariably beautiful and genius level offspring as of course is my own little boy as I wouldn't want to break the trend!

When filling out the *Story* card I did not put my website address as there is a Links card where you can put your social media and website links.

Getting your personalized, custom profile URL

As part of Google+, you can have your own custom URL so you can send an easy link to people to see your Google+ profile or add it to blogs or other social network sites.

Go to your profile and you should see a message pop up suggesting that your profile is eligible for a custom URL. Click on *Get URL* to start the process.

Figure 201 Go to your profile and look for the message to add a custom URL

If the message doesn't appear, go to your profile then click on the *About* tab. Look for the Links card and click on *Get URL* under *Google+ URL* as seen below.

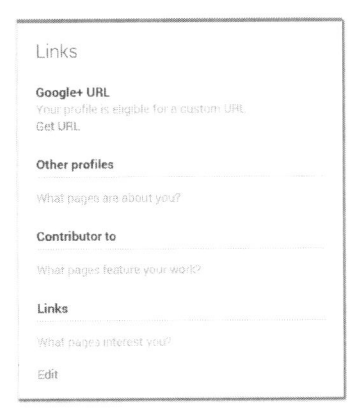

Figure 202 Click on Get URL on the Links card

The URL for your profile that Google+ gives you by default when you open your account is long and complicated, they give you the option to shorten and simplify it.

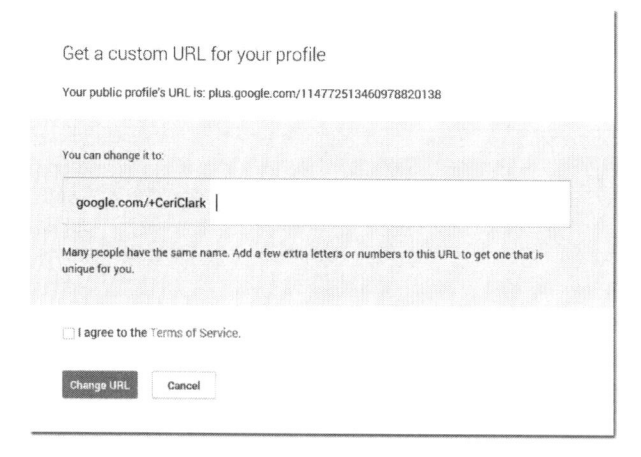

Figure 203 Get your own simplified profile URL

Type in some letters or numbers after the URL they suggest. If you are an author, you could put author after the name. Keep changing the URL until you get the green tick which shows no one else has it. When you are happy click on the *Change URL* button. You now have a new address to get to your Google+ profile. Once you have created your custom URL you will not be able to change it.

Hangouts

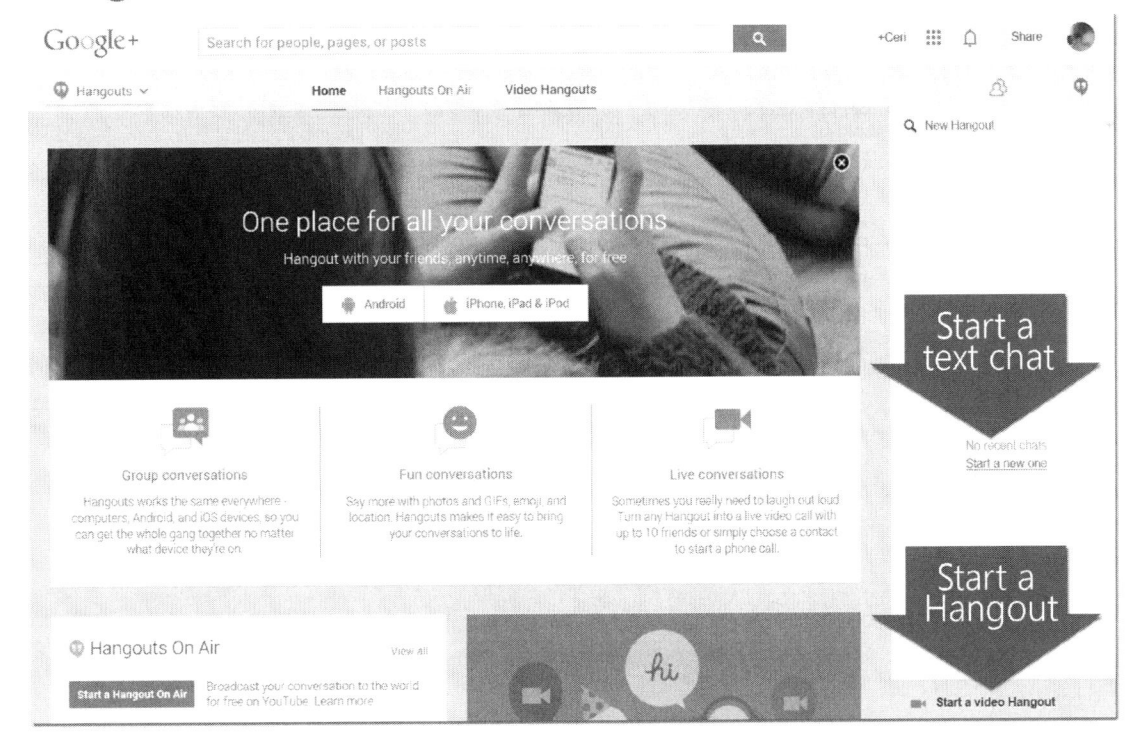

Figure 204 Where to start a text chat or video hangout

This is my favorite feature of Google+. Why restrict yourself to chatting by video to one person at a time? Google Hangouts lets you chat or talk to up to 10 people at the same time using video chat or 100 people using text chat from anywhere as long as everyone who you want to talk to has an internet connection and has installed the plugin.

I personally have had conversations with people from the United States, UK and Australia - all at the same time. This is great for business, book groups and just keeping in touch with family.

Google Hangouts are for text chats and for group video chats. You can chat one-to-one but the fun is in having lots of people chatting together (maximum of ten). It is a free service and very easy to use, simply click on *Start a Video Hangout* on the right of the screen, (please see the arrows on figure 204), allow the plugin to be installed if you haven't already done so and wait for people to join you.

When you start a hangout you can broadcast that you have started one to circles or individuals. It will appear in their streams that you are LIVE and they can join you from there.

- Draw (app)
- Chat
- Screenshare
- Capture
- YouTube
- Google Drive
- Remote desktop
- Add apps

Invite people | Mute microphone | Turn camera off | Adjust bandwidth usage | Settings | Leave call

Navigation options in a video hangout

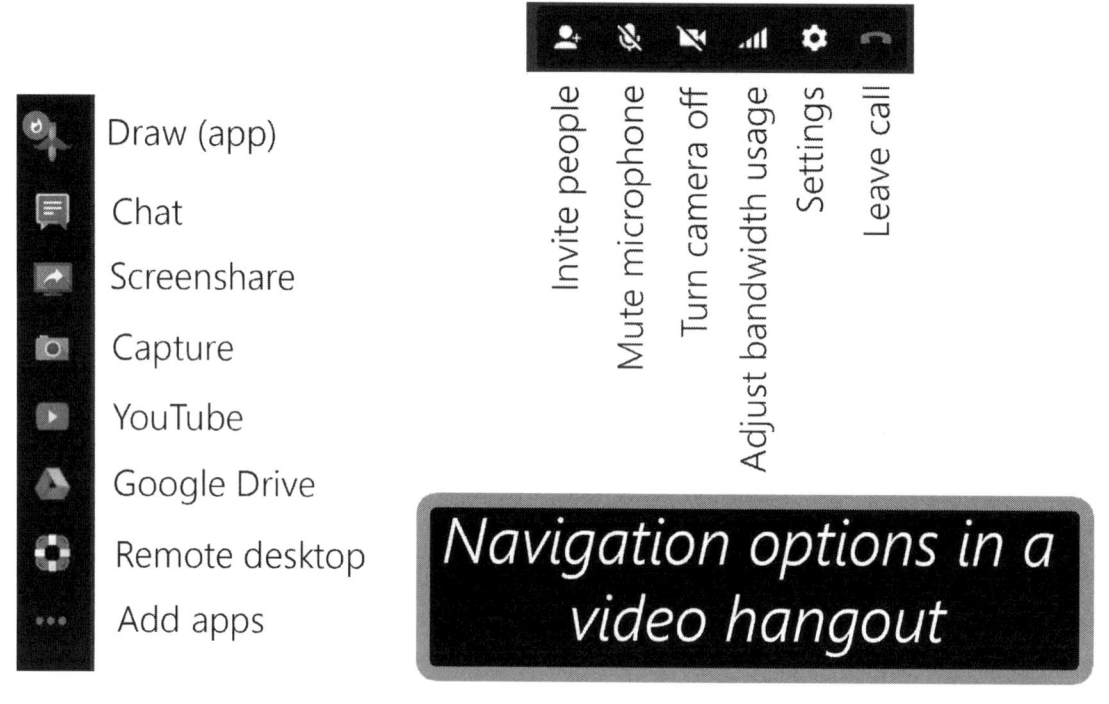

Figure 205 Navigation options inside a video hangout

You can also invite people from inside the Hangout by clicking on the picture of a person with a cross (when your mouse hovers over the picture the words *Invite people* should show) on the top of the hangout screen. You can text chat if someone is having problems with their microphone (*Chat* in left navigation bar) and even watch a YouTube video while you are waiting for people to join you. Please see the graphic above for all the options available on Google+ Hangouts. Please note that if you click on the three dots at the bottom of the left vertical menu, you can install apps on the hangout software. For example the *Draw* app allows you to draw on people and there is an app called Google effects where you can put masks or other strange effects on yourself viewable by other people on the hangout.

Other options at the top of the screen include turning the camera off (if you have a camera shy partner or friend who needs to come in the room) and *Mute*

Microphone (should you wish to shout at your partner down the stairs for a cup of tea), *Settings* and *Leave call*.

Reasons to use Hangouts
- Distance family get-togethers
- Book Clubs
- Watching sports/films/TV shows with friends
- Classes
- Meetings

About Circles

At the heart of Google+ is the Circles system. These are people that you have put into groups that you name. The circle names are private and no one knows what you call them – the people in your circles only know that they are *in* one of your circles.

The first thing you should do after sorting out your profile is to create at least one circle so you can have a stream of information on the homepage that interests you. You never know maybe some of those people will add you back and will see your posts!

This section will show how to find the circles page, how to add people and/or groups of people of the same interests, organize your circles and even share circles that you have created.

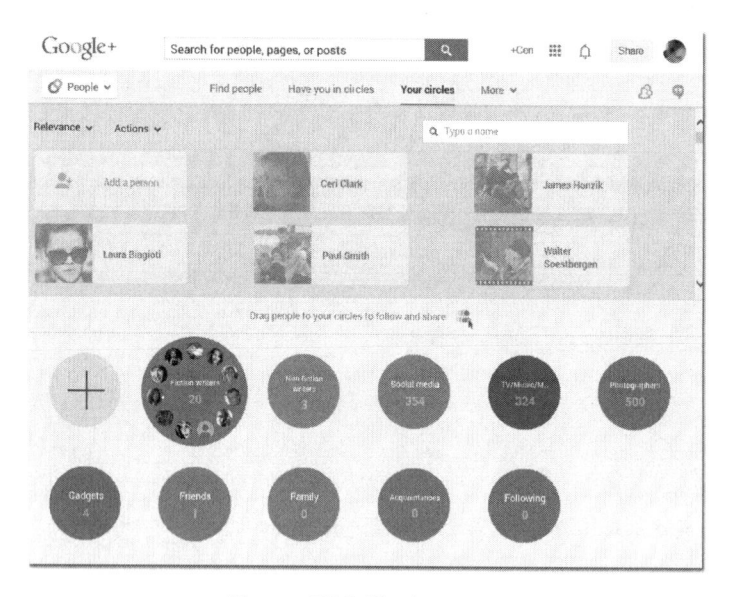

Figure 206 Circles page

The sky is the limit for how many Circles you have or what you want to name them. There is however a limit of 5,000 people that you can add. You can be put in any number of other people's Circles. This means that if you have reached your limit with people in your Circles but you have changed your interests over time, you will have to delete some people in your Circles so you will be able to see the new content in your home stream. With this in mind it is important to keep your circles organized and add people because you know them or they follow/post similar interests.

You don't have to add people who add you and vice-versa, you can block people, talk to individual people or have public posts to have conversations with hundreds of people. Unlike Twitter, all the elements are in one place so you can follow a conversation easily and get notified when something new is said.

Remember whenever you post, you don't have to post to a Circle. You can post to individuals, circles of people, or all your circles. You have complete control over who sees what you say. This is very useful for keeping family and friends informed without everyone else knowing what you post. Just don't post everything to public unless you want everyone and his dog to see it. This is for the most part fine if you make a mistake but bear in mind that future employers may have a quick look at your profile to see what you are like. I can't say this enough but you should only post publicly if you would be happy if people on the street saw it on a billboard standing next to you with a comedy red arrow pointing at you. Public means everyone can see it and make judgments on posts. If you want something to be only shared with your closest friends then make a circle with just those people in it and post to that circle.

Creating a Circle

Google+ will have already created four circles for you which are, friends, family, acquaintances and following. These may be enough for you but if you are using Google+ on a daily basis you will eventually need to categorize further based on the people you follow or the subjects you are interested in. This section will show you how to make a circle from the beginning.

First get to *Your circles* by clicking on *People* from the dropdown menu and then choosing *Your circles* at the top of the screen.

The page is split between profiles you have already added and the circles underneath that you already have. The people in the top half of the screen are in one of the circles in the bottom half and one person can be in more than one of the circles in the lower half.

To create a circle, click on the gray circle at the beginning of your circles. You can also drag one of the profiles from the top of the screen in to the gray circle to put the person into a new circle that you will create.

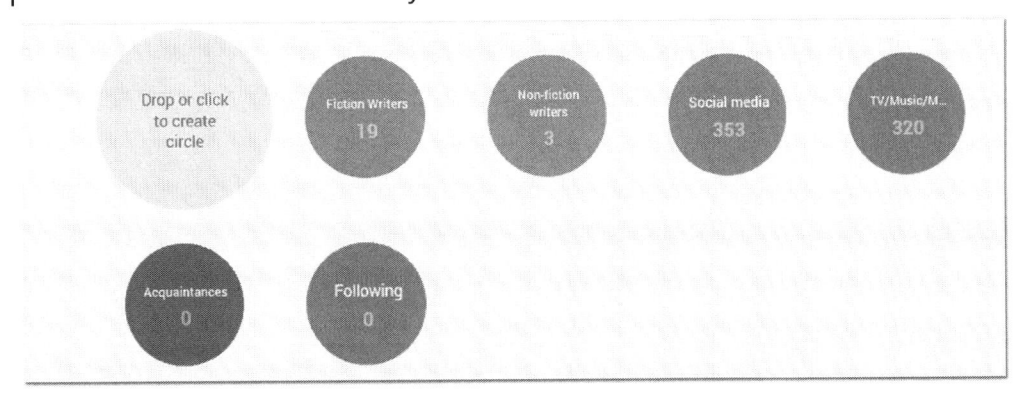

Figure 207 Click on the gray circle to create a circle

If you click on any circle, the profiles of people in that circle will appear in the top half of the screen. If you want to put them into another circle that is already made just click on their profile picture and drag them down the page using your mouse and drop them over the circle you want to add them to.

Once you click on the gray circle, a new page will load overlaying the old asking you what you want to call it. In the example below I have chosen to name my new circle 'Work Colleagues'. You can click on *Add a person* directly from this window.

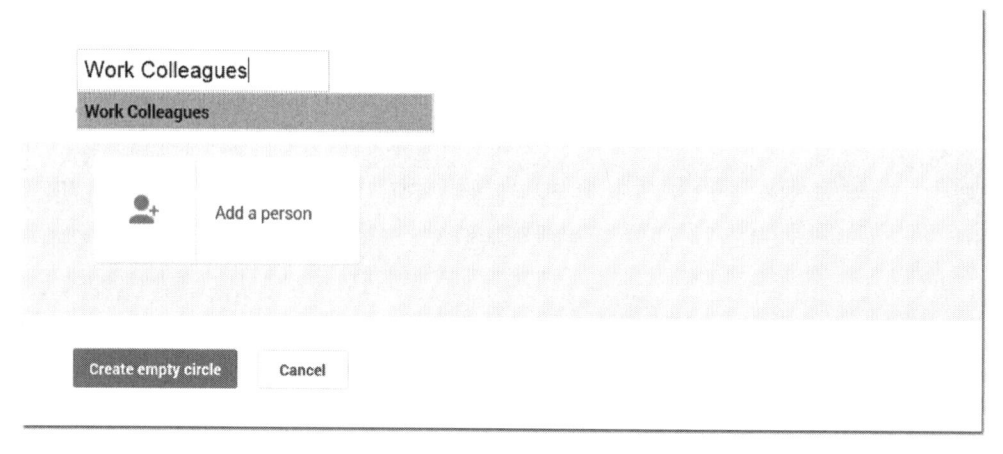

Figure 208 Name your circle and add a person.

You can find a friend, work colleague or other contact by searching for their name in the text box that will appear. Click on their name or profile picture and the contact will be added to the new circle as seen in the next image.

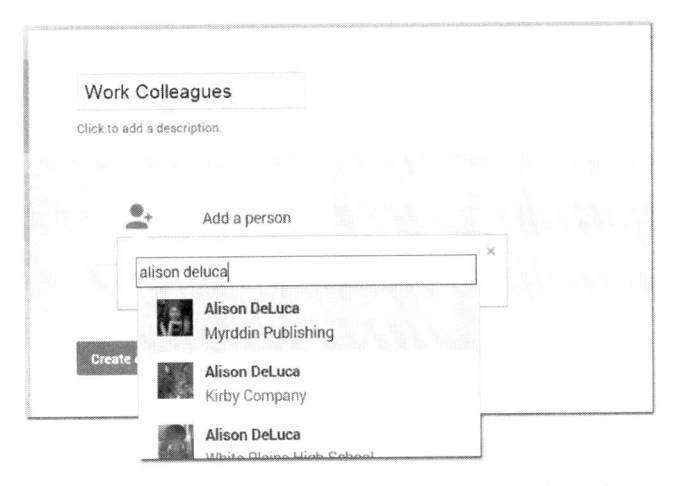

Figure 209 Type your colleague's name to find them

The profile will be added but Google will also suggest other contacts it thinks you might be interested in based on the profile you have just added. Click on any name whose posts you think you may find interesting and then click *Create circle with 1 person/x people*. If you want to remove a person from the list, hover your mouse over the profile picture and a small x will appear in the top right of the tile. Click on this and the card will drop away from the screen.

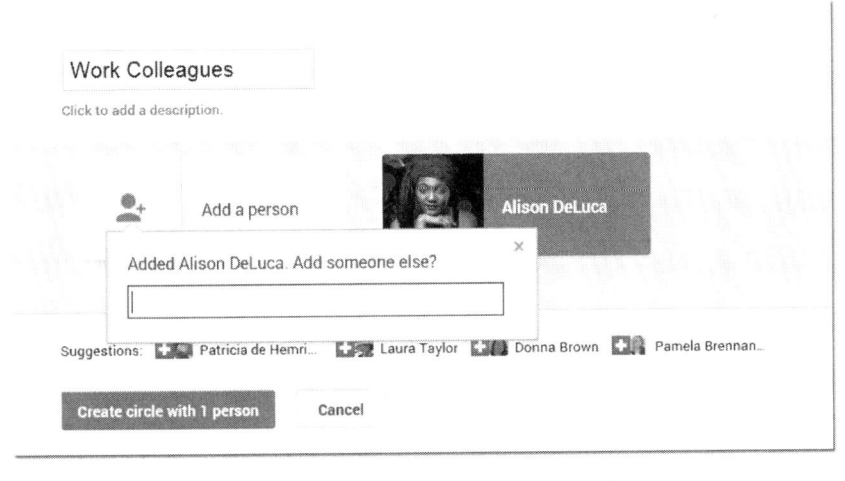

Figure 210 Add another person?

When you are back on the Circles page you will see your newly created circle in the bottom half of the screen with the number of people in it. If there is one circle that you use more than any other, you can reorder the circles to put the one you use the most on the left by clicking on it and dragging it to where you want to put it.

> **Tip**
>
> You can make your contacts or circles section bigger on the Circles page by 'grabbing' the line between the two and dragging up or down.

You can add more people by looking at Google's suggestions. The more people that you add from your own contacts, the better Google is able to suggest other people they think you will be interested in based on their profile information. A quick way to find out what Google suggests is to click on the people icon on the top right of your Google+ screen as seen circled below.

Figure 211 Where to find Google's suggestions for finding contacts

> **Tip**
>
> A good tip to know is to create a Circle with no people in it called Bookmarks. If you find any posts that you think are particularly interesting or useful you can share them with this empty Circle. This then becomes your personal folder that no one has access to but you.

Adding people to your Circles

When you first login, Google will put you through a tutorial where you can add contacts from your email accounts. It uses the email addresses in your contacts to find them within the Google+ system. If you skip this it will then ask if you want to add people that you have contacted through your email. If you have emailed friends or family this is an easy introduction to adding someone to a Circle. If the option doesn't appear you can find the people that Google suggests by clicking on *People* in the dropdown navigation bar on the top left of the Google+ screen.

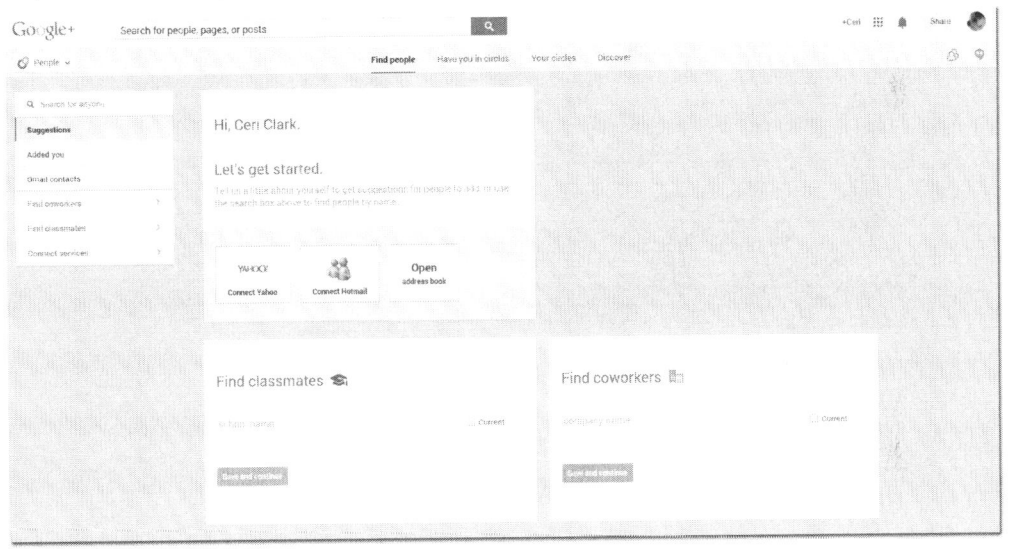

Figure 212 Adding people by email, school and workplace

Next to the picture of the contact Google is suggesting click on *Add to Circles*. A dropdown list will appear. Check the box next to the Group that best describes your relationship or create a new one. You now have your first person in a Circle.

The tutorial will continue to suggest people that you may be interested in, finishing by asking for personal information. Don't feel that you have to fill in all the information. Only put in what you are comfortable with allowing people to know.

Wherever you are in Google+, if you see a post you like, hover over the poster's name and you will have the option to add that person to your circles.

Searching for a name you know

You can also search for people by name in the long search box at the top of the page. For example I searched for the author Alison DeLuca and added her to my circle called 'Authors'.

Type the name you want to search in the long box, click on the magnifying glass. Have a quick look at the information under his/her name and possibly the information in their *About* page, (located in the white bar below the cover photo), to see if you want to add them to your circles.

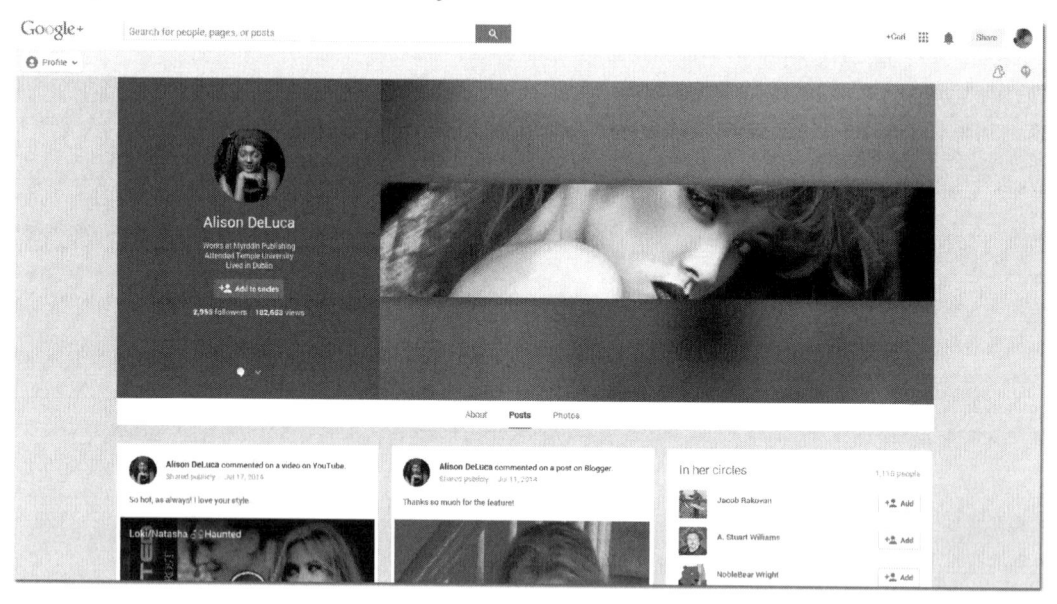

Figure 213 The profile page of a Google+ contact

To add them, click on *Add to Circles* (currently in a red box) as seen in the image above. A little menu will appear where you can check the box next to the group you want to add them in. If there is no suitable group already created, you can go to the bottom of the list and look for the option to create a new Circle.

Searching for people using Communities

Communities are groups of people that get together who have similar interests. You can search for communities in two ways. The first is to put a keyword such as 'cooking' in the search box at the top of the page. Before you finish typing the word, Google should offer suggestions in a little dropdown of suggestions. If

Introduction to Google+

there are any Communities, it will be at the bottom of the list under *Communities* as seen below.

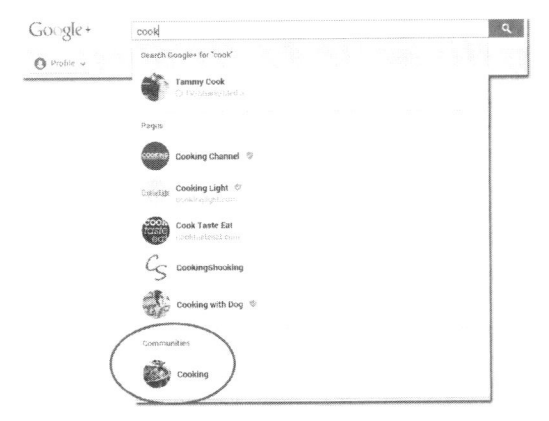

Figure 214 Finding communities by searching

Click on the community you want and you will be taken to the community page.

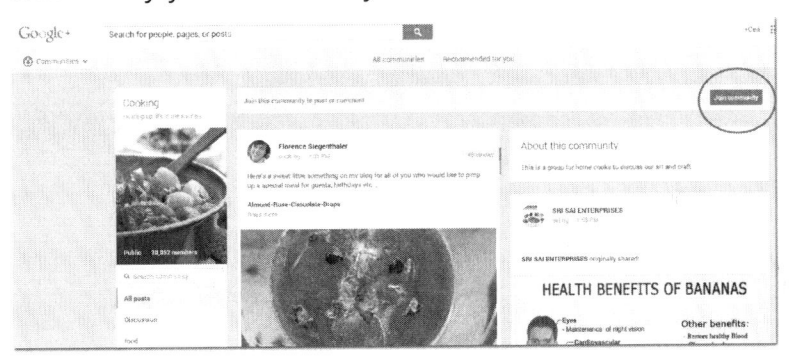

Figure 215 A cooking community

If you join the community by clicking the red button on the top right of the page labelled Join community, you will have all the cooking related posts appear in your stream. However, the people who have joined this community may post other cooking related posts but not post to this page. If you add people to your Circles individually and as long as your contact posts publicly or adds you to the circle they post to then you will see more of their posts. To add them, hover your mouse over their name and a card will appear where you can add them.

You can control if the community posts appear in your home stream by clicking on *Settings* in the dropdown navigation bar and checking the box next to *Show your Google+ communities posts* on the *Posts* tab of your Google+ profile, under *Profile*.

Searching by Tags

If you type a keyword preceded by a hashtag in the search box you will find all the posts that people have labelled with that subject. For example if you want to search for movie reviews, type #moviereview and the following page will load:

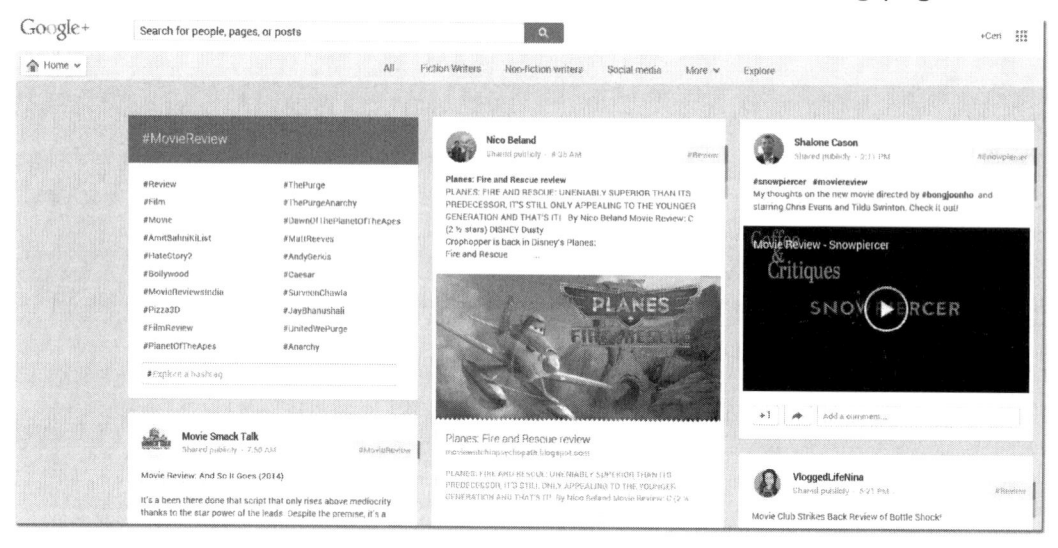

Figure 216 Other tags will be suggested at the beginning of the page

To follow any of the people who have posted, hover your mouse over their names and the option to add them to your Circles will appear. Google+ will also suggest other tags in the first box that you might want to try. Click on the links to find other posts where the authors have used the hashtags shown.

CircleShare

Another way to add people is to use CircleShare. These are groups of people that others have put together and shared as a post. You can add as many as 500 people in one go using this method but I would be careful about which CircleShares you add. Be selective and choose those which align with your interests.

If you type CircleShare into the search box, there is a community where Google+ users solely share their Circles. You can also type #CircleShare in the box to get relevant results. If you already follow a lot of people they can also show up in your news feed/home stream.

Adding a CircleShare

Find a CircleShare (at the time of writing they looked like figure 217). You will see what the group of people have in common by looking at the text in the post preceding the CircleShare. If you are happy to include the contacts in your Google+ account, you can click on *Add people* and choose if you want to add them to a Circle you've already made, make a new one with the name the poster chose or change the name for the Circle to one you prefer.

You add as many of these groups as you want but remember you can only have a total of 5,000 contacts in your Circles and you want to make sure they are people that you want to follow.

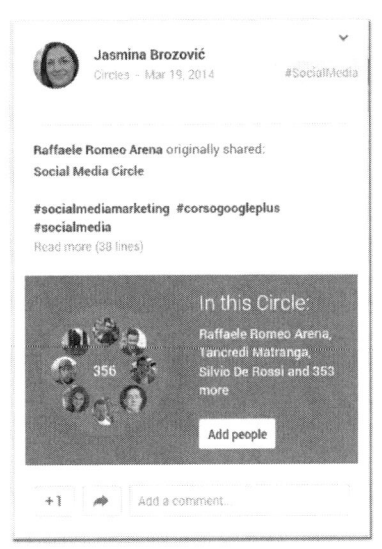

Figure 217 CircleShare

Creating a CircleShare or sharing a Circle

After you have organized all the people into relevant circles you may want to share them with friends. An example of why you may want to do this in my personal experience was a book group I ran using Google+. I put everyone in the book group in a 'BookGroup' Circle. I then shared that circle with everyone in the book group so everyone instantly had the same circle and when they messaged the group all they had to do was put the name for their Circle in to the *To* box and I knew everyone would get the post.

If you want to share your group, find the Circle by going to *People* from the dropdown menu, then select *Your Circles* at the top of the page. Click on the Circle you want to share and choose the arrow pointing right which will appear in the middle of the circle.

If you click on the little pencil you can change the name of your circle and add a brief description and if you click on the trash can/bin icon then you will delete the circle.

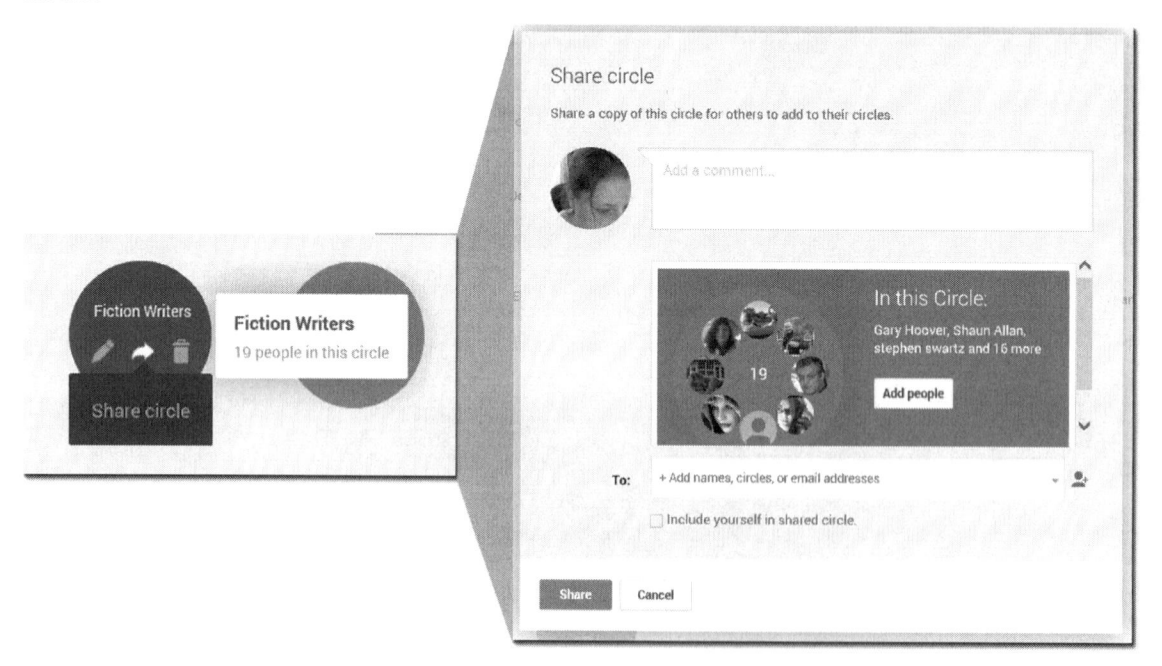

Figure 218 Sharing your Circle

In the comments section let people know what it is about the circle that might interest them. Are they business people? Are they photographers or do they all enjoy gaming? Then make the Circles public if you want all your 'followers' to see them or choose certain circles or even individuals depending on who you want to share with. Click on *Share* and other people will be able to benefit from the collection of profiles you've put together.

Deleting people and/or Circles

You may want to delete people because you no longer share the same interests. It isn't personal as can be the case in other social networks. You may also want to get rid of circles because you are tidying up your profile.

Deleting individuals

To remove someone from your circles, hover your mouse over their picture in the Circles page and click on the little *x* which appears on the top right of the profile photo as seen circled on the next image.

Figure 219 Click on the little x to remove a profile from your circles

Deleting Circles

If you want to delete a circle, all you need to do is right-click on the circle you want to remove and choose *Delete circle*.

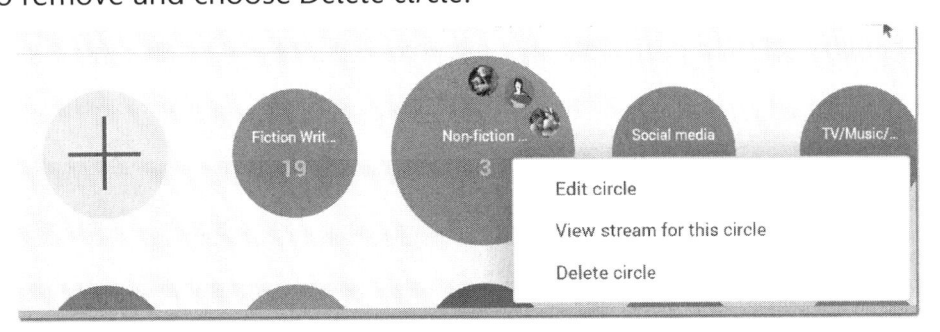

Figure 220 Right-click on a circle to delete it

A message will appear warning you that you will remove everyone in your circle unless you have also put them in another one and of course if you delete the contacts they will not be able to see *anything* you have posted, before or after you click the button.

It should also be noted that once you have deleted a circle and therefore a lot of people *en masse*, then there is no way to get them back unless you can remember each person and add them individually. The only exception to this is if you added them by *CircleShare* and you still have access to it.

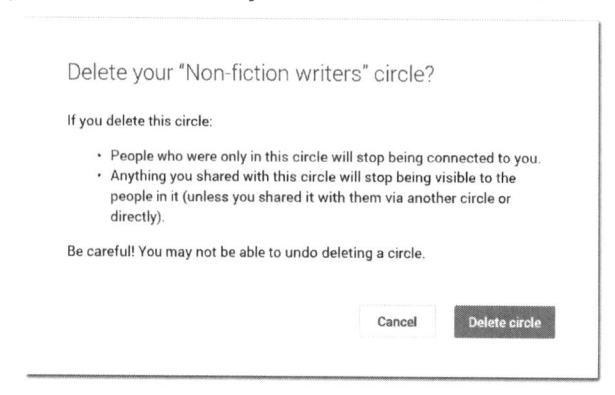

Figure 221 Make sure that you are happy to remove everyone in the circle you are deleting

Being social: liking, commenting and sharing

Google+ is a Social network and like all the other social networks out there you need to comment, reshare and let people know you like their posts. They in turn will reciprocate and a beautiful friendship will begin. Well that is the goal anyway. Google+ may have different terms from Facebook or Twitter but they all do these things in a similar way.

+1 (Like)

As Facebook is to like, Google+ is to +1. If you see any post you think is funny, informative or just interesting to you, like it to let the authors and anyone viewing the post know that it is appreciated.

If you want to remove the +1 for any reason, just click on the +1 button again.

Introduction to Google+

Commenting

Other Google+ users love people who comment on their posts. It is the reason why many people are on the site - to engage with others. It is a compliment to receive a comment, even a not so good one, as someone has gone to the effort of commenting and furthering a conversation.

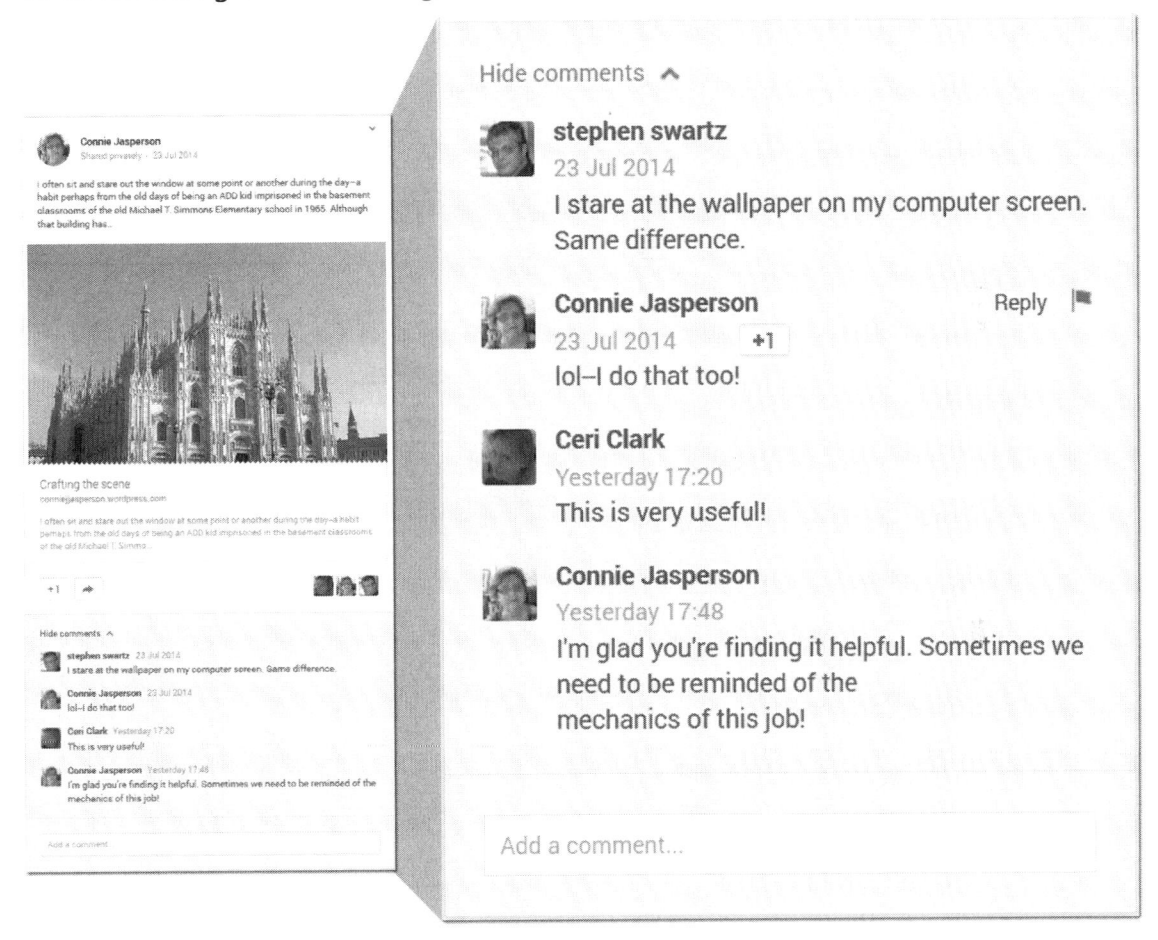

Figure 222 Commenting on a post

If you just want to comment on the post, there is a box below the post which says *Add comment*. Once you start typing, the box will expand and a button will appear giving you the option to post the comment or cancel.

If however you want to reply to a comment already made then if you hover over the comment, the word *Reply* will appear. Click on this and you can comment on the comment. There is also the option to report a comment as spam or even to +1. If the comment adds to the conversation rather than just saying how great the post is, I would recommend clicking the +1 button.

It doesn't really need to be said that when you comment, everyone who can see that post will see that comment. It is best to be super polite at all times as that comment will be there for a long time and people will make judgments on posts and comments they see on Google+.

If you disagree strongly with a post or comment that appears offensive, the best policy is to walk away and pretend you didn't see it. There are trolls out there whose sole aim in life is to annoy people. Don't give them the satisfaction. There is nothing more annoying to *them* if they think no one has noticed their attempts to get attention in a nasty way.

Sharing

While browsing your stream you may occasionally come across some posts so brilliant that you will want to re-share them to your own circles or make them public so that people who have circled you (but you may not necessarily have circled yourself) can see the post. This is really the highest honor. Posts usually state whether they have been re-shared from another Google+ user but it is nice to tip your hat in acknowledgment to the originator of the post. To do this you can simply say *hat tip* and then a + before the originator's name. For example acknowledging Connie Jasperson would look like *Hat tip to +Connie Jasperson*.

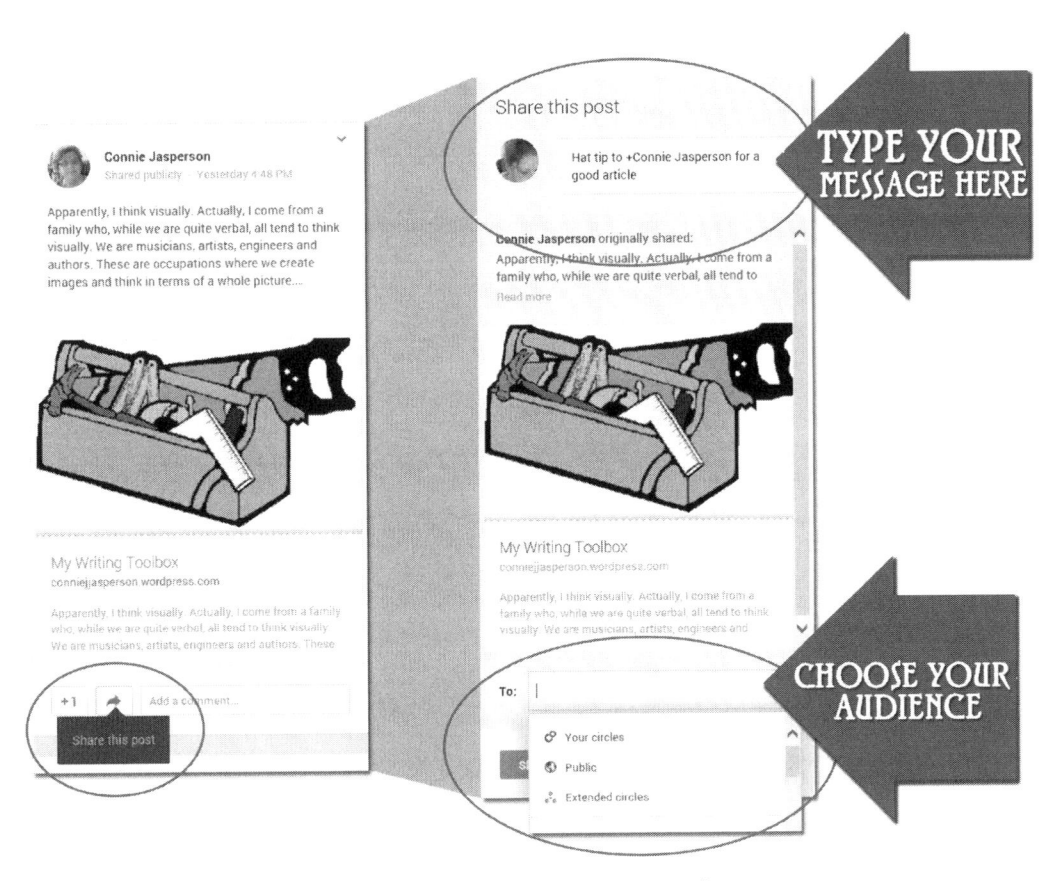

Figure 223 Steps to share someone else's post

If you want to share a post, look for the arrow pointing right (currently at the bottom of the post and click on it. Write your message at the top of the new screen as indicated in the above screenshot and then choose who you want to see the post at the bottom.

Managing your posts

Viewing Posts

You can see all the posts from people in your circles in your Stream as well as your own.

You can see posts by people not in your circle by clicking on their photo and looking in their stream. If they have allowed you to view their posts, you will be able to see them (for example if they posted them to *Public*).

If you want to serendipitously stumble upon an interesting post click on What's hot on the left under your list of Circles to find what Google thinks you might be interested in (although this option may not appear until you have used Google+ for a while, if not click on *Explore* in the top navigation menu).

You can also limit the posts you see in your stream by your circles. Say for example you only want to see posts from the photographers in your Photographers circle then you can do that by clicking on the circle name at the top of the Google+ window.

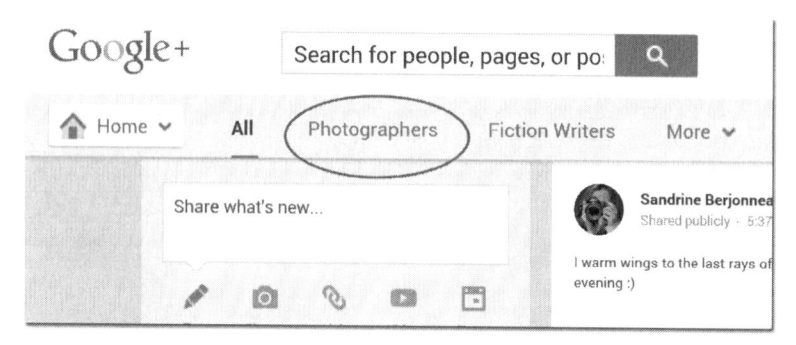

Figure 224 Limit the posts you can see by clicking on one of your circles

If you want to see everything again, just click on *All*.

Another neat trick is that you can also limit or increase how many posts you see from a circle. First you need to click on the circle that you want to change. Then look to the right of the screen to the top right box on the page which is titled *In this circle*. This 'card' contains people in your circle. Click on the gear wheel symbol on the top right of this box and move your mouse down to *Amount Standard* which will then give you the option to either have more posts from the people in that circle in your stream, the standard amount as decided by Google or fewer posts. Please see the screenshot below for an example of the options,

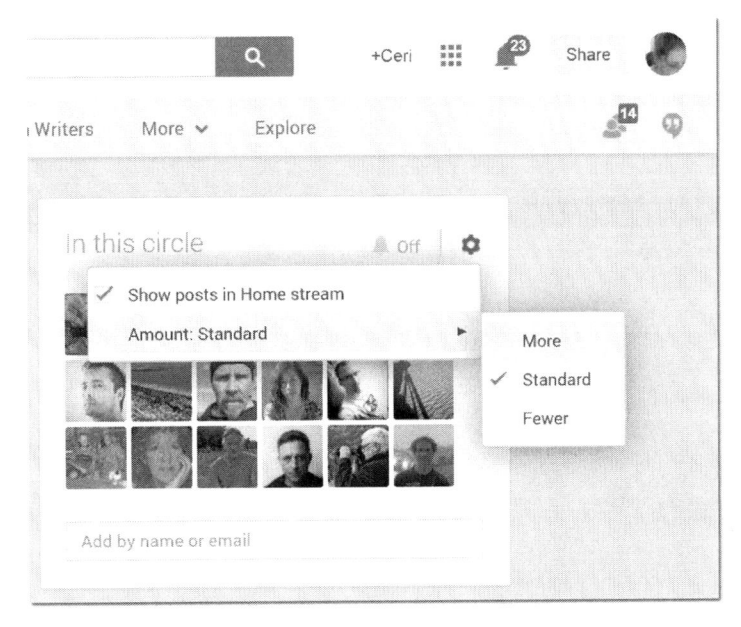

Figure 225 Limiting or increasing posts from a circle

Viewing comments

Comments are always below posts as you would expect but sometimes you need to expand the comments on a post. Just click on the number of comments or the arrow beside it and all the comments will load. If you want to hide all the comments just click on *Hide comments* which will replace the *x comments* which was there before.

Google+ is global and the comments and posts can be in different languages. You used to have to install a special Chrome extension to read them but now a *Translate* link appears on all posts with a language different to yours. They appear directly below the text that is in the different language as seen in the next graphic.

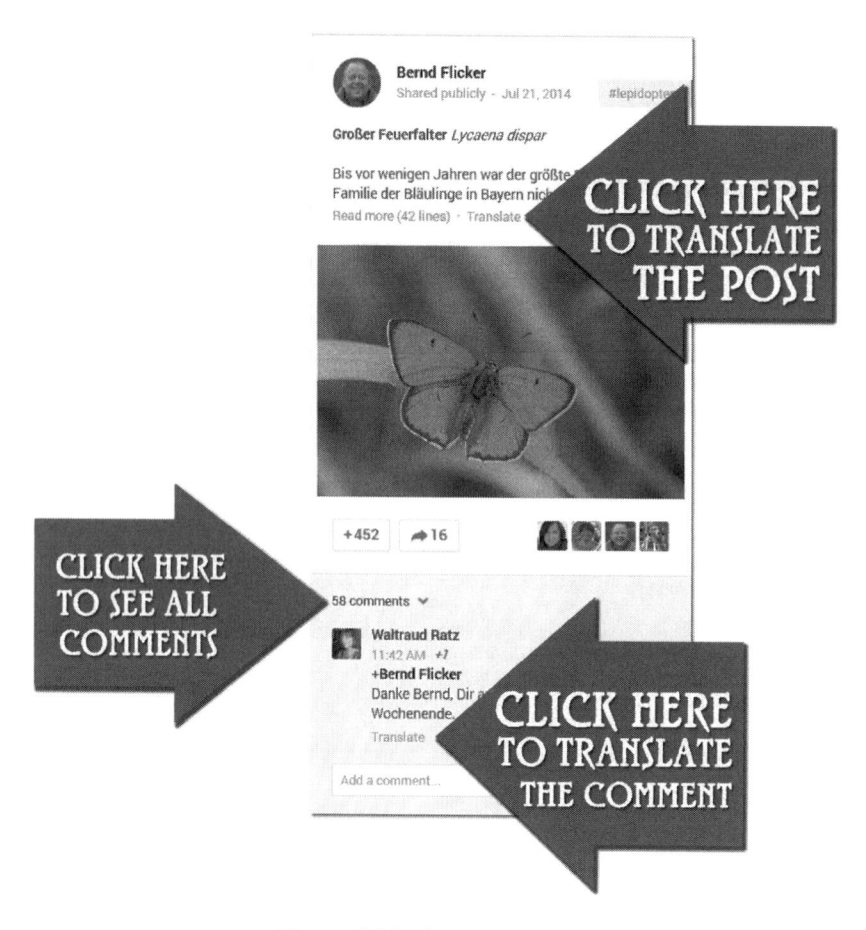

Figure 226 View comments

Posting

Posting on Google+ is as easy as Facebook or Twitter, so if you are familiar with these services you already have a head start. Click on *Home* on the top left of the Google+ screen and start typing your post in the box immediately below the navigation menu in your Stream.

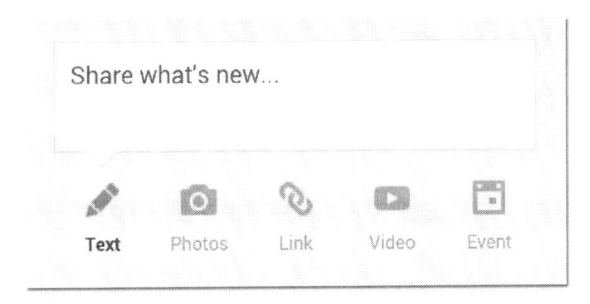

Figure 227 To post, look for this box at the top of your news stream

You have five options once you have put in some text, you can add a photo, insert a video, add a link or put in your location by choosing the icons underneath the text box.

Once you are done you can choose who will see your post. By default your first post will be set to be *Public* which will mean anyone will be able to see what you have said. To remove this, click in the box and press delete or click on the little x to the side of the audience highlighted. A dropdown of all your options will appear. You can choose one of your Circles (groups) to see your post or you can start typing someone's name in if you only want a certain person to see it.

When you are happy with your post, click *Share* and it will go live. To see how it looks, go to your profile and your latest post will always be the top post. Please note that there is an option to *View as: Public* or *View as: Yourself* on the top of the screen. If you view as yourself, you cannot see the posts that you made public and if you choose the option to view as public, you will *only* see posts you have chosen to make public.

Posting privately or publically

You can be as public or private as you want but bear in mind that nothing you post on the internet can ever be totally private as anyone you share it with could copy and paste the text or take a screenshot to re-share if they want to.

I tend to think unless you want to share a holiday or your children's photos with family and friends or it is potentially embarrassing for future employers looking at your profile (with the caveat of my privacy comment above) then you should make everything public, *if you are a business or are promoting a product*. My reasoning is that Google users like to see posts from people that they are considering following. The more content that they can see without having to add you to their circles first, will give them more information to base a judgment on whether you are worth adding. Also if you have a Google+ profile to promote yourself because you are a writer or have a business then the more high quality posts that Google can index in its search engine from your posts will bring more people to your Google+ profile and possibly lead to more sales.

Making your posts more visible

If you want to make your public posts more visible, use hashtags and +mentions. Sometimes posts get lost amid the flow of news. If you use hashtags (a word with # before the word such as #cooking), then your post will be seen alongside others with that hashtag when someone searches for it.

Putting a + before someone's name for example +Ceri Clark will alert that person that you are asking or telling them something. They will get a notification and an email informing them of the mention.

Adding photos to your posts

By adding photos to your posts, they make them seem more interesting and catch the eye of the casual browser.

Click on the camera icon in the share box and you can add a photo from your computer or your Google+ photos.

Please bear in mind the etiquette of photo usage. Photos have copyright attached to them which means that the people who make the images have the right to do with them as they will which includes not allowing others to use them. Have a look at where you found your photo, does it have any licensing information by it. A lot of photographers/illustrators will allow you to use their pictures for non-commercial use as long as they are acknowledged. Using the hat-tip +name format shows how polite you are. You could type something like: Hat-tip to +Ceri Clark for the photo. It not only shows the person borrowing has good manners but it also lets the image creator know that their picture/photo is popular and it is liked.

Deleting posts

Occasionally, you may find that posts you have made in the past are irrelevant, wrong or there was that time you had a few too many rum and cokes and thought that post was *really* funny but it *really wasn't* in the cold light of day and you now want to remove it.

If for any reason you want to delete a post, find the post in your profile and choose *Public* if you posted it as a public post or *Yourself* for anything else. You can also limit it to posts that you sent to specific people or circles by typing their name in the box that appears in the dropdown menu as illustrated below..

Figure 228 See how others view your profile

Once you have found your post, click on the little arrow on the top right of the card and choose *Delete post*. You will then be asked to confirm the deletion and a confirmation will then appear. To get rid of the confirmation, click on *Dismiss*.

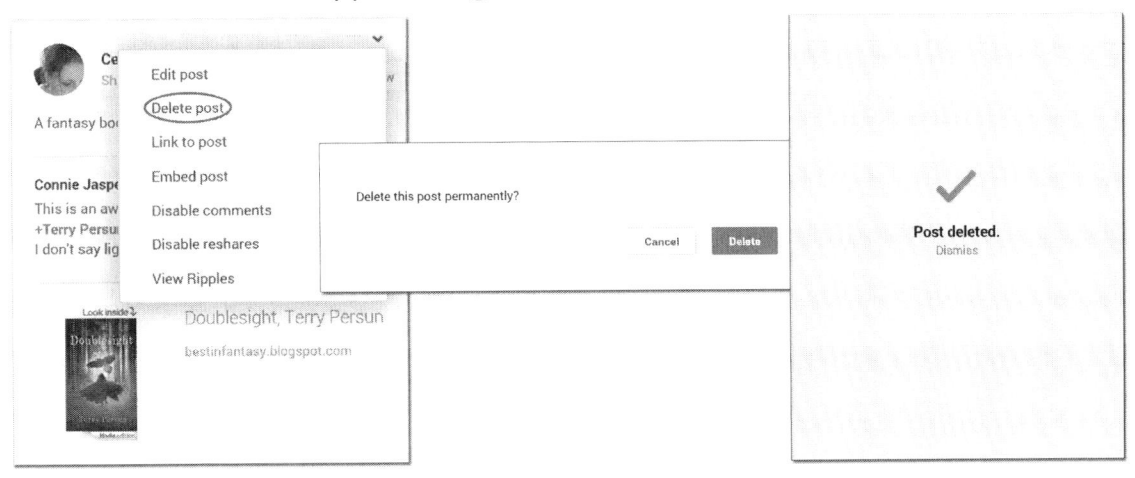

Figure 229 How to delete a post you have made

Disabling Comments and reshares

There may be an occasion where you want to disable comments or reshares on a post. It is very simple to do this. The following steps will walk you through how to do it.

Disabling the features when posting

Beside the *To:* box, you will find a downwards pointing arrow. If you select this, you can disable comments and reshares for your posts as you make them.

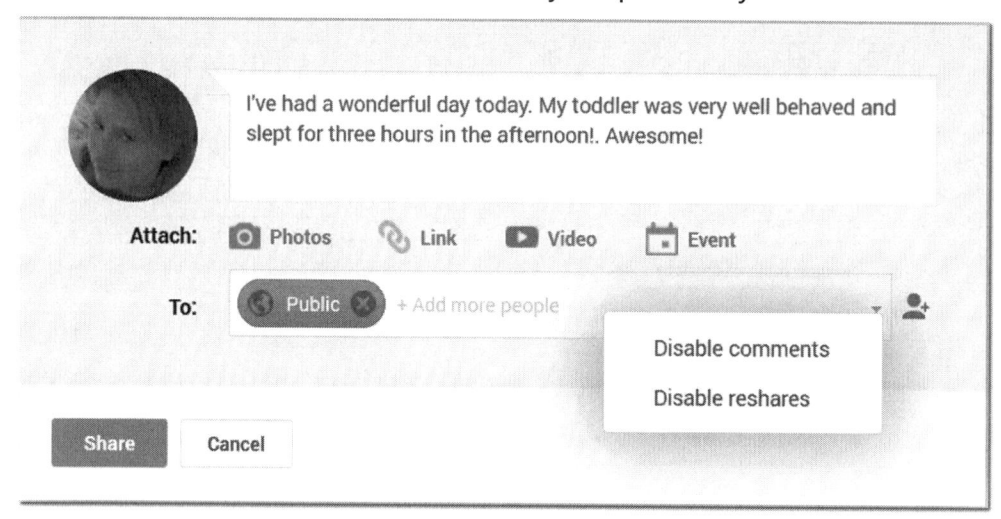

Figure 230How to disable comments or reshares

When you select one or the other, or both, you will see a comments and reshare symbol with a line through it appear in the *To:* box as seen below.

Figure 231 Disabling comments and reshare symbols

If you want to enable comments and resharing, just hover your mouse over the symbols and choose the option to re-enable the feature again.

Disabling comments and reshares after you have already posted

Find the post you want to change. The easiest way to do this is to go to your profile (using the dropdown menu of the top left of the Google+ screen) and choose to view your profile either as Public or Yourself, depending on who your targeted audience was when posting.

Locate the little downwards pointing arrow on the top right of the card and choose *Disable comments* or *Disable reshares* as appropriate.

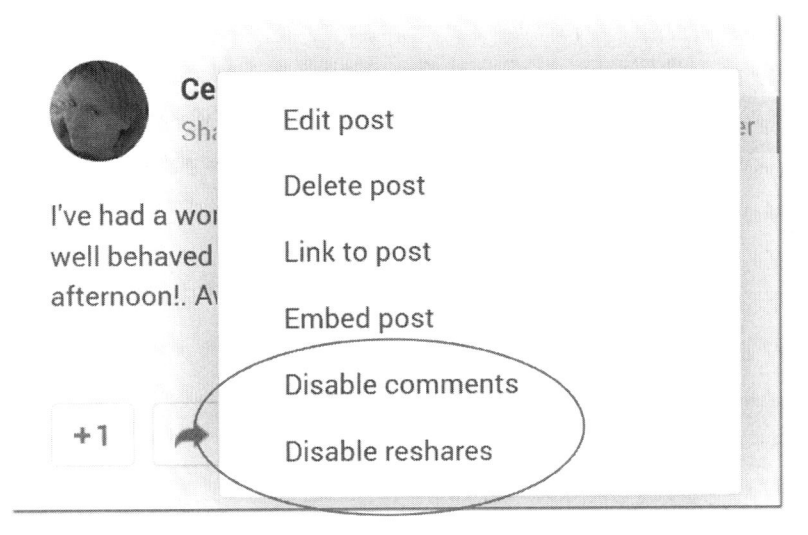

Figure 232 Disabling comments or reshares after you have posted

Notifications

Sometimes you just don't have time to go through your stream but notifications allows you to know if anyone has commented on posts you have created. You will be able to see if there has been any comments on posts you have commented on and who has added you on Google+. Look out for the little symbol of the bell in the top right of the screen and click on it to view all your recent notifications.

If someone puts a + before your name then you will get a notification and an email telling you about the post. This also works the other way in that if you put +Ceri Clark for example then I would get an email and a notification in Google+ of your post.

You can remove certain types of notifications by clicking on the x beside the notice. There is also the option to mute a post or mute a person.

There is a problem with Event notifications. At the time of writing in September 2014 there appears to be no way to stop random strangers from inviting me to events I have no interest in and have no intention of attending.

This has been a problem for years that people who have you in their circles can send you invites even if you don't have them in *your* circles. Another problem is that these invites which you may have no knowledge of, may appear in your Google Calendar. You can turn this off in Google Calendar by not allowing declined events to show but this setting does not apply to other people who are sharing your calendar. For example I share my calendar with my husband. He regularly sees invites from Google+ which I do not because I have disallowed the events to be seen in my calendar. He does not have that option because he was not sent the invite – I was. Meanwhile in blissful ignorance I keep getting bogged down with these erroneous invites in the notifications section of Google+. *Argh* doesn't really convey my frustration with this situation but it will have to do.

This could all be sorted with a simple setting in the *Settings* disallowing event invites from certain people or circles, until then there is one way to stop receiving these event notifications after you have already received one. Unfortunately you will have to do this every time you receive an unwanted invite from people you have not muted yet.

Step 1: Click on the name of the person who sent you the invite or click on the little icon of a calendar which appears on the top right of the event notification (circled in the image below).

Step 2: Click on the downwards pointing arrow in the resulting window in the actual post (also circled below). The two arrows (pointing up and down beside each other above this) are navigation aids for your notifications in general).

Step 3: Click on *Mute* (the name of the poster) as illustrated below.

Introduction to Google+

Figure 233 Muting a person

You will no longer receive posts from the person who sent you the invite. Please bear in mind that doing this step will mean you won't see any of their Google+ invites as future notifications but their invites will appear in your stream as upcoming events and you will see their posts in your stream (unless you remove them from your circles).

Searching on Google+

When you search on Google+, Google looks within public posts, posts from in your circle and the wider internet.

Searching for People

If there is someone you know you want to follow, simply type their name into the search box at the top of Google+. As you type their name, Google+ will give you some suggestions underneath the search box.

In the following example, I searched for Valerie Douglas. I had to type 9 letters of her name for Google to find the person I wanted.

Figure 234 Start typing gor Google+ to suggest people

215

In the next example I searched for Alison Deluca.

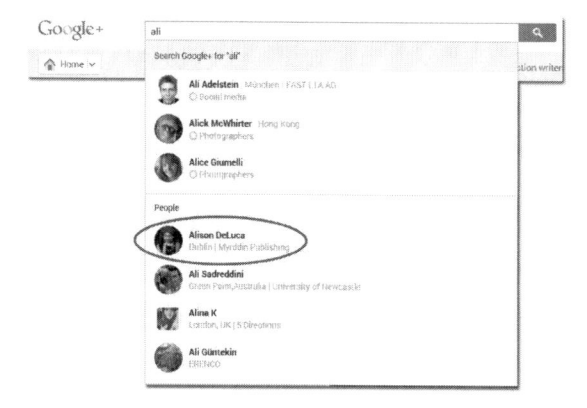

Figure 235 If someone is already in your circles they will appear quicker

As you can see from the image above, I only had to type 3 letters from Alison Deluca's name and it was the first choice in the list. If you already have the person you are looking for in your circles, then Google will put them first in the People section of the [autocorrect] search results.

Searching for subjects

It is possible to just type a subject keyword in the search box and you will get relevant results but if you use hashtags (any word(s) beginning with # for example #cooking) then you will find relevant posts that people have labelled with this tag.

Putting your search with or without quotes yields different results as can be seen in the next images. If you search with quotes you can not only see that you are shown a card with relevant people and places but Google will show you related trending tags. If you search without quotes you will only get related tags. This means if you are interested in seeing what other people like in your topic then using quotes in your searching is the way to go.

Search results with Quotes

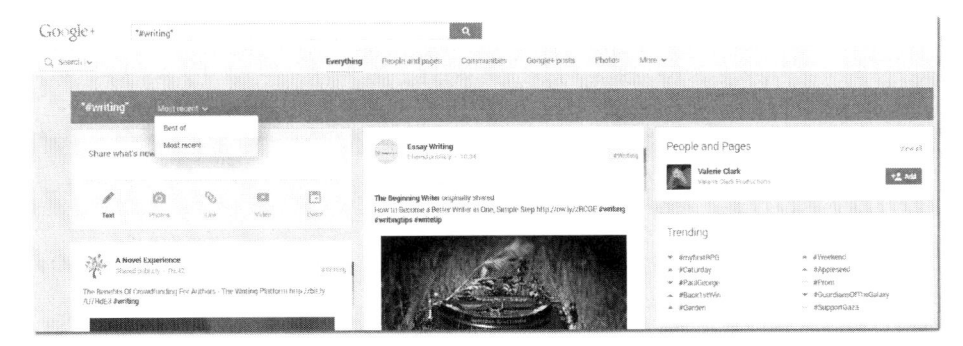

Search results without quotes

Figure 236 Searching with or without quotes

Settings

Having a look at your settings will make your experience of Google+ richer. The easiest way to find your settings is to hover your mouse over the *Home* button to see the dropdown menu and choose *Settings* from the list.

Who can interact with you and your posts

The two options in this section are who can send you notifications or comment on your public posts. You can choose from the usual suspects, Extended circles, Public, Your circles, Only you, (to only receive notifications about yourself) or specific people that you choose.

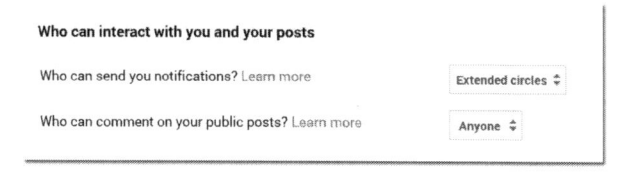

Figure 237 Who can interact with you and your posts

Unless you have set up your Google+ account to talk to a very select number of people that you already know then the selections that Google has provided should be adequate. Extended circles means Google users who are in the circles of the people who have circled you.

Who can Hangout with you

If you want control over who can initiate the video call known as the hangout then you seriously need to look at these settings.

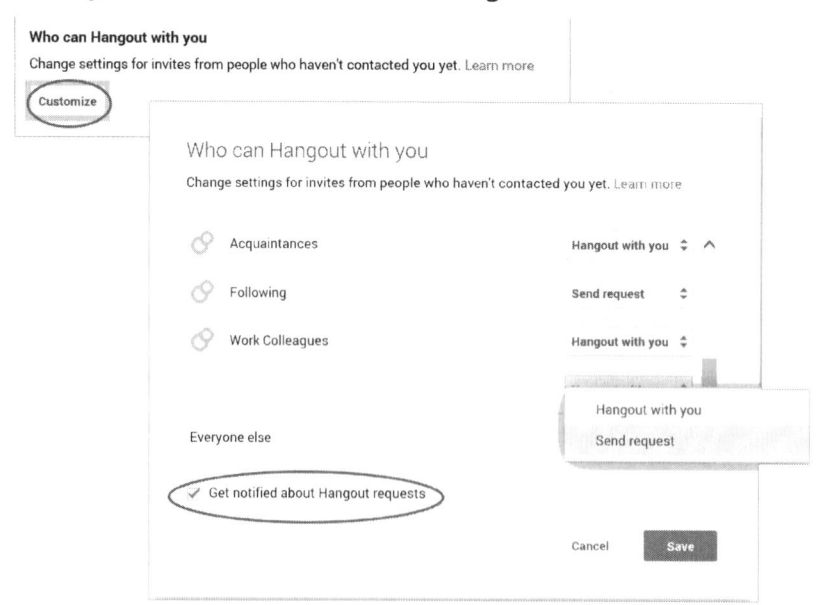

Figure 238 Who can hangout with you

Click on *Customize* and you will be taken to a page where you can choose to allow circles to *Hangout* with you or *Send a request*. There isn't the option of just stopping circles from contacting you so the only option if you don't want to be bothered by Hangout requests from certain circles or people is to choose *Send request* and untick the box that says *Get notified about Hangout requests*.

Shared Endorsements

Shared endorsements are when you or your contacts have clicked on +1 on a post or on the web. They can see what you think is funny or good value if it is a product. I recommend keeping this on - if only to be nosy about what your friends like!

Notification delivery

You can add an email address to be notified about your Google+ notifications or add a phone number.

Figure 239 Get notified by email or phone

If you add your phone number, you will be able to choose receiving notifications through the Google+ mobile app, SMS or not to be notified at all.

Adding your phone number also means that people can find you on Google+ using your phone number. If you add your phone number here it will not be visible to everyone on Google+, that setting is in your general Google account settings. It is just used for people who know your number and you have a popular name like Nick Clark or Tom Smith.

Manage Subscriptions

There is no real reason why you would want to receive occasional updates from people from outside your circles. After all if you were interested in what they had to say or what they were doing, surely you would have added them to your circles. I recommend unchecking these options.

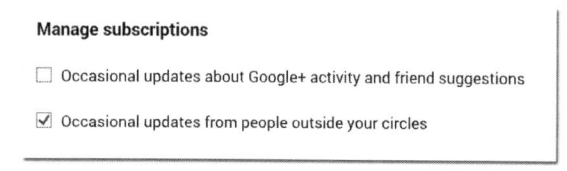

Figure 240 Manage subscriptions

Receive notifications

In this section you can choose how or if you want notifications for categories. The categories are *Posts, Circles, Photos, Hangouts, Events, Communication about Google+ Pages* and *Communities*. You can choose to receive notifications by email and/or your phone, (if you have added it to the settings in *Notification delivery)* for each settings within each category.

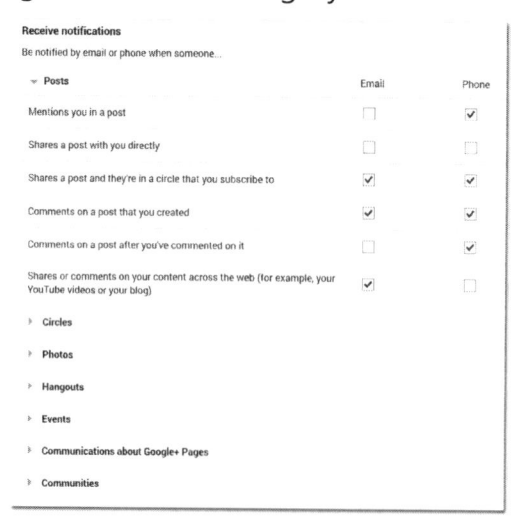

Figure 241 What do you want to receive notification for?

Apps & activities

This setting controls how others can see your activities. Once you have enabled an app, it will appear in a list and you will be able to edit who can view your activities. It also records every time you press +1.

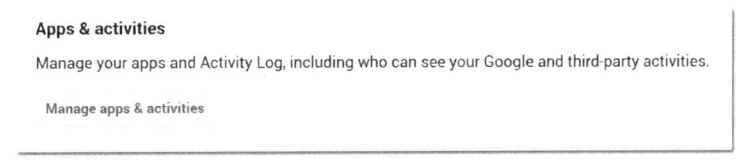

Figure 242 Apps and activities

Your circles

When you share something whether it is a post, comment or reshare, you can choose to send them to *Your circles*. You can control which of your circles are included in this umbrella term. You can have as many circles as you like in your circles or as few. An idea could be that you have a circle for friends and a circle for family and only those two groups could be in *Your Circles*. This would mean that you would only have to type (or at least start typing *Your circles* in the *To:* box and your posts would be seen by those two groups only instead of typing family and friends (or checking the boxes next to the groups in the dropdown options).

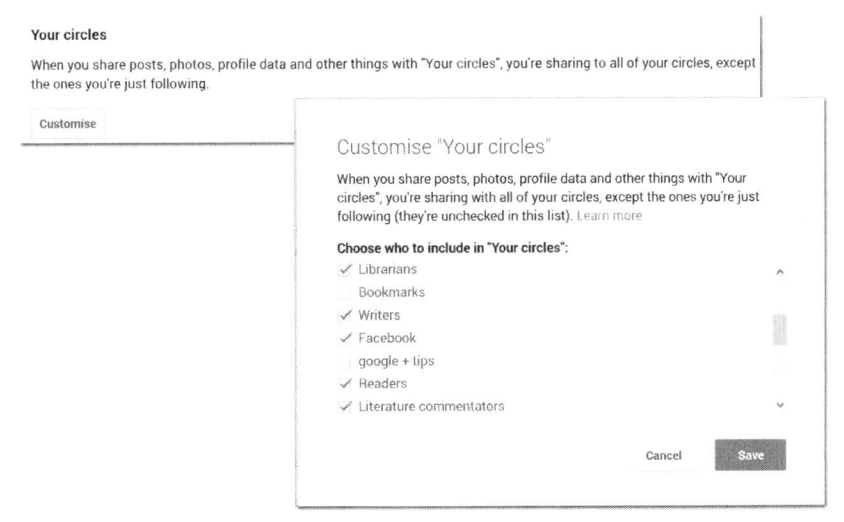

Figure 243 Choose which of your Circles is included in Your circles

Accessibility

Check this option if you use a screen reader or other accessibility tools.

Ceri Clark | A Simpler Guide to Gmail

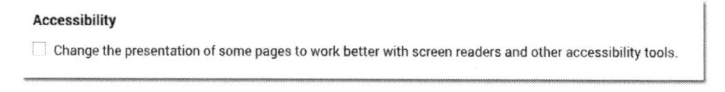

Figure 244 Make Google+ more accessible

Photos and Videos

I would not allow the geolocation of photos and videos if you make those photos public. This is simply for the reason that people will know when you are on holiday and will a) probably know where you live from past photos and b) they will know that your house is probably empty and is just asking to be burgled. Of course this is a worst case scenario but the geolocation of you photos and videos allows people to effectively track where you are.

If you check the box next to Google Drive you will have the option to easily share the pictures in there in your posts. No one will be able to see the photos until you share them.

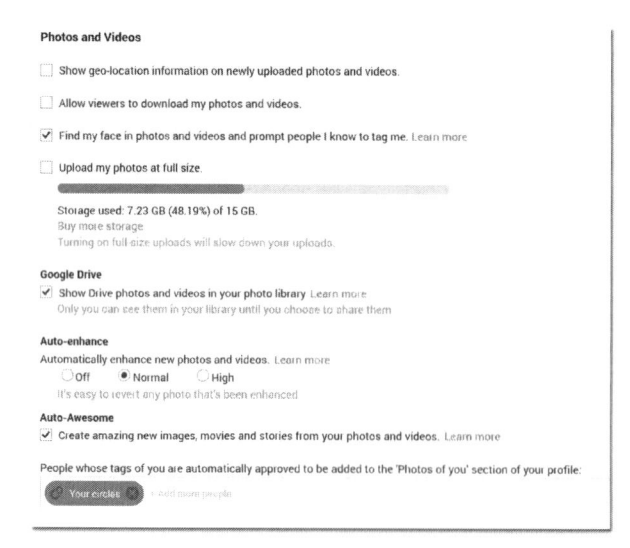

Figure 245 Settings for your photos and videos

You also have the option to auto-enhance your photos by choosing *Normal* and *High*. This will remove red eye and improve the lighting on your photos. If you turn it off then your photos will be the same as they were when you uploaded them.

222

Auto-Awesome as you would expect from the name is Awesome. Google trawls through your uploaded photos and videos and creates new compilations of photos and videos. For example, I have taken quite a few videos of my toddler and Google+ took snippets from several videos and stitched them together with music. It was lovely. Give them a try, you can always delete them if you don't like them.

Profile

These options let you show your Google+ activity so people can see photos, videos, +1s and reviews you've done. If you are promoting yourself or a business then you will want to keep the *Help others discover my profile in search results* option. I would not recommend allowing people to message you from your profile unless you restrict to a circle where you know you want to be contacted from. Allowing extended circles to contact you means that you can be contacted by your circles and those who are in the circles of the people who have circled you).

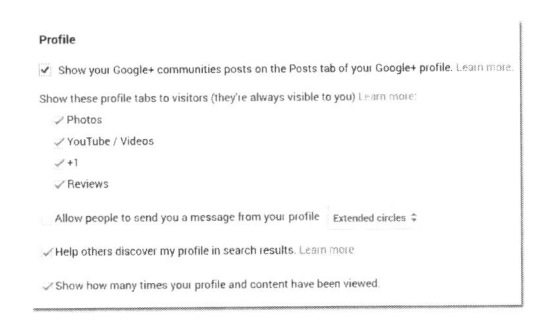

Figure 246 Show how you want the world to see elements of your profile

Hashtags

The option to add related hashtags to your posts is a really useful feature. If your posts are public it means that more people will be able to find what you share without you even thinking about it!

Figure 247 Have hashtags automatically added to your posts

Location Settings

The location settings can track your whereabouts using your mobile devices. In some cases this can be really useful. I allow my husband to see me and I can see where my husband is so I can know when to put the oven on for dinner. However, I would only share this information with a few select people who need to know where you are. Sharing your city is fine but any finer detail I think could be dangerous. For the same reason you wouldn't post your address on Google+, I don't think it would be sensible allowing just anyone to see where you are at all times.

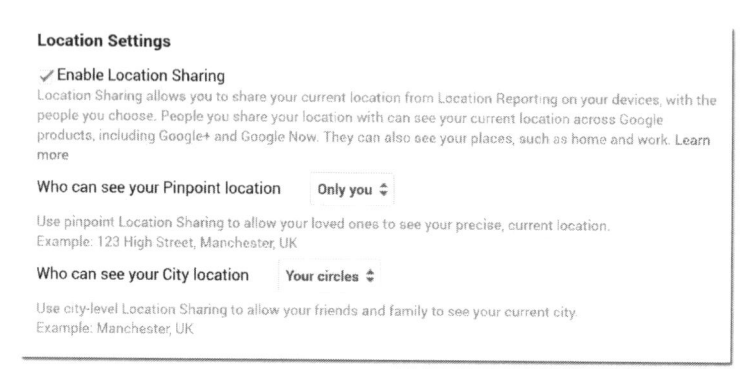

Figure 248 Do you want people to know where you are?

SMS Terms

The SMS terms explains that there are charges for using this service. It also lets you know how you can stop receiving text messages. I can't imagine that anything that happens on Google+ would be so important that you need a text message considering you can use notifications from your Google+ app or view your email.

Disable Google+

If you ever want to delete your Google+ account then this is the place you should visit. Click on the link to remove yourself from Google+.

Privacy

The notion of privacy on any social network is an illusion. As soon as you share anything it can be copied and forwarded by the people you share with. Google+ gives you the ability to stop people resharing and to stop commenting. Don't let this give you a false sense of security. Be aware that anyone can cut and paste or take screenshots. Never put anything on a social network that would devastate you if it got out into the wider internet.

The best way to protect your privacy is to have trustworthy people in your circles (in the case of Google+) and to be selective about what you share. The only caveat I would say to this is if you own a business and want to promote yourself, your products or your work. In this case always be professional and courteous and you will never have to worry about privacy.

With this in mind, Google does have a couple of options for increasing your control over what can be done with what in your post. Please see the section, *Disabling Comments and reshares* in *Managing your posts* for how to stop people 'forwarding' on posts and commenting.

You can view Google's privacy policy by going to your account picture on the top right of the screen and then choosing Privacy as below.

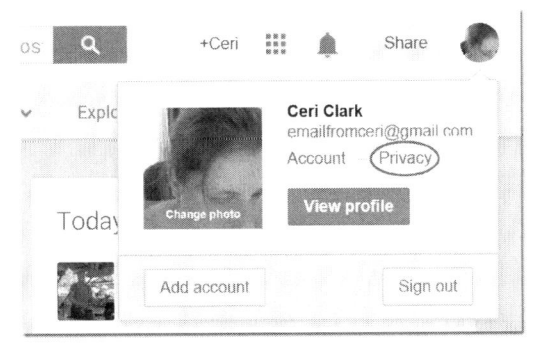

Figure 249 How to find the privacy settings and privacy policy

The page the link takes you to is split into four sections, privacy policy, terms of service, tools and information and the Google Safety Centre. To access your privacy settings, go to your *Google Account Settings* under *Tools and information*. In the resulting page, click on *Google+ settings*.

The section that applies the most to privacy settings is under *Photos and Videos*. I would uncheck *Show geo location information on newly updated photos and videos* unless you want people to know where you live or know when you are on holiday and the best time to burgle your house! Of course if you are not worried checking this will be fine.

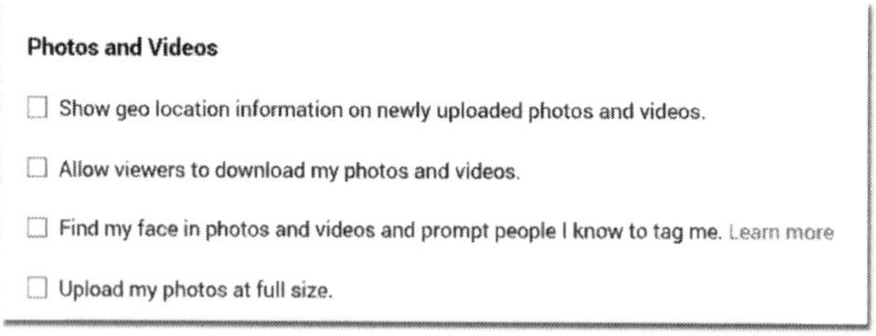

Figure 250 Privacy settings related to photos and videos

If you are sharing photos and videos, think about if you want people who can see them to have the ability to download them. If it is trusted close family and friends that is fine but bear in mind what kind of photos and videos you are sharing. That weekend away on holiday with a few too many beers could be used to embarrass you in the future or then again could be used to throw you a surprise birthday party, you never know!

Google+ app on your phone

If you have an Android phone then Google+ should be on your phone when you buy it. If it isn't or you have an iPhone then go to the app store for your phone and download it.

Having the Google+ app on your phone is really useful. You can receive notifications and share while on the go. Whether you are keeping in contact or just bored and browsing, the app is a must have app for your phone. Please note that Hangouts is not a part of the Google+ app and if you want to do video calling then you will need to download the separate Hangout app.

The placement of the options in the following screenshots may change over time but the options will still be there with a little digging and exploration.

Introduction to Google+

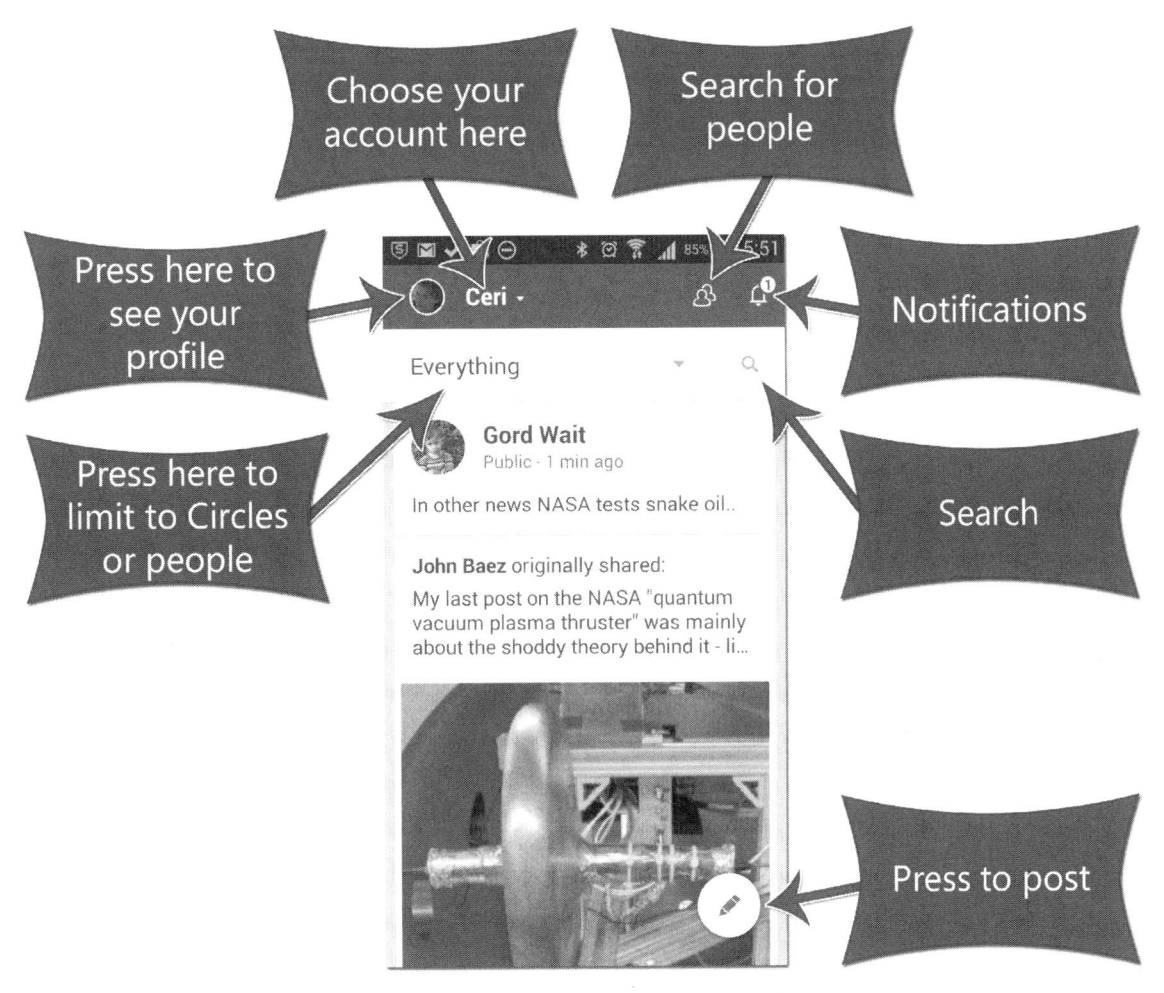

- Choose your account here
- Search for people
- Press here to see your profile
- Notifications
- Press here to limit to Circles or people
- Search
- Press to post

Figure 251 Home screen/Stream options

Viewing your profile

Click on your profile picture on the top left of the screen on your phone to see how your profile looks to others on a phone. Flip through your profile information by pressing on *ABOUT*, look through your posts by pressing on *POSTS* and flick through your photos by pressing on the last tab labelled *PHOTOS*.

When you go into *ABOUT*, you will have the option to edit your information by clicking on the little picture of a pen to the right of each section.

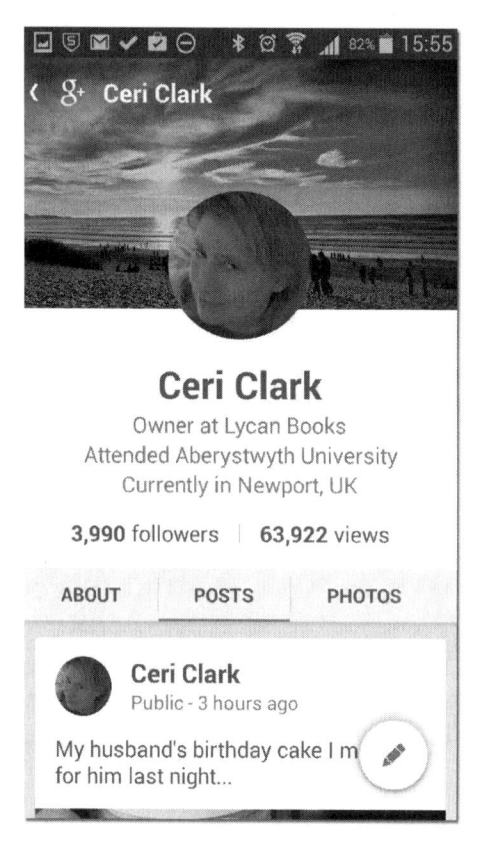

Figure 252 An example of a profile

Choosing your account

Next to your profile photo, you will see your name. Press on this to load your accounts. This is useful if you have any pages but if you only have the one account the option is pretty redundant.

People Search

When you press on the people icon (as seen in the screenshot at the beginning of this section, you will be offered suggestions for who you might want to add to your circles and follow. Press on *Add* and choose which circles you think they are most appropriate for or create a new one.

Introduction to Google+

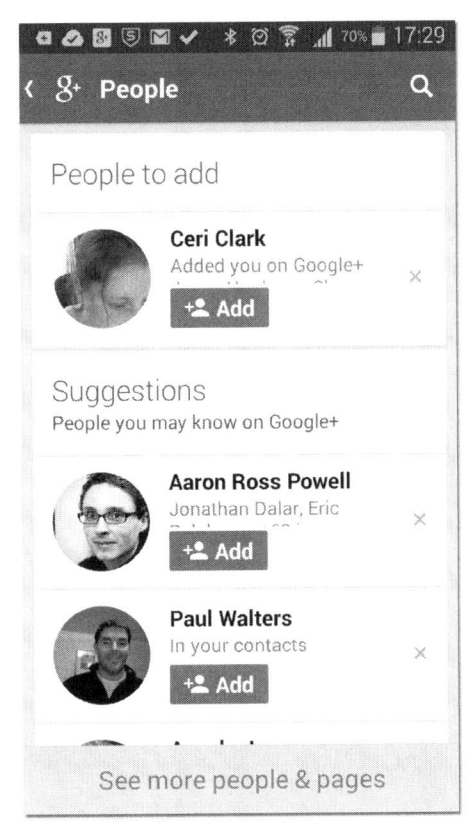

Figure 253 Click the people icon to see Google+ suggestions for people to add

Notifications

Press on the bell icon to see your notifications. You will be told, when people contact you by typing + in front of your name, when other Google+ users +1 your posts, event invites and when people add you to their circles.

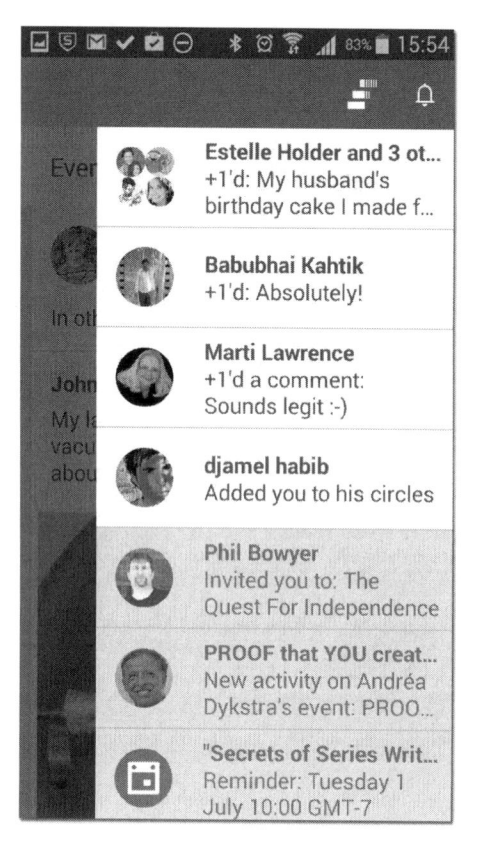

Figure 254 Notification screen

Once you have seen the notification, it will be grayed out.

Limiting the posts you see

As with the desktop version of Google+ you can limit the posts you see by choosing to only see posts from certain circles. Press on the word *Everything* and you press on *My Circles* to get the list of your circles. Choose the one you want and you will only see the posts from the people in that group. You can change the circle at any time by redoing the above steps.

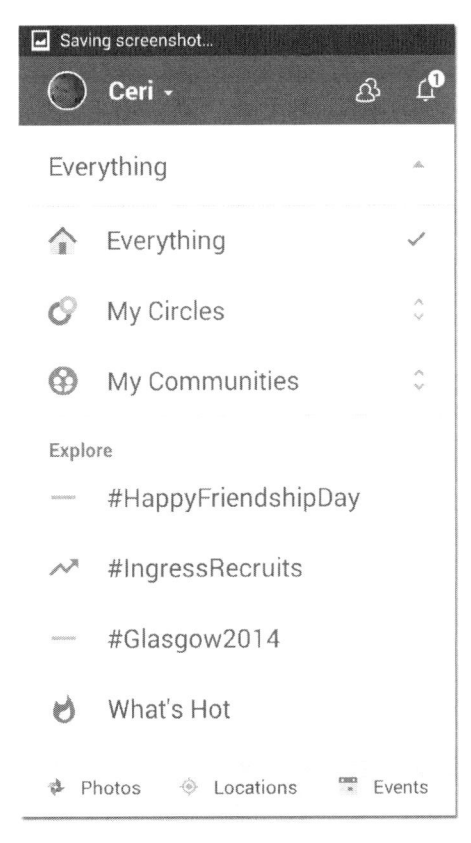

Figure 255 Press on My Circles to get a list of your circles

In the screen where you can select the circles you want to see posts from you can also choose to see posts from communities you have joined but also have a look at what is trending on Google+ by pressing on hash tags or *What's Hot*.

Search

The Google+ app allows you to search for people, posts and photos. Look for the little magnifying glass on the top right of the home screen and type what you want to find. Remember typing in a word with the hash tag (#) in front or even with the #+word in quotes (for example "+cooking") will give you the best results when searching.

Posting

If you want to write a post in the Google+ app, look for the pen symbol in the circle which at the time of writing in 2014 was located in the bottom right of the screen as seen illustrated at the beginning of this section.

If you press your finger firmly on a comment for a couple of seconds you will be given the opportunity to reply to the comment or just reply.

Settings

The Google+ app allows you to change many settings on your Google+ account. Go to the menu button on your phone, then choose settings in your Google+ app. The first screen in the next image will load.

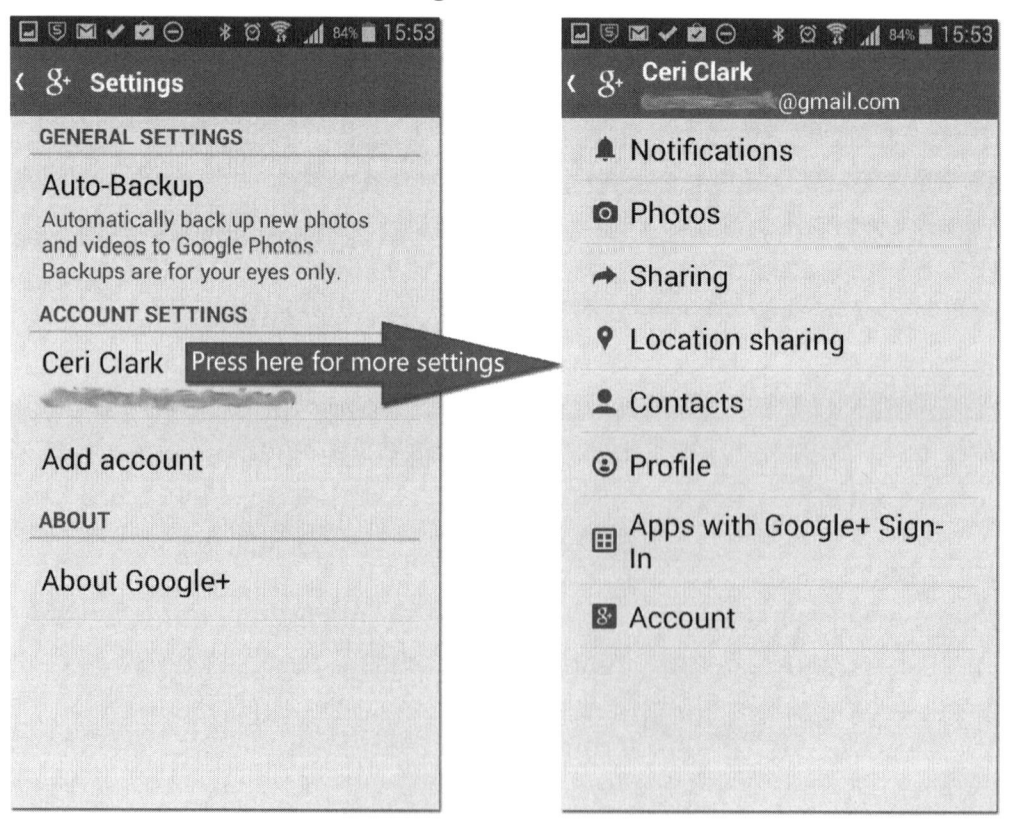

Figure 256 Google+ settings

You have the option to auto-backup your photos, add an account or read about Google+ on the first settings screen. If you press on your account name, you will

Introduction to Google+

get to the settings which are available on the desktop version of Google+. The second screen on the image above shows what settings are available from the app. Bear in mind that not all settings on the desktop are accessible on the app. I recommend using your desktop or laptop to make settings changes. Please see the *Settings* section for more information.

Google+ extensions for the Chrome browser

There are some really useful applications that developers have made to extend what Google+ can do. These have to be installed on the Chrome browser. Here are the best of what is available:

Installing the extensions on Chrome

Please follow the steps below for installing extensions in your Chrome browser:

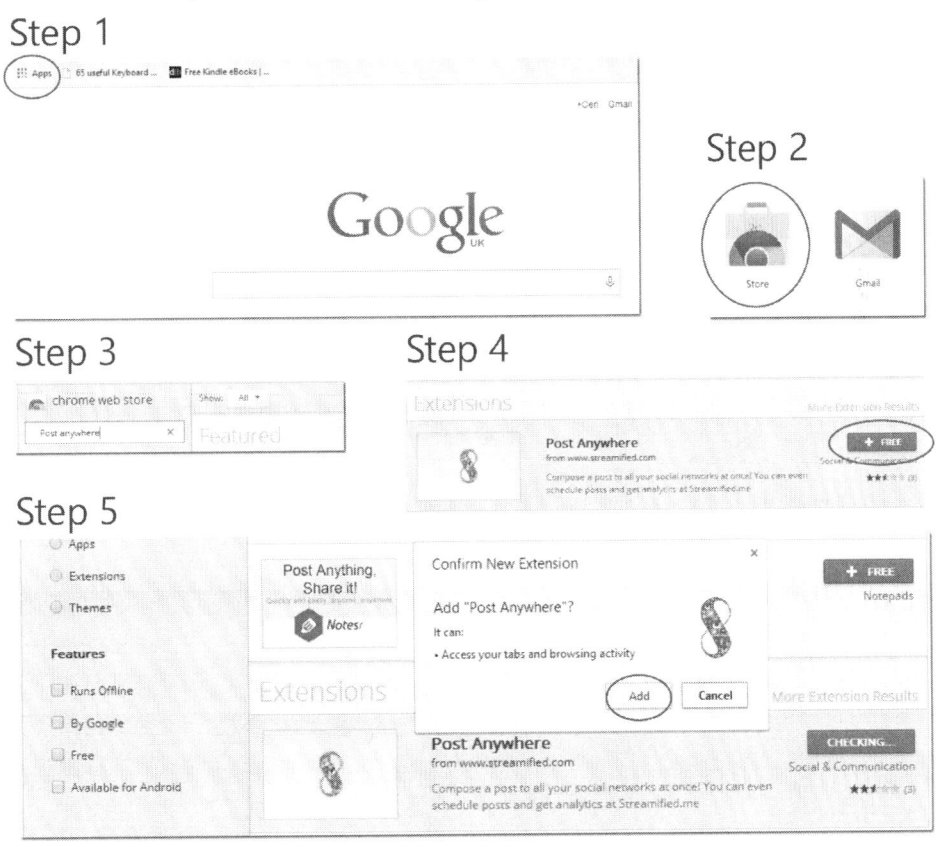

Step 1

Step 2

Step 3

Step 4

Step 5

Step 1: Open your Chrome browser to get to the Google homepage or open a new tab and click on *Apps* (located at the top left of the screen as seen in the screenshot at the beginning of this section.

Step 2: Choose *Store*

Step 3: Type in the name of the extension in the box on the top left of the screen.

Step 4: Click on the button with the *+Free* on. See the screenshots at the beginning of the section for a visual representation.

Step 5: Click on *Add*.

Your extension will then be added to your Chrome browser.

If you want to find your extensions, click on the three horizontal lines on the top right of the Google Chrome browser. Hover your mouse over *Tools* then *Extensions* and all your extensions will load. You can remove an extension on this page by clicking on the trash/bin icon to the right of the extension.

Figure 257 Where to find your extensions in your Chrome browser

Circloscope
Price: Free or $47 per year for more functionality

Google+ will only allow you to add up to 5,000 people to your circles. Circloscope allows you to manage your circles so that you can see and remove people who are not active and who are not following you back. These features are invaluable for freeing up space so you can follow the people you are really interested in.

Replies and more for Google+
Price: Free

The three stand out features of this extension are the *Reply to Author* button (adds the +name automatically to your post), the option to share with Facebook, Twitter and through your email and finally the Google+ icon in your browser tab becomes animated so shows the number of notifications you have. The latter feature means you can be working on a different tab, maybe looking at your email and you will see just by glancing at the tabs that you have a new Google+ notification.

Do Share
Price: Free

Do Share is a Chrome extension that will allow you to schedule Google+ posts. The downside is that your computer must be on and the browser open for the schedule to work but the upside is, *you can schedule posts*!

Google+ Posting Cheat Sheet

Text Styling
Example starring text will bold the words and it will look like **Example**.

Example underscoring text will italicize the words and it will look like *Example*.

-Example- hyphenating on either side of text will strike out the text so it will look like ~~Example~~.

Posting

Add + or @ to mention people in your posts.

Prevent resharing of your posts by clicking the arrow at the top right of each post and clicking 'Disable reshare'.

Google+ Shortcut keys

To view the latest shortcut key combinations while in Google+ press the Shift and the question mark key (Shift+?).

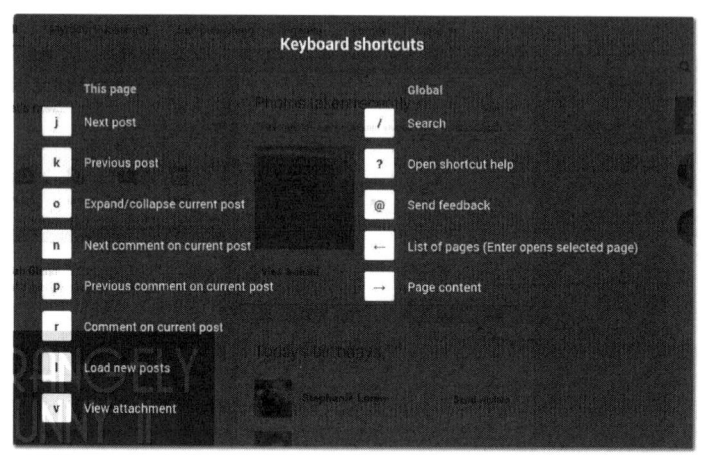

Figure 258 Keyboard shortcuts

J will scroll down one post at a time

K will scroll up one post at a time.

Down and up arrows will scroll down and up the page

L will load new posts

Chapter 15 Chat

What to expect in this Chapter:

- Turning on Chat
- Inviting contacts to chat
- Video, phone or text chat

Gmail gives you the option to chat to your contact. Sometimes you might want to get an answer quickly and if you see that they are online, it can be faster to open a text or video chat rather than send an email and wait for a response.

Turning on Chat

The Chat function can be found in the left navigation bar on your Gmail homepage. You will need to invite someone to chat in the first instance but after that, your contact will be in the chat list.

First, go to the gear wheel at the top right of the screen, this is the main settings button, and then click on *Settings* as in the next figure.

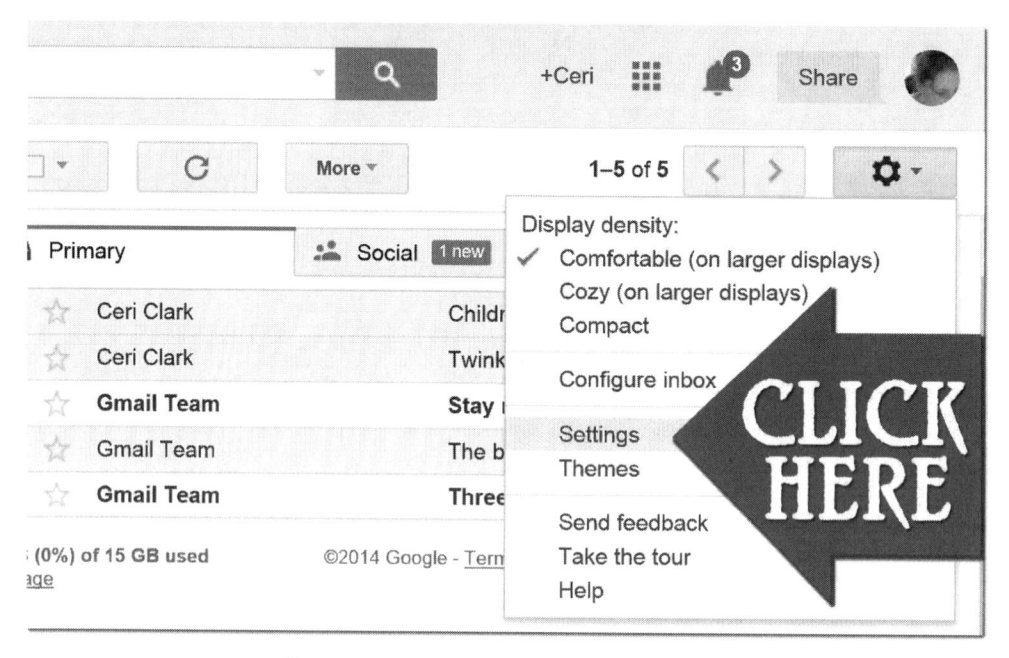

Figure 259 Location of settings button

A dropdown menu will appear when it is clicked on allowing you to choose *settings* to get the following screen.

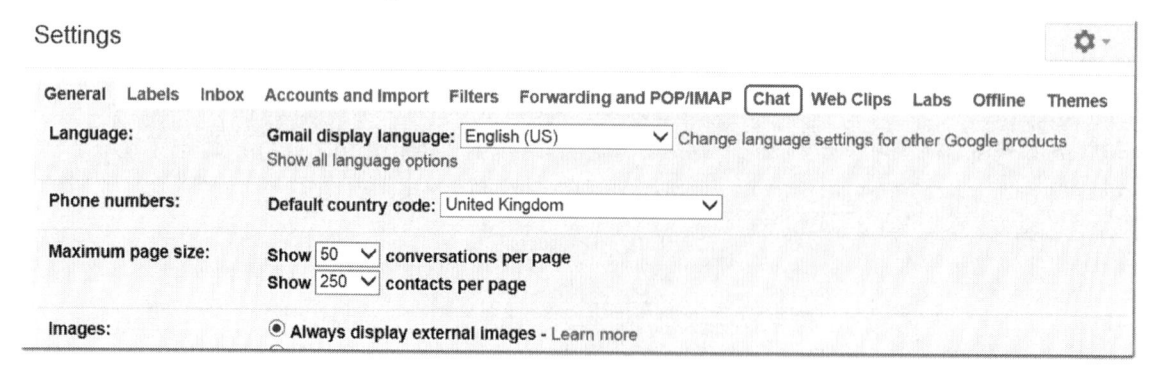

Figure 260 Chat settings

Go to the circled location labelled *Chat* (as above) to get all the settings relevant to it. Turn chat on by choosing *Chat on* and then clicking *Save Changes* at the bottom of the screen.

Inviting a contact to chat

The chat section of Gmail is on the bottom left of the Gmail screen, always available even when you are typing mail! If you can't see your profile picture name and search button, click on the speech button with the quotation marks inside to open the section.

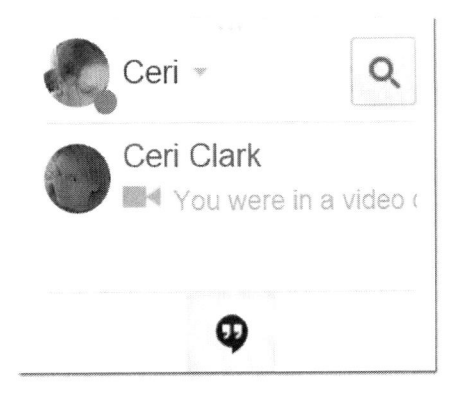

Figure 261 Chat section

Type your contact's email address in the search box which opens when you click on the magnifying glass. Google will look through the contacts in your Gmail account first and then in Google+ for other contacts. It doesn't matter if you do not have a person in your contacts, if they are in Google+, Gmail will still find them for you.

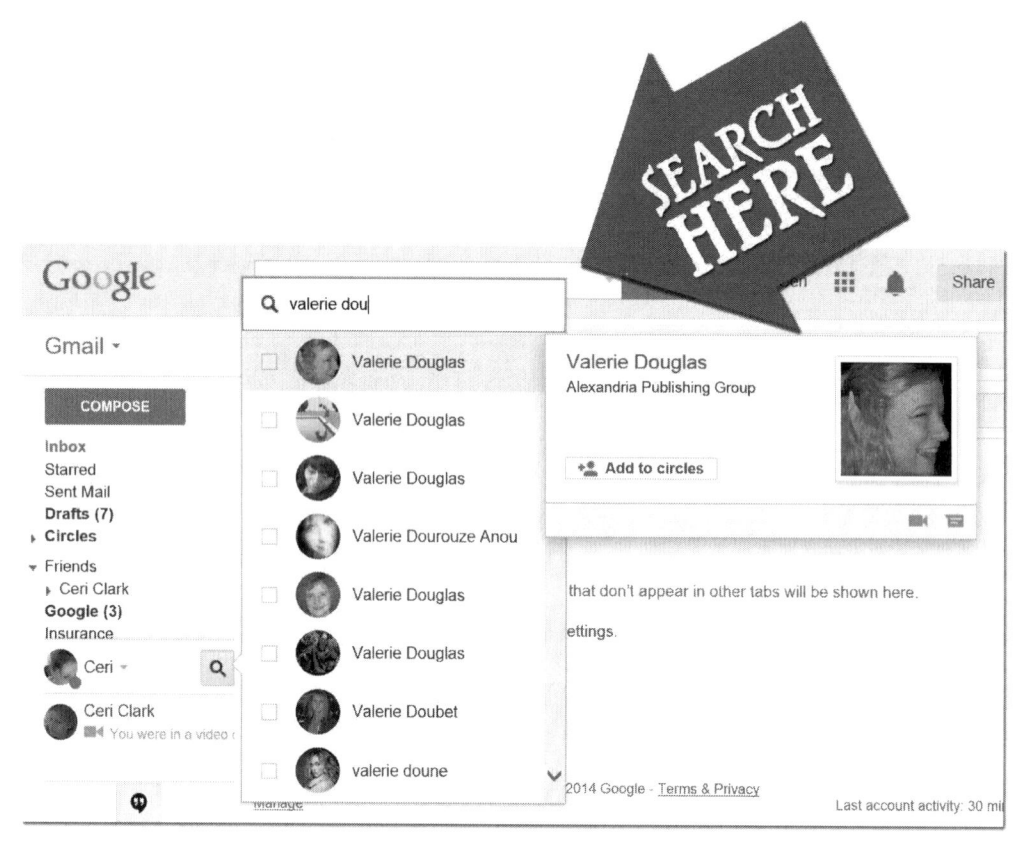

Figure 262 Gmail will search Google+ if our contact isn't in your Gmail account

Before you can contact the person, they will be notified that you are trying to contact them for the first time. They will have to allow this before you can start chatting. Be aware it is possible to disallow people from contacting you at all using the Google+ settings. If you want to do this, click on the little arrow next to your name and choose *Customize invite settings* to change how people can contact you.

It is worth knowing that even if you remove a contact from your contacts and Google+, their name will still appear in the chat list below your name. You can start a video chat by clicking on the little representation of a camera by their name.

Older accounts

Older accounts may look slightly different. My personal account looks like the following image (I have blanked out my contacts). If you like the old system, then for a limited time you can switch to it by clicking on your profile picture/name or downwards arrow and choosing *Revert to old chat*. This is at the bottom of the window, beneath the scroll bar next to *Help* and *Feedback*.

Figure 263 Your contacts will have symbols next to them

As you can see the search box is more obvious under my status. Adding people is the same as in the new style accounts. Just type the name of the person you want to add in the search box and select from the profiles that Google offers.

Contact availability

The symbols next to each contact tell you how they can be contacted. The symbol of the video camera as seen next to the first contact above will allow you to start a video call, the android symbol shows that they can be contacted via their mobile phone (if you enable the green robot lab on old accounts) and the green circle means they are online. If a circle is gray then the person in your contacts is not online, an orange circle which looks like a clock means your contact's computer is idle. If the circle is red with a horizontal white line running through it that means they are busy.

The way to get the chat section to appear on new or old accounts is to look for the speech bubble at the bottom and click on it. Clicking it again will hide it.

The notable difference between the two chat setups is that in the older one you can set a little custom/status message. I've got mine as *do not disturb – working hard* on mine but I love my friend's status message which reads: *Tragically an only twin*. It's a great way to show your personality!

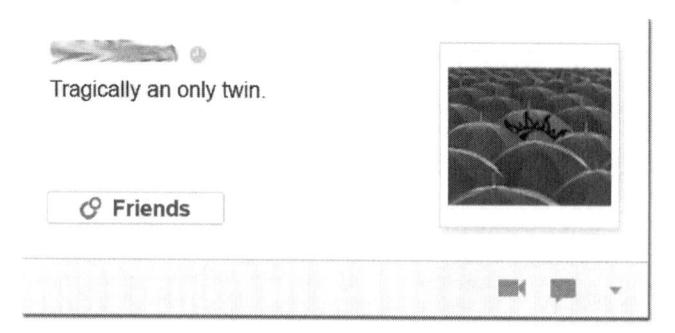

Figure 264 Example of a person card with status message and circle information

By clicking on the little downwards pointing arrow beside your name, you can get to the Chat settings quickly.

Blocking contacts

If you would like the option of blocking a person you are chatting to, particularly useful for ex-boyfriends/girlfriends you can do this by the following two methods depending on if you have a new account or an older account:

New account

1. Start a hangout with the person by clicking on their name, (they won't be alerted until you start typing). The hangout will appear in a box on the bottom far right of your screen
2. Click on the gear wheel on the top right of the box.
3. Choose the option to *Block*.

Older account

Bring up your contact's card by clicking on their name and select the arrow on the bottom right of the card.

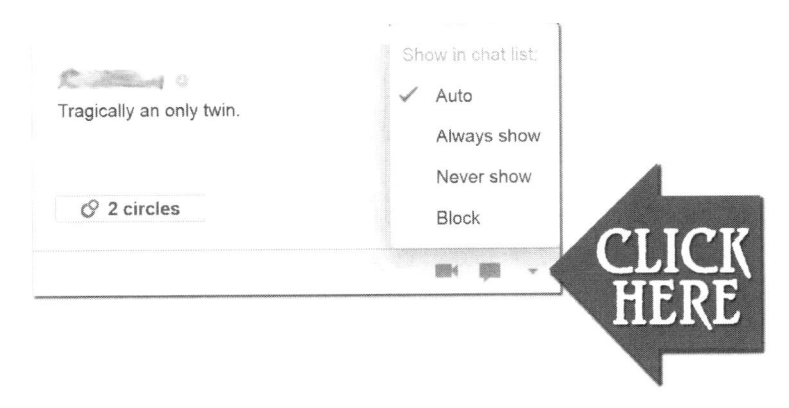

Figure 265 Blocking a contact or removing it from your chat contacts

You can then select *Block* if you want to stop them contacting you. You can stop their name appearing in the list of your chat contacts here or, alternatively, if you contact them a lot you might want to choose *Always show*.

Video, phone or text chat

To video, phone or text chat depends on the circumstances at the time you are trying to contact them. This could be anything from having a *bad hair day*, a *work from home and forgot accidentally-on-purpose to take off my pajamas and wear work clothes day* or more seriously, the other person is busy and you can type a message and you don't mind waiting for an answer. People will usually respond to chat messages a lot quicker than email.

If you click on the video icon then the hangout window will load. This is the same as in Google+, rather than write the instructions again, please see *Chapter 14 Introduction to Google+*.

Chapter 16 Tasks

What to expect in this Chapter:

- Getting the most out of tasks
- Creating tasks
- Deleting tasks
- Organizing tasks

Tasks are a great way of remembering lists of things to do. As long as you have access to the internet you can add, edit and delete from your task list wherever you are. Whether on your smartphone or on your computer at home, use tasks to organize your life.

Where to find Tasks

Tasks can be found on the left navigation bar in the top left corner of your screen as seen in Figure 266.

Figure 266 Where to find Tasks

By clicking on Tasks a popup will appear on the bottom right of the screen which looks like this:

Figure 267 Tasks window

The buttons on the top of the task window do three things:
1. minimizes the window
2. pops the window to a larger, new browser window
3. Closes the Task window completely

The options on the bottom of the screen are (from left to right):

4. *Actions:* These include moving tasks in a list, emailing, printing, viewing, sorting and clearing tasks in a list.
5. The plus sign adds a new task
6. Clicking on the trash can/bin symbol deletes a task
7. The lists options include refresh, rename, delete and create a new list.

Adding a task

To add a task, click next to the little white box and start typing. After you've made the first task you can then click on the + button at the bottom of each window to make another.

Other ways to start a new task:

- Pressing enter after you have finished typing a new task will start a new one
- Clicking directly under the last task in the list will also create a new task.

If you want to add more details to a task (such as a due date) click on the arrow pointing right, on the line of the subject and the page in the next figure will load:

Figure 268 Adding details to a task

Click on *Back to List*, and the main tasks window will appear again. All the information is then displayed under the task subject. There is no need to save, Google will automatically do this for you.

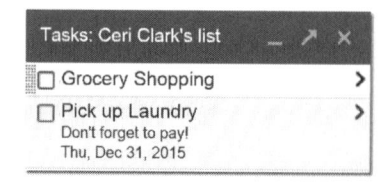

Figure 269 Example of a tasks list

Completing a task

To complete a task simply check the box next to the subject. The text will have a line through it so you know you've done it.

Deleting or removing a task

To remove a task, click on the subject and click on the trash can (bin) symbol at the bottom of the task window.

Actions

Clicking on *Actions* as seen in figure 270 can give you more options.

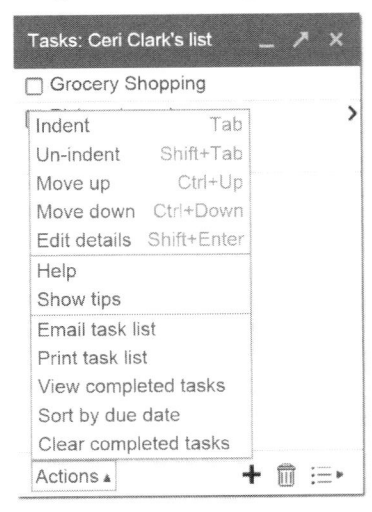

Figure 270 Actions available in Tasks

Indent and Unindent

These options will allow you to move dependent tasks as if you were using Tab in a word processor. Click on the subject, then *Actions*, then *Indent*. The subject will then move a little to the right. For an example of how this might work see the next figure.

Figure 271 Task indenting in action

Clicking on the indented item and then *Actions* > *Un-indent* will send the item back to the left.

Move up or down
Similar to indenting, click on the subject > *Actions* > *Move up/Move down.*

Edit Details
This option will bring up the details page again. Clicking on the arrow next to each task will do the same thing.

Help
Clicking on this will send you to Google's help pages on using Tasks.

Show tips
This will show you tips in the Tasks window.

Email task list
Have a list which you want your partner or friend to see? Email them the list.

Print task list
This sends your list to your printer.

View completed tasks
This is useful if you just want to see what you have completed/organized by date.

Sort by due date
If you have put dates to your tasks, see what you need to complete first.

Clear completed tasks
Just have your uncompleted tasks in your list.

Organizing lists

On the bottom bar of the task window click on ≡▸ to bring up some options for creating and editing task lists. Please see the next figure for the list of options.

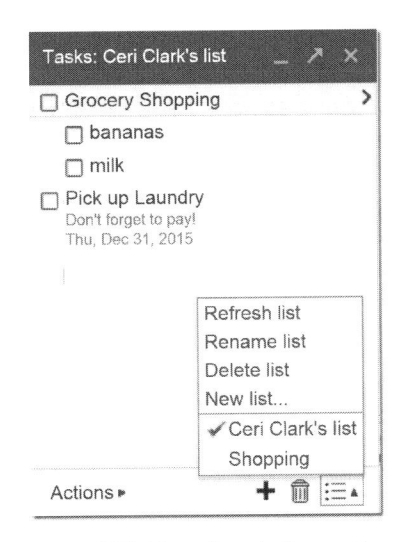

Figure 272 List of task list options

These options are *Refresh list, Rename list, Delete list, New list* and then the lists you have already made.

You can have more than one list, choose the list you want from the bottom of the options that appears when you click on the three lines icon, as seen above.

Chapter 17 Netiquette

What to expect in this Chapter:

- Traditions of communicating over the internet
- What to do with trolls

If this is your first email account you may not be familiar with some of the traditions of Netiquette. Here are the top rules of email etiquette.

1. Never type your emails ALL IN CAPS LOCK! IT WILL SEEM TO THE READER THAT YOU ARE SHOUTING AT THEM.
2. If you use abbreviations or acronyms, write them out in full during first use. After that you don't need to explain it in the same email.
3. Don't remove previous messages from your email thread when replying. The person you are emailing may have deleted your previous emails altogether and if you reply with no history they may have no idea what you are talking about.
4. When replying, start your message at the top of the thread. This is so your friends, colleagues and other contacts don't have to scroll down an exceedingly long list just to find out what you have to say.

5. If you have a long reply, try to put a summary of the most important items at the beginning of your email. Most people scan-read emails when they are busy and if you want them to do something make sure it is obvious at the beginning of the email.
6. Use a meaningful subject. Should I bother to read this email? If it just says "Howdy", the recipient might think its spam. And at the same time don't send emails with a blank subject either!
7. Don't forward chain-emails, unless it's a *really* funny one, then share it on Google+!
8. Read the email before you send it. What sounds perfectly reasonable when you are writing can seem really insulting after ten minutes – and that's when you are not trying to be insulting!
9. Be careful when replying to mailing lists. Remember that email can go to hundreds if not thousands of people.
10. Don't make personal remarks about people in jest. The reader can't see the glint in your eye as you are being ironic.
11. Don't post your email address on websites unless you want to be sent a lot of spam.
12. Be respectful, imagine you are talking to someone you know. Sending an email can seem anonymous, but people's feelings can still hurt.
13. If you don't know the person you are contacting, make an extra effort to make your emails as clear and concise as possible.
14. Keep your fonts and language simple. Make sure you do not use yellow, grey or light colors when emailing people. They are difficult to see, why make life hard for people? You may think it looks cool, but if your contact has to highlight, copy it, then paste it into word, change the color and make it bigger just to read it, let's just say your email just may go unread.
15. If someone comments on one of your posts on social networks and it appears malicious, they are most probably a troll. They are posting to get a response. In this situation, ignore them. Nothing annoys a troll more than if they think someone hasn't noticed a comment designed to infuriate.

Chapter 18 Gmail on Your Android Device

What to expect in this Chapter:

- The Gmail app overview
- Reading and writing emails on your Android device
- Searching your emails
- A look at the settings

With an ever growing number of new smartphones and tablets available there is no excuse to be without your email. Gmail is so simple to set up with an Android device. At the time of writing this book I have a Samsung Galaxy Note so these instructions are designed with that phone in mind but the instructions should be similar across all Android phones and tablets.

Gmail should already be installed on your Android device. Browse your Apps list and find the (envelope) icon for Gmail. Your account will have already been set up when you set your Google account on your phone. The screen when you launch the app will look like this:

Ceri Clark | A Simpler Guide to Gmail

Overview

Annotations on screenshot:
- Press here to search your messages
- Press here for the Gmail menu
- Other inbox notifications
- EMAILS
- Press here to compose a new message

Figure 273 Gmail app overview

The Gmail menu

Tapping on the three horizontal lines will take you to the Gmail settings (at the bottom of the list, just below Help & feedback). In the top bar of the main screen you will also find a magnifying glass which will allow you to search your messages. To start a new message press the pen symbol in the circle on the bottom right of the screen as seen above.

Gmail on Your Android device

Your emails will be displayed in the order Gmail received them and notifications will appear every now and again to let you know if any new email has arrived in your other inboxes (if they are activated). In the screenshot above, the Social, Promotions and Updates inboxes are at the top of the screen. When a new email arrives in one of the other inboxes, the notification jumps to the top of the screen with the total amount of unread emails in the 'bar'. When a new email from the Primary inbox arrives it will appear above the other inbox emails, unless of course you get another email in one of your other inboxes and so on. This means your latest messages will always be at the top.

Checking mail in the Gmail app

If your phone hasn't sync'd, press on your phone's screen and draw your finger down. A circling arrow will appear near the top of the screen to let you that Gmail is checking for new messages.

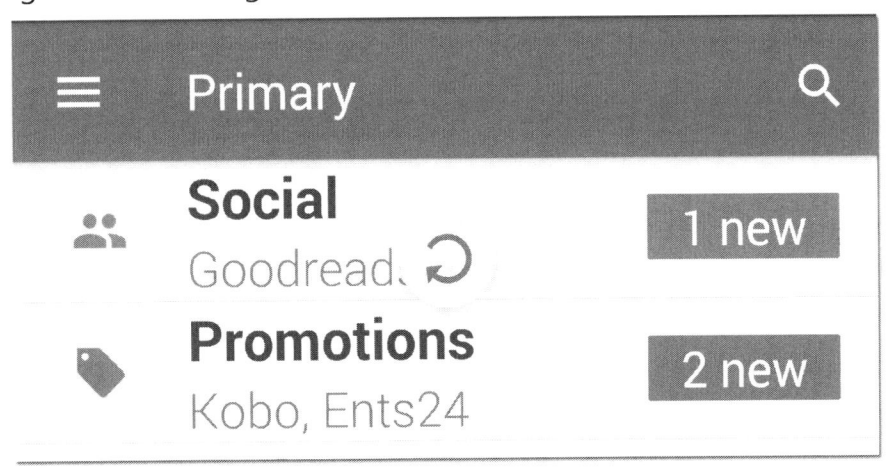

Figure 274 The circling arrow lets you know Gmail is checking for emails

Composing mail in the Gmail app

- Tap on the pen symbol in the circle located on the bottom right of your device's screen.
- Tap on *To (the email address you are sending from will appear at the top. You can choose a different one if you have set more than one up in your phone's account options).*

- Type in the first few letters, if you have already sent an email to that person from your phone before, Gmail will give you suggest that person below where you are typing. Select the person by tapping on them.
- Add a subject.
- Type your message.
- Tap on the arrow at the top right of the screen.

Replying and forwarding to mail in the Gmail app

- Open an email.
- Click on the arrow pointing left (circled below) on the right of the screen beside your contact's name and fill in the boxes as necessary.

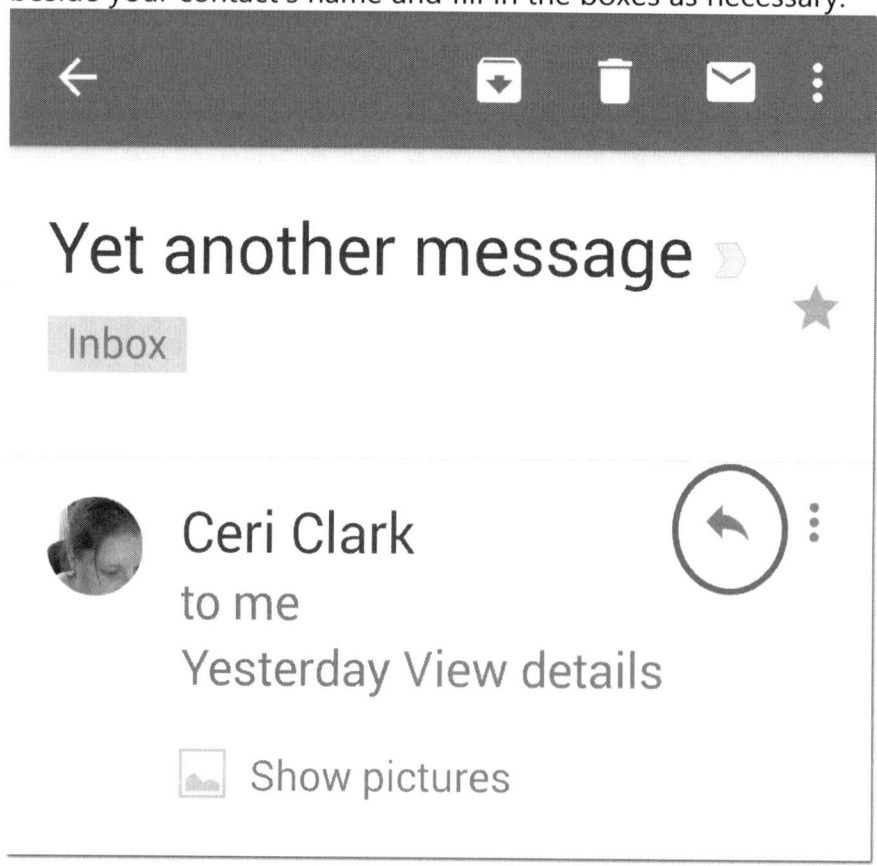

Figure 275 The arrow pointing left will allow you to reply to an email

Gmail on Your Android device

- Clicking on the three vertical dots will give you the option to *Reply all*, *Forward*, *Remove star* and *Print (the message)*.

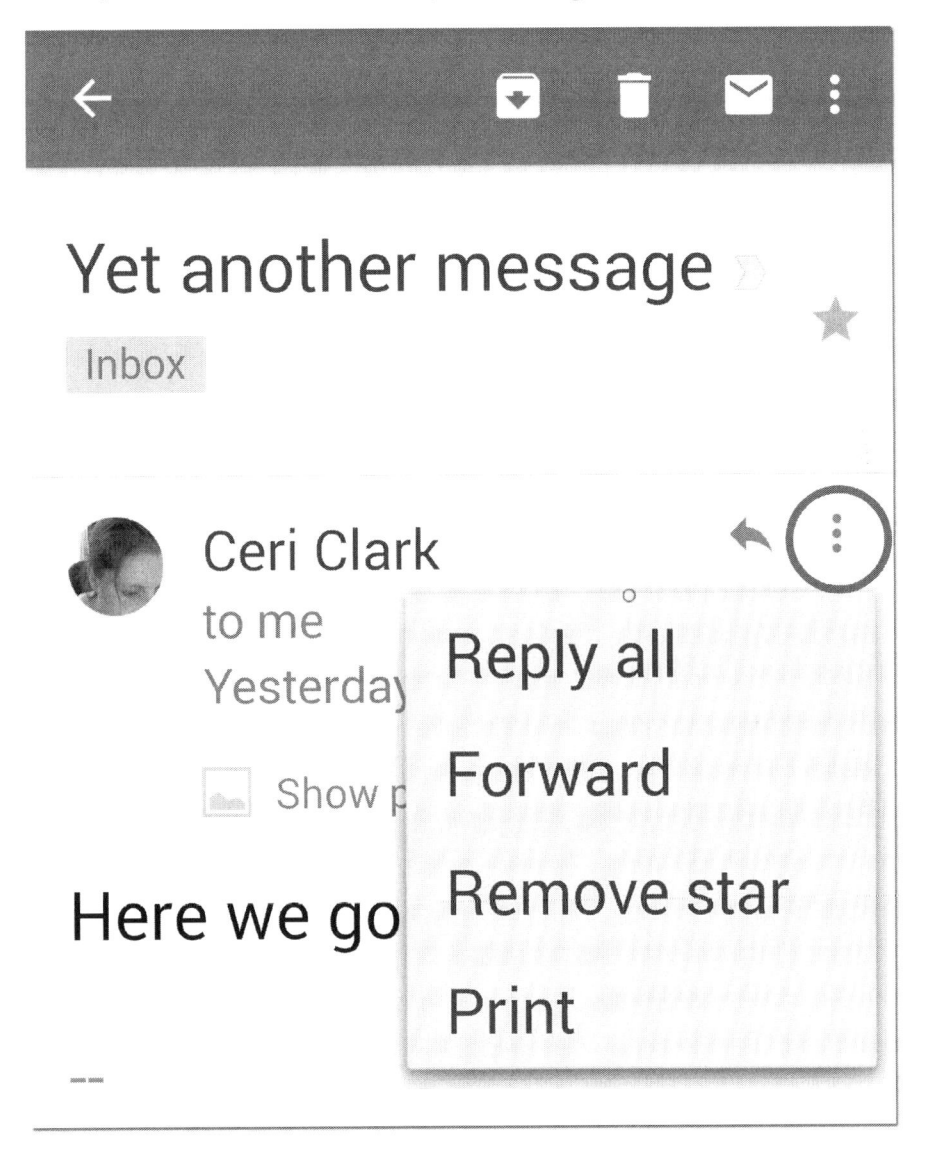

Figure 276 Press the three vertical dots for more options

Browsing your email using Labels

- Tap on the top left of the Gmail app (three white lines).

- Scroll down to the label you want then,
- Tap the Label you want.

Search your email

- Tap on the magnifying glass on the top right of the screen.
- Type in your search term and tap on the magnifying glass on your keyboard (or return depending on your keyboard). You will get a list of emails with the search words in them. For tips on searching Gmail please see *Chapter 9 Searching For, and In, Emails*.

Settings

You can get to the settings by tapping on the three lines button on the top left of the main screen.

In the top right of the screen there is the three vertical dots menu button. Here you can Manage your Account (takes you to your phone's settings) or you can access Help & feedback.

General settings

There are several settings within this section which, once set, will apply to all your Gmail accounts that you use with the Gmail app.

Below are a closer look at the options in the main window but you can get a couple more by clicking on the menu button (three vertical dots). These options are:

Manage Accounts: This takes you to your phone's settings.

Clear search history: Clears your search record.

Clear picture approval: Stops pictures showing in your emails which you may have approved previously. This will stop all pictures showing automatically so you would have to go and approve them all again if you just wanted to stop getting pictures from one sender!

Help & feedback: Access help from Gmail and provide feedback on their service.

Gmail default action (Archive and delete options)

This setting will determine if your email will be deleted when you swipe or archived. I always choose archive as it is easier to find the emails if they are mistakenly archived than if they are deleted.

Swipe actions

This is a great time saver. If this setting is activated, swipe your finger to the left or right on the email you want to archive or delete depending on how you set the previous option and it will go. You will have the option to undo for a couple of seconds if you made the gesture by mistake.

Sender image

If you have this setting on, you will see the picture of the sender of the email in the information when you are browsing your emails. If you turn it off you will be able to see more of the message on the home screen as it will expand to fill the space the picture took up.

Reply all

I do not recommend that you have this setting on. Replying to all is very dangerous if you are in a hurry. The email may go to people you do not intend it to. You can always choose to *Reply all* to each message as you reply but having a blanket settings could cause problems.

Auto-fit messages

If you have messages that don't wrap easily, this option will shrink it so it fits in the window. You can then zoom in to read the text.

Auto-advance

When you archive or delete you can choose here whether you want to go to a newer or older message or go to the conversation list.

Confirm before deleting, Confirm before archiving and Confirm before sending

These options are self-explanatory. If you want Gmail to ask whether you are sure that you want to delete, archive or send your message then turning this on will help you.

Email settings

These settings apply to the email address you specify.

Inbox type

By choosing this option you can make the *Priority inbox* your default inbox. I would recommend you do this only after a couple of months of using your email and you are sure that Google is tagging the right emails as important.

Inbox categories

This is where you choose which inboxes you want the emails to be filtered by in your Gmail. These are *Primary, Social, Promotions, Updates* and *Forums*. You can also drag all your starred emails in to the primary inbox here as well no matter how old they are.

Notifications and Inbox sound & vibrate

Control if and how you get notifications with this setting.

Signature

The Signature you created on the web version of Gmail does not apply on your smartphone. You must create another one here.

Vacation responder

You can set up a vacation/holiday responder here. If you do set one up I would advise that you check the button for it to work with your contacts only. Burglars have been known to break into houses when they know the owners are on their vacation/holiday.

Sync Gmail and days of mail to sync

If you are going to use this app, you need to sync your Gmail but you can choose how many of those emails you want on your phone by choosing how many days of your messages you want on there.

Manage labels

This is where you can turn on syncing for individual labels. It is not for creating/editing or deleting labels.

Download attachments

Choose whether you want attachments to be auto-downloaded.

Images

This is where you can get Gmail to ask before showing you images in your email or to always show them. It is best to have the setting on *Ask before showing*. There are a couple of possible reasons for this.

1. A spammer can use an image to see if your address is real. When you open an email, images are drawn from across the web. Spammers can record that it has been seen. The spammer can then sell your email or try to send emails to him/herself knowing that there is a possibility the spam message could be read.
2. Another reason could be that in the past viruses were hidden within images. This has for the most part been stopped as Google will block those they know about and spammers/hackers have now moved on to other means of harm or easier targets but there is still the possibility. If you only allow images to be shown from trusted sources then this threat is pretty much eliminated.

Tip

There are several other email applications available in the *Play Store* as well as pre-installed on Android devices. If you are finding the text too small on the Gmail app, I recommend having a look at the K9 app. You are able to make the text bigger in the settings. In previous editions of this book, I recommended MailDroid, but software changes, features are added and taken away and of those tested, K9 appears to be the most customizable.

Adding another email account

You can add an account in two places the first is by pressing on the menu button on the top left of the screen on the main window and then pressing on your face or email address or going to *Settings* and pressing on *Add account*.

In each location you will be given the option to choose *Google, a Gmail address* or *Personal (IMAP/POP)*, Yahoo, outlook etc. In each case follow the on screen instructions.

Chapter 19 Advanced Features - Google Labs

What to expect in this Chapter:

- What are Labs
- What else can you do with Gmail using Labs

Google Labs are experimental features that Google are testing. They may disappear at any time or if they become popular, appear as standard options later. I'm going to go through a few select labs which you may find useful. To find the labs, click on the gear wheel at the top right of Gmail and then go to *Settings > Labs*.

A lab which is not detailed below as it does not appear to new accounts is *Green Robot!* I recommend enabling this if it appears in your labs page as it tells you how people are contactable. For example if an Android symbol shows next to their name, they are on their mobile phone and if they don't answer straight away you know they might be at work, shopping or they may even be driving!

Apps Search

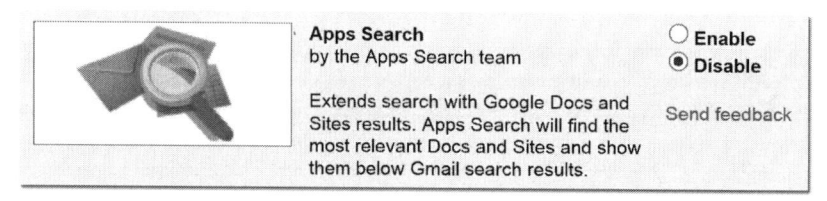

Figure 277 Labs - Apps search

If you use your email as a way of saving information in addition to Google Docs and find yourself searching two different places for something, why not combine your search into one easy search? Enabling this lab will mean that your search will include your docs and it will appear along with your email results.

Authentication icon for verified senders

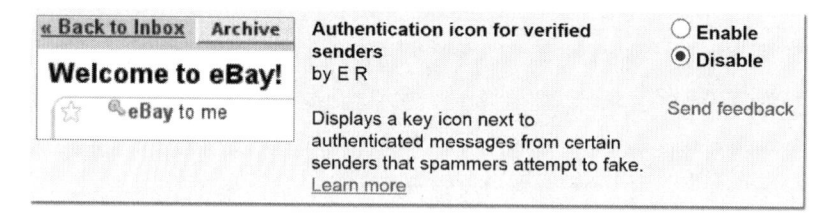

Figure 278 Labs - Authentication icon for verified senders

If you are worried about phishing emails for your eBay and PayPal accounts then you HAVE to enable this lab. A small icon will appear next to genuine emails from eBay and PayPal so you don't have to worry that someone is trying to make you click on a link to a fake site.

Auto-advance

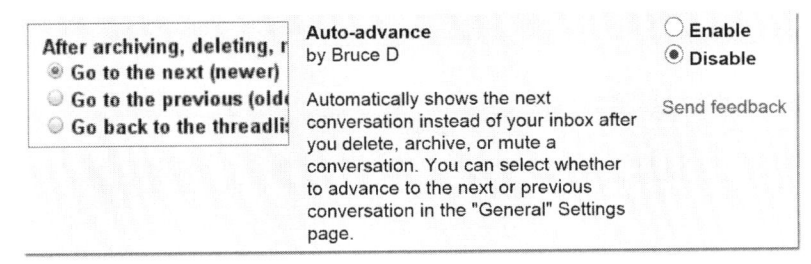

Figure 279 Labs - Auto-advance

This lab is great for busy Gmailers. If you are tired of going back to the inbox just to get to the next email then enabling this lab will mean you automatically go to it after you delete, archive or mute the email you are reading. When it is enabled you can choose whether to go to an earlier or later conversation.

Canned Responses

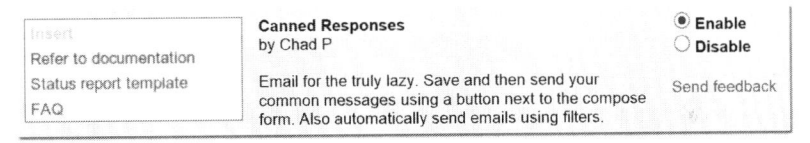

Figure 280 Labels - Canned Responses

Canned responses can save you time by automating your email. Please see *Chapter 13 Keeping Your Email Under Control* for more information.

Custom keyboard shortcuts

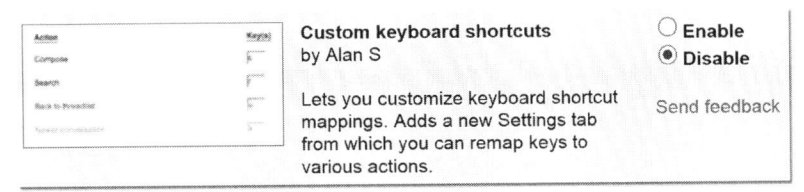

Figure 281 Labs - Custom keyboard shortcuts

Change or make your own keyboard shortcuts, Simply enable this lab (clicking save changes at the bottom of the page) and then go to *Gear wheel > Settings > Keyboard Shortcuts*.

These are the options available:

- Compose. Compose in a tab (new compose only),
- Search mail
- Back to threadlist
- Newer conversation
- Older conversation
- Select conversation
- Rotate superstar
- Remove label
- Mute conversation
- Delete
- Previous message
- Next message
- Reply
- Reply in a new window
- Reply all
- Reply all in a new window
- Forward
- Forward in a new window
- Search chat contacts
- Go to Inbox
- Go to Starred conversations
- Go to Sent messages
- Go to Drafts
- Go to All mail
- Go to Contacts
- Move focus to toolbar
- Select all conversations
- Deselect all conversations
- Select read conversations

Advanced Features – Google Labs

- Select unread conversations
- Select starred conversations
- Select unstarred conversations
- Update conversation
- Remove label and go to previous conversation
- Remove label and go to next conversation
- Archive and go to previous conversation
- Archive and go to next conversation
- Undo last action
- Open "more actions" menu
- Mark as read
- Mark as unread
- Mark unread from the selected message
- Mark as not important
- Open keyboard shortcut help
- Archive
- Open "move to" menu
- Open "label as" menu
- Open conversation
- Focus last mole (mole is a name for a chat window)
- Mark as important
- Teach Gmail
- Go to next inbox section
- Go to previous inbox section
- Go to Tasks
- Add conversation to Tasks
- Go to Label
- Show menu
- Show Archived Hangouts
- Show Hangout requests
- Focus on the Conversation list
- Open phone

Google Calendar gadget

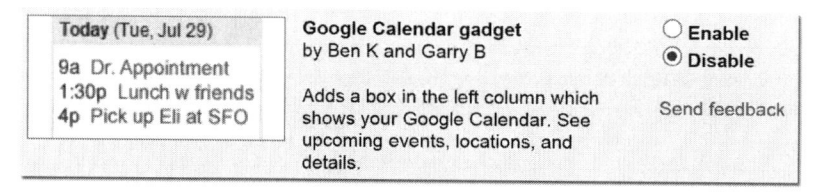

Figure 282 Labs - Google calendar gadget

The Google calendar app will save you time by showing you your calendar events in the left column.

Google Maps preview in mail

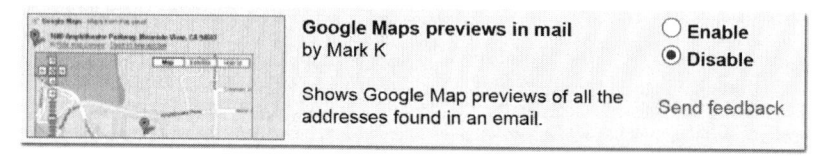

Figure 283 Labs Google maps previews

If this is enabled, when someone send you an address in an email, a Google Map will automatically load showing where the address is.

Google Voice player in mail

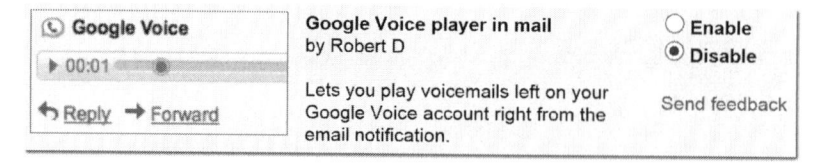

Figure 284 Labs - Google voice player in mail

Don't you wish you could play your voicemails from your computer? With this lab you can. Enable this and when someone leaves you a voicemail in your Google Voice account, you can play it from the email.

Mark as Read button

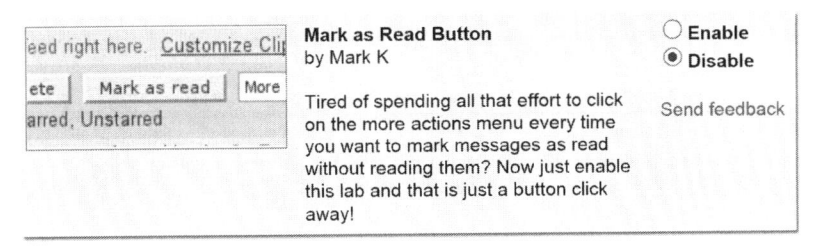

Figure 285 Labs - Mark as read button

This is an essential lab if you want to mark an email read and keep it in your inbox. It could also be used if you receive an email reply to another email which you were cc'd. You haven't read the original email as you saw the reply first. You read the reply but the original email is still unread in your inbox. Check the box next to it and click on the button *Mark as read* to solve this (or you could just open the email).

Multiple inboxes

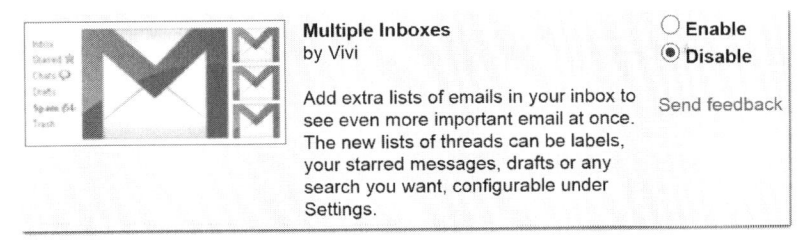

Figure 286 Labs - Multiple inboxes

This lab can keep your emails organized if you do not use the recommended Gmail inboxes. You can choose to have lists of email such as by label, archived or keyword. Once enabled go to the Multiple Inboxes in settings (*Gear wheel > Settings > Multiple Inboxes*) to set your preferences.

Some examples of new inboxes:

- Label:Shopping – This will show emails which have had the label Shopping applied to them.
- is:unread – This will show only unread messages.

- is:starred – This will show only starred messages.
- is:sent – This will show emails that you've sent.

Please note if you have enabled your inbox tabs, you must go to *inbox* in *settings* and uncheck all the inboxes you can, otherwise it will not work.

Warning, check to see if the settings button is on the top right of your screen when you enable *Multiple Inboxes*. If it is no longer there, go back using your browser buttons and re-enable the Gmail inboxes. You don't want to be left without the ability to get to the settings options!

Picasa previews in mail

Figure 287 Labs - Picasa previews in mail

This will allow you to see images from Picasa when someone sends you a Picasa link in an email. Click on *Enable* then *Save Changes* at the bottom of the email.

Pictures in chat

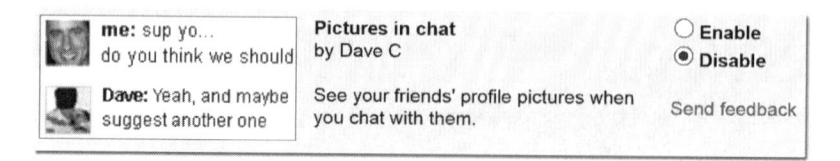

Figure 288 Labs - Pictures in chat

Chat can be pretty boring with just text. Enable this lab to see your friend's pictures while chatting to them. Click on *Enable* then *Save Changes* at the bottom of the email.

Preview Pane

Figure 289 Labs - Preview pane

Do you miss the preview pane in Outlook and other traditional email programs? This lab allows you to get the familiar style inside Gmail. When you check a box in your list view you will be able to see the contents of the email in the new Preview Pane.

Once you have enabled the Preview, you need to use the dropdown button on the top right of the screen and choose vertical or horizontal view as seen at the top of the next figure.

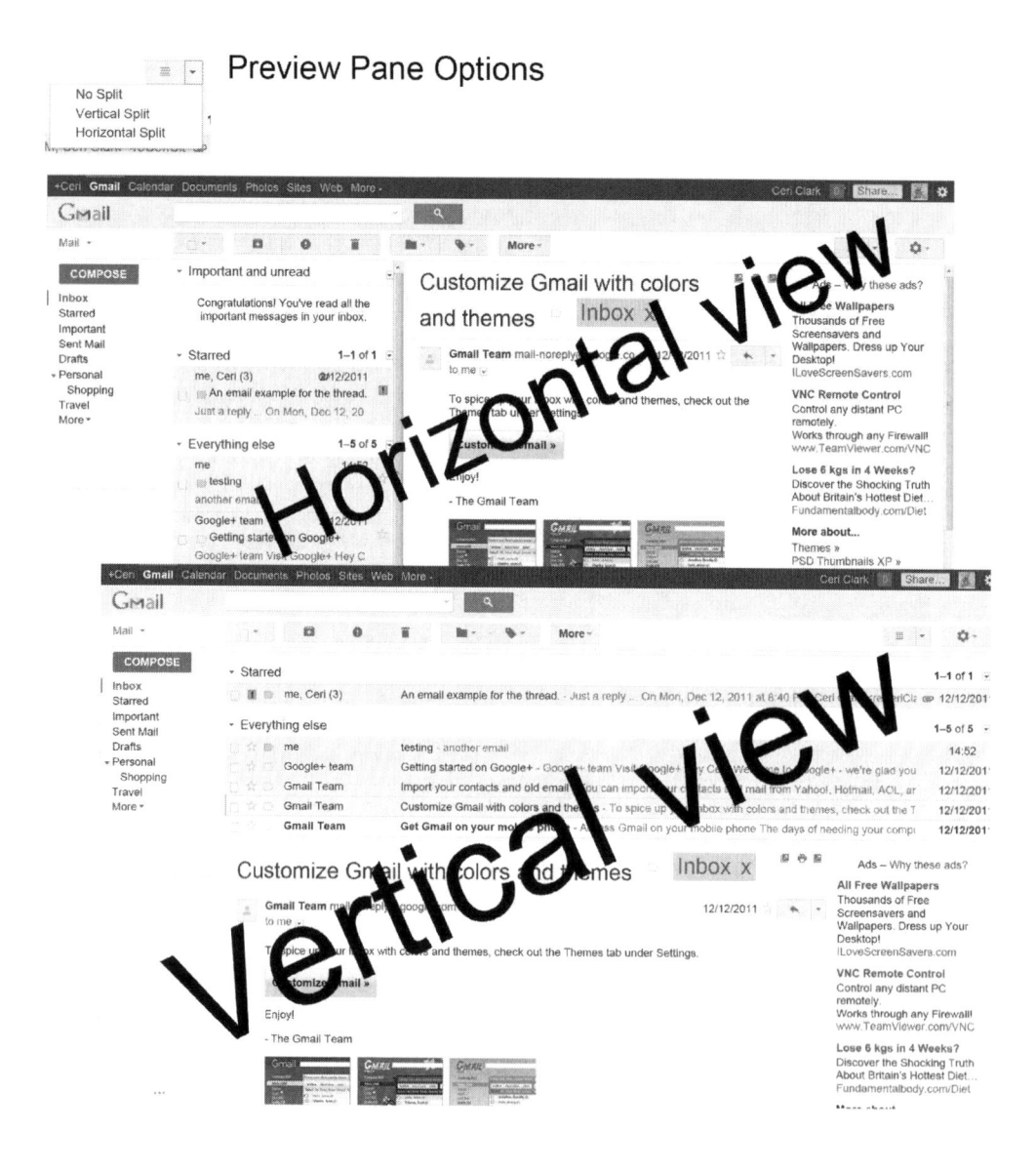

Figure 290 Labs - Preview pane options

Quick Links

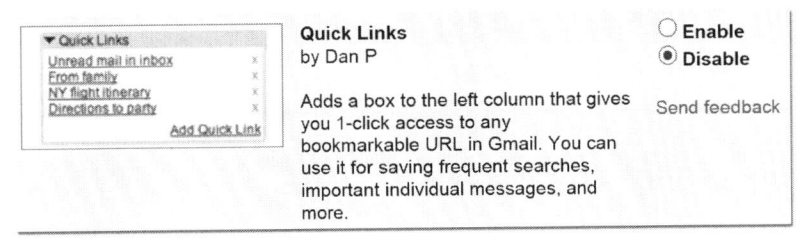

Figure 291 Labs - Quick links

Quick links will save URLs that appear in your Gmail. To turn it on, click on *Enable* and then *Save Changes*.

Quote selected text

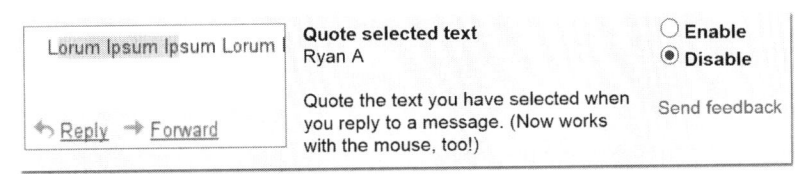

Figure 292 Labs - Quote selected text

Once you have enabled this lab, highlight the text you want to quote and then click reply. The text you highlighted will appear in the new email.

You *can* just cut what you want to quote out of the email (Ctrl + C) and paste it in a reply (Ctrl + V) to do the same thing if you end up inadvertently quoting text you don't mean to and disabling the lab.

Right-sided chat

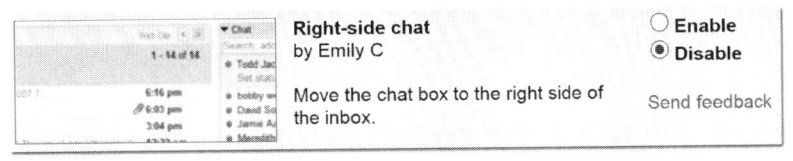

Figure 293 Labs - Right-sided chat

As is suggested by the title you can move the chat from the left column to the right with this lab.

Smartlabels

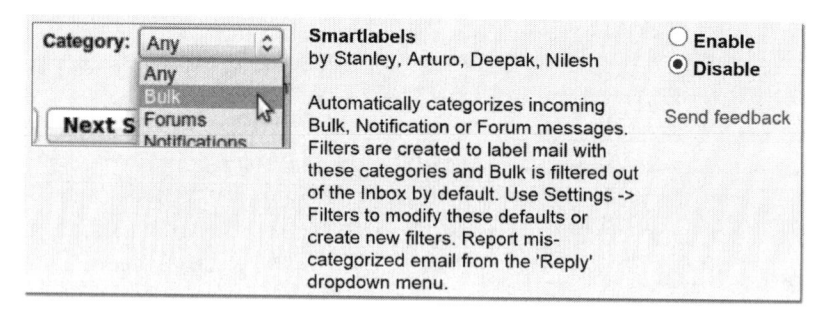

Figure 294 Labs - Smartlabels

This app automatically labels your emails based on what you've done before. Each time you open an email there will be a dropdown box where you can choose a category. After a while Gmail will learn what to label and you won't have to do it (much) anymore!

Undo Send

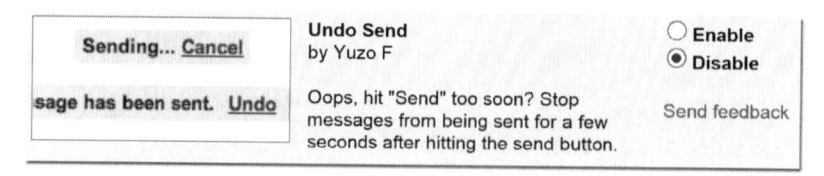

Figure 295 Labs - Undo send

This is a lab I could have done with a few times in my life but it only works for a couple of seconds. Stop that email from leaving your account. Click on *Enable* then *Save Changes* at the bottom of the email.

Unread Message Icon

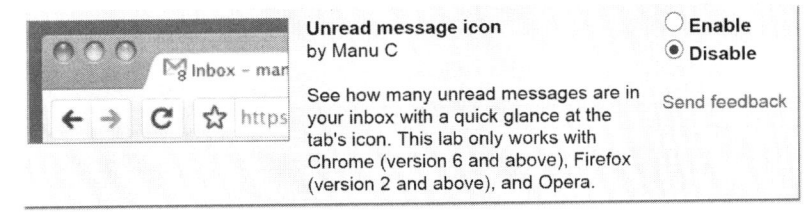

Figure 296 Labs Unread message icon

Are you constantly flicking between tabs on your browser to see if you have any new emails? This lab can solve this problem but only if you use Chrome, Firefox or Opera. It will put a little unread message count number on the tab where you have your email open so you can just glance up rather than having to open the tab all the time.

Yelp previews in mail

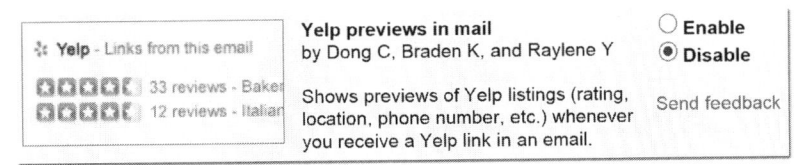

Figure 297 Labs - Yelp previews in mail

This lab shows information about Yelp listings.

Chapter 20 Frequently Asked Questions (FAQ)

What to expect in this Chapter:

- How to get to Gmail
- Recovering or change a password
- How to print emails from Gmail
- Using or removing the extra inboxes in Gmail

What was the address again to login to Gmail?

http://mail.google.com or http://gmail.com

Help I've lost my password, what do I do now?

You've been on holiday or have had better things to do than check your email. You've opened up Gmail and you can't remember your password. Please use the following instructions to get your password sent to you:

Ceri Clark | A Simpler Guide to Gmail

Step 1

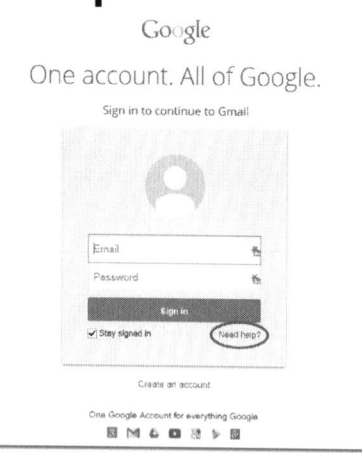

Google
One account. All of Google.
Sign in to continue to Gmail

Email
Password
Sign in
☑ Stay signed in   Need help?

Create an account
One Google Account for everything Google

Step 2

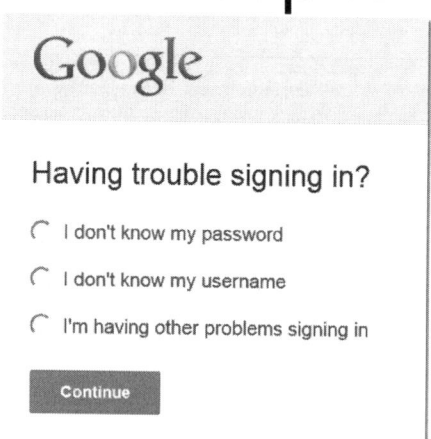

Google

Having trouble signing in?

○ I don't know my password
○ I don't know my username
○ I'm having other problems signing in

Continue

Step 3

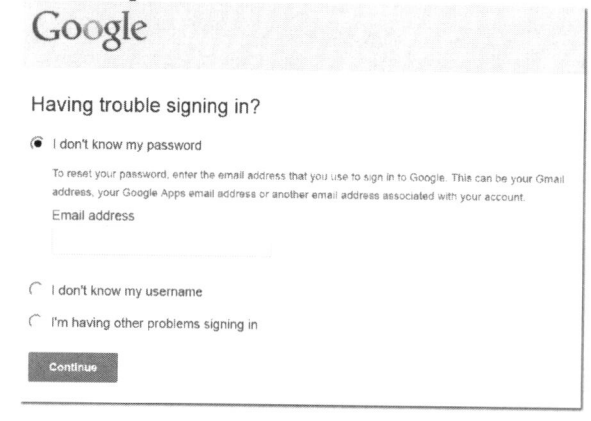

Google

Having trouble signing in?

● I don't know my password

To reset your password, enter the email address that you use to sign in to Google. This can be your Gmail address, your Google Apps email address or another email address associated with your account.

Email address

○ I don't know my username
○ I'm having other problems signing in

Continue

Step 4

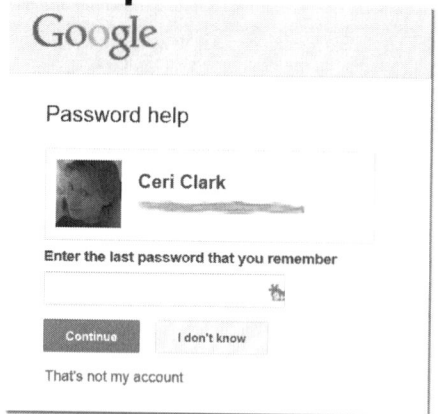

Google

Password help

Ceri Clark

Enter the last password that you remember

Continue   I don't know

That's not my account

Step 5

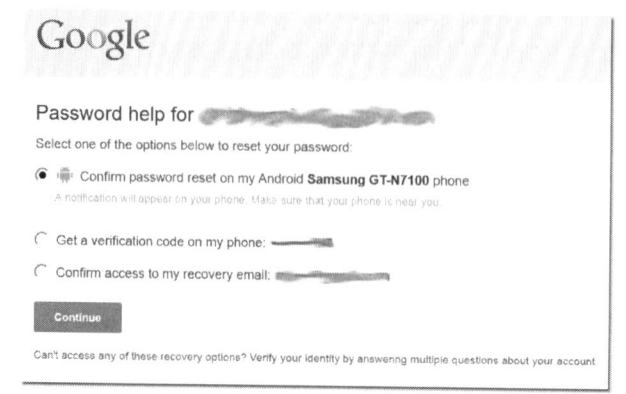

Google

Password help for

Select one of the options below to reset your password:

● Confirm password reset on my Android **Samsung GT-N7100** phone
   A notification will appear on your phone. Make sure that your phone is near you.

○ Get a verification code on my phone:
○ Confirm access to my recovery email:

Continue

Can't access any of these recovery options? Verify your identity by answering multiple questions about your account.

Step 1: Go to http://mail.google.com if you are not already on the login screen. Click on *Need help?* as seen in *step 1* of the graphic above.

Step 2: Choose *I don't know my password* and then click on *Continue*.

Step 3: Type in your email address in the box provided.

Step 4: If you remembered your password you wouldn't be looking for it right? I would click *I don't know* here.

Step 5: Choose an option from the suggestions. You can choose to use your phone to reset your password or it can be reset by clicking on a link sent to an alternative email address. This can be yours or a trusted family member.

Where do I go to change my password?

Go to *Settings* > *Account and Import* > *Change password.*

Do I need a special browser to use Gmail?

Gmail runs on most browsers including Internet Explorer, Firefox, Chrome and Safari.

How do I print email?

This is easy. Enter the email you want to print. Look for the gray box on the top right of the email. Click on the arrow next to reply and select *Print.*

How do remove the 'extra' inboxes like updates, social and promotions?

Removing the extra inboxes can be done in two places. The easiest to do this is to click on the plus sign at the end of the tabs row as seen below:

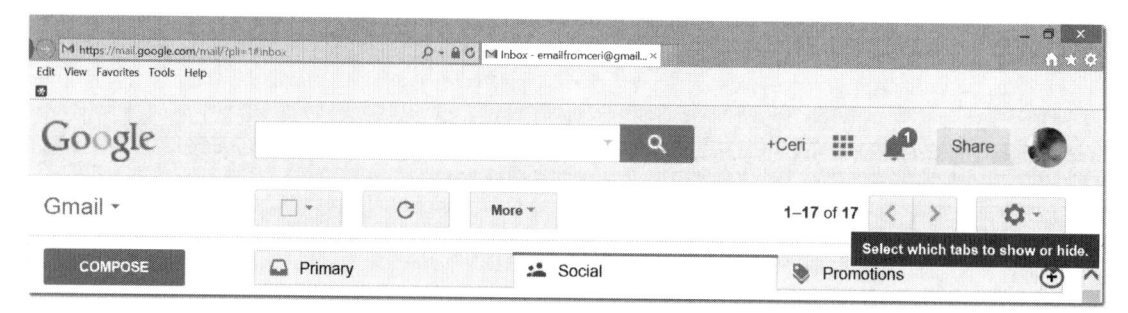

Figure 298 How to get to the inboxes screen

In the page that loads, uncheck all the tabs you can (you won't be able to get rid of the Primary inbox as it is the main one). Once you click *Save* all your tabs will disappear leaving you with the one inbox.

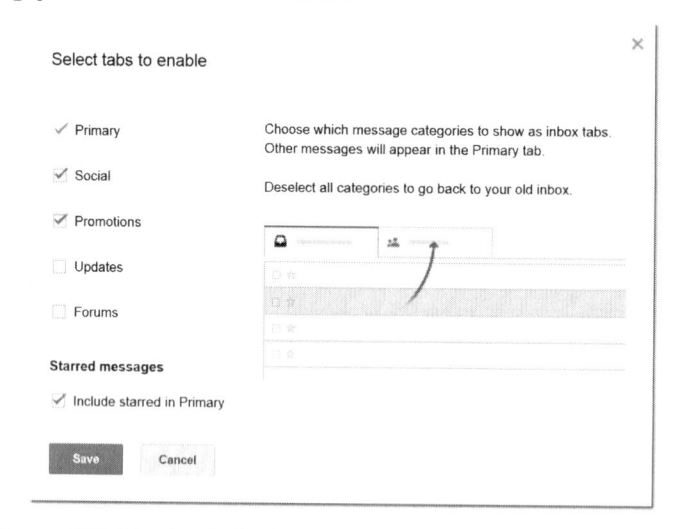

Figure 299 Uncheck the boxes to get rid of the extra inboxes

The other way to turn off the other inboxes is to go to the gear wheel on the top right of your screen then *Settings > Inbox*.

Frequently Asked Questions (FAQ)

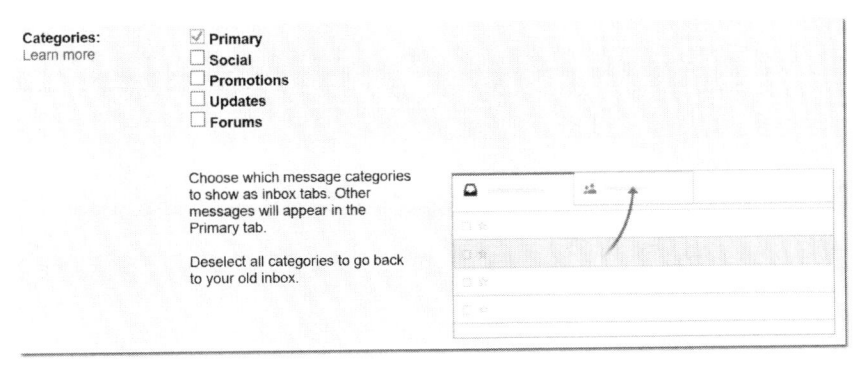

Figure 300 Uncheck the boxes to remove the extra inboxes

In the *Categories* section, uncheck all the boxes bar Primary and then click on *Save Changes* at the bottom of the screen.

How do I remove email addresses when I Reply to All?

The way to remove email addresses when you reply to more than one person is to click on the email addresses to expand them and click on the X beside each address to remove them one-by-one.

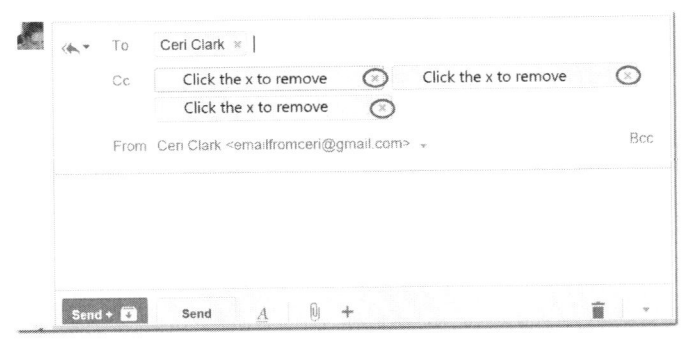

Figure 301 Click on the x to remove an email address

283

How do I increase the size of the text in my browser and my Android phone?

To make anything bigger in Internet Explorer, you can change the text size by clicking on View in the top navigation bar and choosing Text size. You can change it in *any* browser by pressing down on the *Ctrl* key and then pushing away on your scroll wheel to make the page bigger or closer to you to make it smaller.

On your Android device you can make the text size bigger by changing them in your phone's main settings. These can be found at *Settings > My device > Display > Font size* and you can also pinch and zoom inside emails.

If there are any questions you would like answered about Gmail that you think should be in this guide, visit http://www.CeriClark.com and have a look at my contact page. I will update the e-book with the new addition to the FAQ.

Glossary

2-step verification A security feature where two items are needed to log in to a website. This is usually a password and some other form of identification such as a code from a mobile device.

Address bar The box at the top of your browser where website addresses show, for example http://gmail.com

Address book Similar to an old-style book where addresses were written in a book but held electronically in Gmail.

Adobe Flash This is software which operates in browsers that is created by Adobe to view interactive elements on a webpage.

Android device These are smartphones and tablets which run on Google's operating system, Android.

App Short for application, these are small programs which run on mobile devices such as smartphones and tablets

Archive Archiving emails means in the strictest sense that the label inbox has been removed from an email and is no longer in your inbox. You can find any email in All Mail unless it has been deleted.

Attachment This is a document, picture or anything that can be 'attached' to an email.

Browser This is a computer program that allows you to view webpages.

Calibre This is a free e-book management program created by Kovid Goyal which will allow you to organize, convert and read e-books on your computer.

Captcha Also known as word verification, this box, usually containing letters or numbers is used to prove that people submitting to a website are not robots.

Chat In Gmail, this can be talking using text or your webcam.

Circles These are groups of people you put together in Google+ to organize your contacts on the social network.

Contacts People you have connected with by Gmail or Google+.

CSV This is a type of document known as a spreadsheet.

Discussion thread A number of emails grouped together with a common subject.

Drive Drive is Google's free online storage of files and photos. It is also the place where you can create free spreadsheets and documents.

Export This is a feature where you can download some data or a document that can be saved on your computer which can then be used on a different account or application.

File Explorer An application on your computer which allows you to find files, folder, and software on your PC or Mac.

Filters A feature of Gmail that sorts your email by predetermined elements. This can be for example filtering your email so all emails from a certain address will all go into a Finance folder (label).

Gear Wheel The symbol located on the top right of Google pages that will take you to the settings for that service.

Gigabytes A unit of computer storage. At the time of writing Google gives you 15 Gigabytes of space. This is roughly equivalent to 200,000 emails.

Gmail The free email service provided by Google.

Hackers There are good or bad hackers but for the purposes of this book, I refer to those nefarious people who have devoted their lives to harming you or others by breaking in to computers.

Glossary

Hangouts Hangouts refer to connecting to people by both instant messaging (text chat) and video chats with webcams.

Hashtags These are words preceded by the # symbol. For example #cooking is a hashtag.

Homepage The start page of a website, also known as the main page.

Icon A picture or symbol which when pressed takes you to another webpage or function (such as a Google Hangout).

Images Photos, pictures and graphics.

Import This is a feature where you can upload some data or a document to a web service like Gmail or Google+.

Inbox This is an electronic folder which holds your emails. Traditionally your inbox was one folder where all your emails first arrived. Gmail now provides several inboxes which sort your emails into categories.

Kindle This is a device produced and sold by Amazon which uses the AZW or Mobi e-book formats.

Labs Google Labs are experimental features that Google are testing. They may disappear at any time or if they become popular, appear as standard options later.

Labels Labels are what folders are in other programs. You assign a label to an email to sort them. Click on a label to find other emails of the same type.

LastPass This is a service from lastpass.com where you can store all your passwords in the cloud which is protected by one password and 2-factor authentication for extra security. Use this service to generate a different password for every website you sign up to but you will only have to remember the one.

Nested label A nested label means that a label will appear under another in the label list.

Password A string of letters and numbers which can be a phrase or random which allows you access to a website or service.

PC A computer that runs the Windows operating system.

Phishing This is where criminals will try to get your personal information from you by sending emails that appear to be from people or organizations you trust. This can be usernames, passwords and/or credit card information.

Profile In the context of this book this is your information held by Google.

Scams Schemes designed to commit fraud.

Signature Text that finishes off an email. This is usually your name but can include your address, email address, phone numbers and images.

Spam Irrelevant, unwanted and unasked-for emails.

Stream In Google+ this is in your homepage where a constant 'stream' of news flows.

Subject The subject of your email should be a short description of the contents of the email.

Two-factor authentication *See 2-step verification*

URL URL is short for Uniform Resource Locator. It is a quick way of saying web address.

Unsubscribe Get rid of emails you no longer want by following the instructions at the bottom of emails to unsubscribe from future emails.

Username A unique piece of information used as a means to identify you to Google.

vCard This is a way of sending contact information in the form of a document. Import vCards to Gmail to fill in details of a contact.

Webcam A video camera which will enable you to talk face-to-face in Google Hangouts.

Word Verification *See Captcha*

Index

A

Address book
> *See also* Chapter 6 Address Book (Google Contacts) 65-76
> adding contacts 65-68
> adding groups 71-73
> adding pictures to contacts 69
> adding a contact using an email address 67
> editing contacts 70
> manually adding a contact 67-68

Android phone, *see* Gmail app

Appearance
> *See also* Chapter 10 Changing the Look and Feel 103-108
> display density 104-105
> themes 106-108

Attachments
> searching for emails with 100-101
> viewing 27-29

C

Canned Responses, *see* Organizing emails

Changing appearance, see appearance

Chat
> *See also* Chapter 15 Chat 237-243
> availability 241-242
> blocking contacts 242-243
> inviting a contact to chat 239
> phone chat 243
> reactivating 31
> settings, *see* settings
> text chat 243
> turn off 29-30
> turn on 237-238
> video chat 243

Composing
> *See also* Chapter 5 Sending and Receiving emails 51-63
> adding a link 61

289

formatting 59-61
spell check 61-63
Contacts, *see* Address book

D

Definition 2
Deleting email 63
Discussions 52-54

E

Etiquette *See Netiquette*
Exporting
    contacts 73-75
    exporting filters 94-95

F

Filters
    See also Chapter 8 Filters 89-95
    adding filters from friends, *see* Importing
    creating a filter 90-92
    deleting a filter 94
    editing a filter 93-94
    location of filter settings 93
    settings, *see* accounts and import *under* Settings
    sharing filters, *see* exporting
Fonts
    default text style 113
    formatting emails 59-61
Forwarding
    an email 54-57
    settings, *see* forwarding and POP/IMAP *under* Settings
Frequently Asked Questions
    See also Chapter 20 Frequently Asked Questions (FAQ) 279-284
    browser requirement 281
    password
        changing 281
        lost 279-281
        reply-to-all, removing email addresses 283
    text size, increasing 284
    website address 279

G

Glossary 285-288
Gmail app
    See also Chapter 18 Gmail on Your Android Device 255-264
    browsing using labels 259
    checking email 257-260
    composing mail 257-258
    forwarding mail 258-259
    menu 256-257
    replying 258-259
    searching mail 260
    settings 260-264
        adding another email account 264
        auto-advance 261
        auto-fit messages 261
        confirming actions 262
        download attachments 263
        Gmail default action 261
        images 263
        inbox categories 262
        inbox type 262
        manage labels 263
        notifications 262
        reply all 261

Index

sender image 261
signature 262
swipe actions 261
sync Gmail 263
vacation responder 262-263

Google+
See also Chapter 14 Introduction to Google+ 175-236
cell app, *see* phone app
cheat sheet 235-236
chrome extensions 233-235
circles
adding people to Circles 195-201
commenting 203-204
creating a Circle 191-194
deleting Circles 201-202
deleting people to Circles 201
liking (+1) 202
sharing 204-205
disabling Google+ 224
hangouts 187-189
homepage 177
location 176
navigating 177-179
notifications 213-215
phone app 226-233
choosing account 228
limiting the posts you see 230-231
notifications 229-230
posting 232
search 231
searching for people 228-229
settings 232-233
viewing your profile 227-228
posts
deleting posts 211
disabling comments and reshares 212-213
posting 208-210
viewing 205-207
privacy 225-226
profile, setting up 180-186
searching 215-217
settings 217-224
accessibility 221-222
apps and activities 220-221
disable Google+ 224
Gmail app settings, *see* settings *under* Gmail app
hashtags 223
interacting with you 217-219
location settings 224
manage subscriptions 219
notification delivery 219
photos and videos 222
profile 223
receive notifications 220
shared endorsements 219
SMS Terms 224
your Circles 221
vanity URL 185-186

I

Importing
contacts during setup 21
contacts after setup 75-76

filters 94-95
mail 18-21
settings, *see* accounts and import under Settings

Inbox
See also Organizing emails

L

Labels
See also Chapter 7 Sorting Emails – No More Folders with Labels 77-87
applying a label from the email list 83-84
applying a label from an opened email 85-86
circles 83
creating a label 79-82
settings, *see* Settings

Labs
See also Chapter 19 Advanced Features – Google Labs 265-277
See also Settings
Apps Search 266
Authentication Icon for Verified Senders 266
Auto-advance 267
Canned Responses 267
Custom Keyboard Shortcuts 267-269
Google Calendar Gadget 270
Google Maps Preview in Mail 270
Google Voice Player in Mail 270
Mark as Read Button 271
Multiple Inboxes 271-272
Picasa Preview in Mail 272
Pictures in Chat 272

Preview Pane 273-274
Quick Links 275
Quote Selected Text 275
Right-sided Chat 275-276
Smartlabels 276
Undo Send 276
Unread Message Icon 277
Yelp Previews in Mail 277

Logging in 21-25
going directly there 21-23
adding as homepage 23-25

N

Netiquette 253-254

O

Opening a new Account *See* Chapter 2 Opening Your Account 5-16-

Organizing emails
See also Chapter 13 Keeping Your Email Under Control 161-173
canned responses 164-166
customized inboxes using labels/folders 166-167
inbox tabs 166
filters, using with labels 168
folders 167
labels, *see* Labels
prioritize 162
replying to messages 162-164
Roll.me 169-173
starring emails 162
time management 161-162
unsubscribing 169-172

Index

P

Passwords
    See also Chapter 4 Security 33-50
    choosing passwords 9-11
    changing password 33-34
Phishing, *see* Spams, scams and phishing
Profile
    adding a profile picture 13-15
    creating 13-16
    Google+, *see* Google+
    public profile 157-160

R

Reading emails 25-27
    See also Chapter 5 Sending and Receiving Emails 51-63
Replying
    See also Chapter 5 Sending and Receiving Emails 51-63
    replying to a person 54-57
    replying to a group 58-59

S

Searching
    See also Chapter 9 Searching For, and In, Emails 97-101
    by date 101
    by size 101
    for emails from a person 99
    in chats 101
    in labels 99
    in sent emails 99
    keyword searching 100
    subject searching 99-100
    with attachments 100-101
Scams, *see* Spams, scams and phishing
Security
    See also Chapter 4 Security 33-50
    passwords, see Passwords
    two-factor authentication, *see* Two-factor authentication
Sending emails, *see* Composing
Settings
    See also Chapter 11 Under the Hood – Settings 109-153
    General 109
        button labels 117
        conversation view 113
        create contacts for auto-complete 118
        default 132-135
        default reply behaviour 112
        default text style 113
        desktop notifications 115-116
        email via Google+ 114
        images 111-112
        important first 135-136
        important signals for ads 118-122
        inbox 131-132
        keyboard shortcuts 116
        labels 131
        language 111
        maximum page size 111
        my picture 117-118
        outgoing message encoding 131
        people widget 118

personal level indicators 129
phone numbers 111
priority inbox 139-140
send and archive 114-115
signature 122-129
snippets 130
starred first 137-138
stars 115
unread first 136-137
vacation responder/out of office 130-131
Accounts and Import 141-147
    add additional storage 147
    change account settings 141-142
    check mail using POP3 144-146
    grant access to your account 147
    import mail and contacts 142
    send mail as 143-144
    using Gmail for work 146
Filters 147-148
    See also Chapter 7 Sorting Emails – No More Folders 77-87
Forwarding and POP/IMAP 148-150
    forwarding 149
    IMAP access 150-151
    POP download 149-150
Chat 151
Web Clips 151
Labs 151
    See Labs

Offline 152
Themes 152-153
Sorting out emails, *see* Organizing emails
Spam, *see* Spams, scams and phishing
Spams, scams and phishing
    See also Chapter 4 Security 33-50
    bank emails 49
    bad grammar and spelling 49
    email from yourself 48-49
    friend in trouble 48
    marking email as spam 86-87
    stranger sob story 48
    too good to be true 48
    unsubscribe link 49-50

T

Tasks
    See also Chapter 16 Tasks 245-251
    actions 249-250
        clear completed tasks 250
        edit (change) details 250
        email task list 250
        help 250
        indent and unindent 249
        move up or down 250
        print task list 250
        sort by due date 250
        tips 250
        view completed task 250
    adding tasks 247-248
    completing tasks 248
    deleting or removing tasks 248
    organizing lists 250-251
    location 245-246

Index

Tour 17-21
Two-factor authentication
    accessing after setup 43
    backup access 38-39
    on your mobile device 40-47
    setting up 2 step verification 34-37
    verification codes using Android apps 43-47

U

URL, *see* going directly there *under* logging in
Username 8-9

About the Author

Ceri Clark is a full-time author and mother. She was a Librarian with over eleven years of experience in corporate, public and private libraries culminating in a Library Manager position at the ill-fated English Audit Commission. Following the closure of the library (and the future demise of the organization) she began to utilize her skills for searching, writing and advising with her A Simpler Guide Series.

Other books from Ceri Clark

A Simpler Guide to Calibre: How to organize, edit and convert your eBooks using free software for readers, writers, students and researchers for any eReader

A Simpler Guide to Finding Free eBooks: A step-by-step guide to discovering and downloading free e-books for the Kindle, Kindle Fire, Android, iPad and other e-readers

Children of the Elementi

More from Lycan Books & Myrddin Publishing:

A Simpler Guide to Finding Free eBooks by Ceri Clark

After Ilium - Seduction, betrayal, and foreign adventure by Stephen Swartz

Brawn Stroker's Dragula by Nicole Antonia Carro. When the Vampire Queens battle, who will win?

Charm City Chronicles: Ednor Scardens, The Body War, The Hurting Year & On Gabriel's Wings by Kathleen Barker. Young adult romance.

Children of the Elementi by Ceri Clark YA fantasy. Five children must discover their powers and unite to save their world.

Crown Phoenix Series: The Night Watchman Express, Devil's Kitchen, The Lamplighter's Special & South Sea Bubble – Steampunk fantasy by Alison DeLuca.

Dark Places by Shaun Allan: 13 stories. 13 poems. 13 doorways of the mind for the demons to enter through.

Darkness Rising: Chained, Quest, Secrets & Loss - Epic fantasy by Ross Kitson.

Emeline & the Mutants - a post-apocalyptic horror set in Australia with zombies and vampires by Rachel Tsoumbakos.

Heart Search Series: Lost & Found - Fate toys with mortals and immortals alike in this Paranormal Romance series by Carlie Cullen.

Hearts and Minds - Poetry of Love, Loss, and Life by Maria V.A. Johnson.

More from Lycan Books & Myrddin Publishing

Hired by a Demon - paranormal fantasy by Gypsy Madden.

Land Of Nod Trilogy: The Artifact and *The Prophet* - Scifi adventure by Gary Hoover.

Sax and the Suburb by Marilyn Rucker. Why is someone killing the community band geeks of Richland, Texas?

Silent No More by Krista Hatch. Trapped in 1942 Munich by a freak twist in time, two strangers must navigate their way to safety with only each other and the help of a group of university kids hell-bent on taking down Adolf Hitler and the entire Third Reich.

Sin: Horror and humor by Shaun Allan. People die around Sin. He doesn't like it and there's nothing he can do about it. But someone else knows, and Sin has to stop them... and himself.

Sons of Roland - A Rock Odyssey by Nicole Carro.

Tales from the Dreamtime: a novella of 3 fairy tales, by Connie J. Jasperson.

The Dream Land Trilogy - Interdimensional intrigue and alien romance by Stephen Swartz.

The Infinity Bridge: A Sci-fi steampunk adventure set in modern day York, replete with androids, airships... and Merlin by Ross Kitson.

The Guardian Series: The Last Guardian and *Burdens of a Saint* by Joan Hazel - Paranormal Fantasy Romance. Without a Guardian, Haven will destroy itself.

The Ring of Lost Souls: A spooky paranormal gothic tale set in Australia by Rachel Tsoumbakos

Tower of Bones Series: Tower of Bones & Forbidden Road. Epic fantasy, by Connie J. Jasperson. The Gods are at war and the land of Neveyah is the battleground. Magic and destiny lie waiting in the Tower of Bones.

What the Heart Sees by Joan Hazel – Romance. Two brothers, one chance for happiness.

Yum - A yummy horror story. George Orwell meets George Romero! By Nicole Carro.

Made in the USA
Middletown, DE
05 May 2015